The Forty-second Ohio infantry: a history of the organization and services of that regiment in the war of the rebellion; with biographical sketches of its field officers and a full roster of the regiment

Frank H. 1840-1916 Mason

Nabu Public Domain Reprints:

You are holding a reproduction of an original work published before 1923 that is in the public domain in the United States of America, and possibly other countries. You may freely copy and distribute this work as no entity (individual or corporate) has a copyright on the body of the work. This book may contain prior copyright references, and library stamps (as most of these works were scanned from library copies). These have been scanned and retained as part of the historical artifact.

This book may have occasional imperfections such as missing or blurred pages, poor pictures, errant marks, etc. that were either part of the original artifact, or were introduced by the scanning process. We believe this work is culturally important, and despite the imperfections, have elected to bring it back into print as part of our continuing commitment to the preservation of printed works worldwide. We appreciate your understanding of the imperfections in the preservation process, and hope you enjoy this valuable book.

To Gen'l Jas Barnett

Compliments of
  C E Henry
Cleveland Ohio
  October 1st 1878

THE NEW YORK
PUBLIC LIBRARY

ASTOR, LENOX AND
TILDEN FOUNDATIONS

THE
FORTY-SECOND OHIO
INFANTRY:
A HISTORY

OF THE

ORGANIZATION AND SERVICES OF THAT REGIMENT

IN THE

WAR OF THE REBELLION;

WITH

BIOGRAPHICAL SKETCHES OF ITS FIELD OFFICERS AND A FULL
ROSTER OF THE REGIMENT

COMPILED AND WRITTEN FOR THE VETERAN'S ASSOCIATION OF THE
FORTY-SECOND OHIO, BY

F. H. MASON,
PRIVATE OF COMPANY 'A'

CLEVELAND
COBB, ANDREWS & CO., PUBLISHERS
1876

Cleveland, Ohio:
PRESS OF LEADER PRINTING COMPANY.

DEDICATION.

TO THE
WIVES AND MOTHERS
OF THE FORTY-SECOND,

THE LOYAL, DEVOTED WOMEN WHO GAVE THEIR HUSBANDS AND SONS

TO THE REGIMENT,

SENT IT FORTH WITH THEIR BLESSINGS,

FOLLOWED IT WITH THEIR PRAYERS,

SYMPATHIZED IN ITS SUFFERINGS,

AND

WEPT OVER ITS DEAD,

THIS BRIEF AND IMPERFECT RECORD IS RESPECTFULLY

DEDICATED

INTRODUCTORY

When in 1864 and '65 the bronzed and war-worn regiments of the Union army returned from the field, reduced to half their original numbers by battle and disease, there was a feeling among the veterans and their friends that it would be a luxury to forget, amid the comforts of home, the long story of their perils and sufferings. The joy of return to home and friends, with the reflection that the army of right had triumphed and saved the Republic which Slavery would have destroyed, made the weary veteran too happy in his new comfort and freedom to care whether his own personal part in the great struggle were recorded or forgotten. The volunteers were weary with fighting and marching, the people were cloyed and oppressed with the excitement, the waste and the anxieties of war. The blessed benediction of Peace seemed for the time to rise like an obscuring mist between the war and the people who had given the flower of their youth and manhood to the struggle. In a contest in which whole armies had done so nobly, the achievements of particular regiments, companies, or individuals did not seem, either to the veterans or their friends, to demand especial record.

But as the years went by, and the vast importance of the results attained by the war began to grow apparent, there arose a new interest in the minor actors in the struggle. Time had begun to heal the wounds which the close of hostilities had left bleeding, and through the lengthening vista of years the sufferings of the people and their army seemed chastened and exalted to a holy sacrifice

The graves of soldiers, dotting the churchyards and cemeteries of the North, or collected in great National burial grounds by the liberal care of the government, became the shrines of reverent gratitude, and each recurring Spring saw those graves decked with flowers and consecrated anew with formal prayer and eulogy. During these same years there has arisen a new interest in the more minute details of the great conflict, a desire that before the colonels, the captains and the enlisted men who served in the Union armies pass away, the story of their specific parts in the war be placed upon record To the friends of those who wore the blue, to the States which armed and sent them forth, and to posterity which will read the great history of the Rebellion yet to be written, it is due that while the opportunity lasts the records of individual organizations be made as far as possible complete.

It is these considerations which have prompted the preparation and publication of this brief narrative of the organization and services of one of the two hundred and thirty military organizations which Ohio sent into the field Not that there is claimed for its members any greater courage or patriotism than inspired the other two hundred and ninety thousand sons of Ohio who bore arms in the mighty struggle, but because they answered promptly when danger threatened, marched and fought when and where duty called, fulfilling their three years of service with patient, hopeful enthusiasm, their story is worthy of preservation, not merely as a memorial for their own descendants but as a fragment of material for ultimate history

CHAPTER I

THE FIELD OFFICERS OF THE REGIMENT

In no episode of American history have there been greater opportunities for men of high character and ability to wield a strong and controlling influence over large numbers of their fellow citizens, than were given to the officers who organized and commanded the Volunteer regiments of the Union army during the first two years of the war. The rank and file were then far above the ordinary intelligence of common soldiers; they were earnest, patriotic, respected and self-respecting men. They formed a material out of which, in proper hands, would naturally grow the most competent and intelligent citizen soldiery of which history makes mention. Their very intelligence, however, made the Union volunteers exacting and critical as to the qualifications of their superiors, and where, as in the case of the Forty-Second, there has existed, not only through its three years of service, but during all the years which have intervened since the close of hostilities, a firm, abiding sentiment of respect and affection between officers and men, it may be safely assumed that on part of the higher officers at least, that esteem has been well deserved. In the characters of its field officers, the Forty-Second was peculiarly fortunate; and any adequate record of the services of the regiment must naturally begin with some account of the men who assembled the organization, gave it its inspiration and made it what it was.

JAMES A. GARFIELD,

The first Colonel of the Forty-Second, was born in Orange, Cuyahoga County, Ohio, November 19th, 1831. His parents were of New England extraction, and his father dying in 1831, left the mother with four small children and scanty fortune, on a meagre farm in what was then a thinly settled district. JAMES, the youngest of the children, worked on the little farm during the Summer, attending during the Winter the neighboring district school. To further fit himself for the life struggle which had begun so early, he learned, during his fifteenth and sixteenth years, something of the trade of a carpenter, but this not proving remunerative, he left home and secured employment as a driver and afterwards boatman on the Ohio canal. The malaria that overhung the canal in those days finally overcame him, and the autumn of 1848 brought him back to his mother's home for a three months' siege with fever and ague. He remained at home during the following winter and attended a high school in an adjoining county, known as "Geauga Seminary." He found in his studies a new and unexpected source of enjoyment, and when the Spring found him still in uncertain health, he decided to defer until Fall his purpose of shipping as a sailor on Lake Erie, and meanwhile to attend school during the Summer term. That decision may almost be said to have shaped the whole subsequent course of his life. Those nine months at school awakened the intellect that has since made General GARFIELD one of the foremost men of this country, and from that time no obstacle was permitted to thwart his purpose.

Working as a carpenter during summer vacations, teaching when his scanty funds ran low, he managed to attend school most of the time until 1851, when he removed to Hiram and became a student in the "Institute" over which he was eventually to preside. He soon became the most accomplished Latin and Greek scholar that the school had ever produced, and as he was an earnest, self-reliant Christian, whom to know was but to respect, he naturally soon became the oracle and wonder of his classmates. After extraordinary exertions in earning means, he finally entered Williams College, in the fall of 1852, graduating after two years study with the Metaphysical honor, one of the highest gifts of Williams College to a graduating class. He returned home in the Summer of 1856, and became teacher, and the following year President of Hiram Institute, which position he filled with extraordinary ability until politics and the war drew him into more active and public walks of life. In 1859, while still at Hiram, he began the study of law, for which his temperament and attainments gave him rare qualifications. He was already an earnest, powerful, magnetic speaker. He had all the qualities of an orator, fervid, spontaneous sympathies, high convictions, earnestness of purpose, and rich exuberance of language, moulded and chastened by classical study. He was in fact too large and strong a man to be hidden under the Presidency of an incipient College, and in 1859, when men of zeal and courage were wanted in the fight against Slavery, the people of Portage County chose the President of Hiram Institute to represent them in the State Senate. There, during the winter of 1860 and '61, Mr. GARFIELD, with Hon. J. D. Cox and Prof. MONROE, of Oberlin, formed a radical triumvirate in the Ohio Senate, which controlled the sentiment of the Legislature and ripened Ohio for her noble part in the war. National politics growing out of the Slavery question engrossed the attention of the Ohio Legislature to an unusual extent in 1861, and in all the debates of that session, Senator GARFIELD was the leader. The Assembly remained in session until late in the

Spring, weeks after the torch of rebellion had been lit at Fort Sumter and the Governor of Ohio had begun to officer the regiments which flocked to Columbus, and send them into the field. The most powerful and popular man in the Senate, Mr. GARFIELD might have had a Colonelcy at any time for the asking, but he never thought of himself. He went off some where to a Western State after arms with which to equip the Ohio Volunteers, and on his return would have doubtless accepted a lieutenancy had there been a vacancy in that grade without a ready and competent applicant. It was thought at that time that Mr. SEWARD had measured accurately the coming struggle when he predicted that it would "be over in ninety days."

But July brought the disaster at Bull Run, and it became apparent that the nation must strip itself for a life and death struggle. On the 27th of July, Governor DENNISON addressed Mr GARFIELD as follows

THE STATE OF OHIO.
EXECUTIVE DEPARTMENT,
COLUMBUS, July 27th, 1861.

DEAR SIR

I am organizing some new regiments. Can you take a Lieutenant-Colonelcy? I am anxious you should do so. Reply by telegraph

Cox has entered Charleston and is doing nobly. I have sent him my congratulations.   Yours Truly,

W DENNISON

This letter, which reached Hiram during a two weeks absence of Mr GARFIELD, was finally received by him on the 7th of August. He immediately replied that if the proffered position were still vacant and the Colonelcy of the regiment filled by a graduate of West Point, he would accept. The reply was favorable, and on the 15th Mr GARFIELD reached Columbus and on the following morning was mustered into the service as Lieutenant Colonel. He was immediately assigned to duty at Camp Chase, under an order from Adjutant-General BUCKINGHAM to "report in person to Brigadier-General HILL, for such duty as he may assign to you in connection with a temporary command for purposes of instruction in camp duty and discipline." With his arrival at Camp Chase on the 16th of August, the military career of the future Major-General of Volunteers may be said to have fairly commenced

After a few weeks of general service, at Camp Chase, he was detailed on recruiting duty, and aided in raising six of the ten companies which formed the Forty Second O. V. I. No Colonel having yet been appointed, on the 5th of September he was commissioned by the Governor of Ohio, as Colonel of the Forty-Second Regiment. He established a School of Instruction for the officers of the Regiment, requiring two hours of recitation and examination in the morning of each day, and continued the work of drilling, arming and equipping the Regiment, during the months of October, November and the first half of December.

The Roster of the Field and Staff, as mustered in, in November, 1861, was as follows:

Colonel,	JAMES A GARFIELD
Lieutenant-Colonel,	LIONEL A SHELDON
Major,	DON A PARDEE
Adjutant,	WM W OLDS
Quartermaster,	J D STUBBS
Surgeon,	JOEL POMLRENL
Assistant-Surgeon,	JOHN W HARMON
Chaplain,	Rev J H. JONES

On Saturday, December 14th, a telegram came from General D C. BUELL, commanding the Department of the Ohio, at Louisville, Ky., ordering the Regiment to proceed with all possible dispatch to Prestonburgh, Floyd County, Ky At nine o'clock Sunday morning, December 15th, the Regiment left Camp Chase for the railroad depot at Columbus, and before three o'clock p.m., that day, was on the way to Cincinnati, where it arrived at nine in the evening. There Col. GARFIELD received a telegram from General BUELL, directing him to send the Regiment by steamer to Cattlettsburg, Ky., at the mouth of the Big Sandy, and to report in person at his headquarters.

On the evening of the 16th Col. GARFIELD reached Louisville, and sought Gen. BUELL at his headquarters. He found a cold, silent, austere man who asked a few direct questions, revealed nothing, and eyed the new comer with a curious, searching expression as though trying to look into the untried Colonel and divine whether he would succeed or fail. Taking a map, Gen. BUELL pointed out the positions of MARSHALL's forces in Eastern Kentucky, marked the locations at which the Union troops in that district were posted, explained the nature of the country and its supplies, and then dismissed his visitor with the remark: "If you were in command of the sub-department of Eastern Kentucky, what would you do? Come here at nine o'clock to-morrow morning and tell me." Col. GARFIELD returned to his hotel, procured a map of Kentucky, the last census report, paper, pen and ink, and sat down to his task. He studied the roads, resources and population of every county in Eastern Kentucky. At daylight he was still at work, but at nine o'clock he was at Gen. BUELL's headquarters with a sketch of his plans. BUELL read it and made it the basis of his Special Order, No. 35, Army of the Ohio, December 17th, 1861, by which the 18th Brigade, Army of the Ohio, was organized, consisting of the 42d O. V. I., Col. J. A. GARFIELD commanding brigade; 40th O. V. I., Col. J. CRANOR; 14th Kentucky V. I., Col. L. D. F. MOORE; 22d Kentucky V. I., Col. D. W. LINDSAY; a squadron of Ohio Cavalry, two companies, under Major MCLAUGHLIN, and three squadrons, (six companies) of the 1st Kentucky Cavalry, Lieut.-Col. LETCHER commanding. The following autograph letter of instructions was issued to him on the evening of the 17th:

HEADQUARTERS DEPARTMENT OF THE OHIO,
LOUISVILLE, KY., December 17th, 1861.

SIR:

The Brigade organized under your command, is intended to operate against the Rebel force threatening, and indeed, actually committing depredations in Kentucky, through the Valley of the Big Sandy. The actual force of the enemy, from the best information I can gather, does not probably exceed two thousand, or two thousand five hundred, though rumor places it as high as seven thousand. I can better ascertain the true state of the case when you get on the ground.

You are apprised of the position of the troops under your command. Go first to Lexington and Paris, and place the 40th Ohio Regiment in such position as will best give a moral support to the people in the Counties on the route to Prestonburgh and Piketon, and oppose any further advance of the enemy on that route. Then proceed with the least possible delay to the mouth of the Sandy, and move, with the force in that vicinity, up that river and drive the enemy back or cut him off. Having done that, Piketon will probably be in the best position for you to occupy to guard against future incursions. Artillery will be of little, if any, service to you in that country. If the enemy have any it will encumber and weaken, rather than strengthen them.

Your supplies must mainly be taken up the river, and it ought to be done as soon as possible, while the navigation is open. Purchase what you can in the country through which you operate. Send your requisitions to these headquarters for funds and advance stores, and to the Quartermasters and Commissary at Cincinnati for other supplies.

The conversation I have had with you will suggest more details than can be given here. Report frequently on all matters concerning your command.

Very Respectfully,
Your Obedient Servant,
D. C. BUELL,
Brigadier-General Commanding.

The campaign in the Sandy Valley, the battle of Middle Creek, the capture of Pound Gap, and the part taken by Col. GARFIELD in the operations of that Winter, form an important chapter in the body of this narrative. During the Winter he was promoted to a Brigadier-Generalship of Volunteers, his commission to date from the 10th of January, the date of the victory at Middle Creek.

The campaign in the Valley of the Big Sandy being completed, Gen. GARFIELD with the Forty-Second and two other regiments of his brigade returned by way of the Ohio river to Louisville, reaching that city on the 1st of April. He received an order assigning his command to the Seventh Division, Army of the Ohio, then assembling under Gen GEO W. MORGAN at Cumberland Ford, and directing Gen GARFIELD to report in person to Major-Gen. BUELL, commanding the Army of the Ohio. BUELL was then *en route* with his army from Nashville to join the forces of Gen GRANT near Corinth, and Gen GARFIELD reported for duty to that officer while on the march, thirty-three miles beyond Columbia. He was at once assigned to the command of the Twentieth Brigade, Army of the Ohio, and though feeling severely the affliction of being separated from his own regiment, which he had done so much to create and inspire, he swallowed his disappointment and, with the hope that the fortunes of war might yet bring himself and the Forty-Second into the same army if not into the relation of commander and command, he took his place at the head of his new brigade, which included the following regiments: 64th Ohio Infantry, 65th Ohio Infantry, 13th Michigan Infantry, and 51st Indiana Infantry.

The command made forced marches to Savannah and proceeded thence by steamers to Pittsburgh Landing, where it arrived at one o'clock, p m., of the second day of the battle. Gen GARFIELD'S brigade reached the front about three o'clock in the afternoon, an Iowa regiment being temporarily assigned to it, by order of Gen. GRANT. On the 8th of April his brigade was detailed with other forces to make an advance on the Bark road towards Corinth, and had a sharp encounter with the enemy's rear guard. It took part in all the operations near Corinth and the brigade was among the earliest to enter that place.

In the month of June he marched Eastward from Corinth to Decatur with his command and rebuilt the bridges and trestlework that had been destroyed on the railroad between those two points. It crossed the river at Decatur, and encamped at Mooresville, Ala, early in July.

By Special Order No 15, 6th Division Army of the Ohio, of June 15th, 1862, Gen GARFIELD was made President of the General Court Martial for the trial of Lieut JOSEPH GRANT, 58th Indiana Volunteers.

By Special Order, No 93, Army of the Ohio, of July 5th, 1862, he was made President of the General Court Martial for the trial of Col TURCHIN, of the 19th Illinois Volunteers, and others, Capt. P. T. SWAIN of the 19th Infantry, Judge Advocate The Court held its sessions at Athens, Ala.

During the Summer, he had suffered for several weeks with chronic diarrhoea, and by Special Order, No 118, Army of the Ohio, of July 30th, 1862, went home on sick leave. Shortly after his arrival in Ohio, he received a telegram from the Secretary of War, directing him to proceed to Cumberland Gap and relieve Gen MORGAN of his command. But he was unable to obey the order, being confined to his bed by serious illness.

Soon after this he received a telegram from the Secretary of War, as follows:

WASHINGTON, September 1st, 1862.

Brigadier-General J A GARFIELD,
       Hiram, Ohio

As soon as your health permits you will report in person to this Department for orders.

E M STANTON,
Secretary of War

In accordance with this order, he reported to the Secretary of War in person, late in September, 1862

By Special Order of October 25th, 1862, he was detailed as a member of the Court of Inquiry in Gen. McDOWELL's case.

By Special Order of November 8th, 1862, he was ordered to report to Gen. HUNTER for duty on a contemplated expedition to

South Carolina. This order, however, was subsequently superseded, and by Special Order, No. 362, of November 25th, 1862, he was detailed as a member of the General Court Martial for the trial of Major-General FITZ JOHN PORTER, and served on that Court during its sessions.

By Special Order, of January 14th, 1863, Gen. GARFIELD was assigned to duty in the Army of the Cumberland, under Major-General ROSECRANS. He reached the headquarters of that Army at Murfreesboro, near the end of February.

By Department General Orders of February 28th. 1863, he was assigned to duty as Chief of Staff of the Army of the Cumberland, in place of the lamented Col. GARESCHE, who had been killed in in the battle of Stone River. Early in the Spring of that year Capt. D. G. SWAIN, his Adjutant-General since the previous April, was directed to organize a Bureau of Military Information. By a system of police and scout reports, very full and trust-worthy information was obtained of the organization, strength and position of the enemy's forces.

Early in June the General Commanding required each General of a Corps and Division of the Army of the Cumberland, to report his opinions in writing in reference to an early or immediate advance against the forces of Gen. BRAGG. Seventeen general officers submitted written opinions on that subject. Most of them were adverse to any early movement and nearly all advised against an immediate advance. Gen. GARFIELD presented to the Commanding General an analysis and review of these opinions, and urged an immediate movement against the enemy. For more than five months the Army of ROSECRANS had lain inactive at Murfreesboro while the Commanding General had haggled and bandied words with the War Department. As Chief of Staff, Gen. GARFIELD did all that adroit diplomacy could do to soften these asperities, and meanwhile gave all his energy to the work of preparing the Army for an advance, and ascertaining the strength of the enemy.

His Bureau of Military Information was the most perfect machine of the kind organized in the field during the War. When at last June came, the Government and the people demanding an advance, and the seventeen subordinate generals of ROSECRANS advising against it, the analysis of the situation drawn up and submitted by Gen. GARFIELD, met and overthrew them all. Speaking of this letter, Mr. WHITELAW REID in his " Ohio in the War," says: " This report we venture to pronounce the ablest military document known to have been submitted by a Chief of Staff to his superior during the War.' This is high praise, but it is history.

Twelve days after it was submitted the Army moved—against the will and opinion of Gen. CRITTENDEN and nearly all ROSECRANS' leading officers. It marched into the Tullahoma campaign, one of the most perfectly planned and ably executed movements of the War. The lateness of the start, caused by the objections which Gen. GARFIELD'S letter finally overcame, alone saved BRAGG'S army from destruction. There was a certain work to do, which might as well have been begun on the 1st of June as the 24th. Had it been begun on the first of these dates, BRAGG'S army might in all probability have been destroyed. As it was, the heavy rains intervened and saved him from pursuit.

With his military reputation thus strengthened, Gen. GARFIELD went with his chief into the battle of Chickamauga. His influence over ROSECRANS had by this time become almost supreme. His clear and comprehensive mind grasped every detail, and his opinions were invariably consulted on all important questions. He wrote many orders upon his own judgment, submitting them to ROSECRANS for approval or alteration. On the field of Chickamauga he wrote every order except one, and that one was the fatal order to Gen WOOD which ruined ROSECRANS' right wing and lost the battle. The order from ROSECRANS to WOOD, as the latter interpreted it, required him to move his command behind another division, leaving a wide gap in the line of McCOOK's Corps, which held the right. WOOD says that he knew this move would be fatal, but it was ordered and he felt impelled to execute it LONGSTREET saw the blunder, hurled HOOD's division into the gap, and within an hour McCOOK's Corps was broken and streaming, a disorganized mob of men, back to Chattanooga. Trying vainly to check the tide of retreat, Gen GARFIELD was swept with his chief back beyond Rossville. But the Chief of Staff could not concede that defeat had been entire He heard the roar of THOMAS' guns on the left, and gained permission of ROSECRANS to go round to that quarter and find the Army of the Cumberland While the Commander busied himself with preparing a refuge at Chattanooga for his routed army, his Chief of Staff went back, accompanied only by a staff officer and a few orderlies, to find whatever part of the army still held its ground and save what there was left. It was a perilous ride Long before he reached THOMAS one of his orderlies was killed Almost alone he pushed on over the obstructed road, through pursuers and pursued, found the heroic THOMAS encircled by fire but still firm, told him of the disaster on the right and explained how he could withdraw his right wing and fix it upon a new line to meet LONGSTREET's column, which had turned the right of THOMAS' position and was marching in heavy column upon his rear The movement was made just in time, but THOMAS' line was too short, it would not reach to the base of the mountain. LONGSTREET saw the gap, drove his column into it and would have struck THOMAS' line fatally in the rear, but in that critical moment Gen GORDON GRANGER came up with STEADMAN's division, which moved in heavy column, threw itself upon LONGSTREET, and after a terrific struggle drove him back. The dead and wounded lay in heaps where those two columns met, but the Army of Gen THOMAS was saved As night closed in around the heroic Army of the Cumberland, Gens GARFIELD and GRANGER, on foot and enveloped in smoke, directed the loading and pointing of a battery of Napoleon guns, whose flash, as they thundered after the retreating column of the assailants, was the last light that shone upon the battle field of Chickamauga The struggle was over, and the Rebels retired repulsed. Had the two shattered corps of McCOOK and CRITTENDEN that night been brought upon the field and enabled THOMAS to hold his ground, there might have been a second day to that battle which would have changed its complexion in history.

The battle of Chickamauga practically closed Gen GARFIELD's military career About four weeks after the engagement he was sent by ROSECRANS to Washington to report minutely to the President and the War Department the position, needs, resources and capabilities of the army at Chattanooga. He went, had frequent lengthy interviews with the President and Secretary STANTON, and thus, point by point, made a most thorough and satisfactory report. Meanwhile, Gen GARFIELD had been promoted to a Major-Generalship of Volunteers "for gallant and meritorious services at the battle of Chickamauga," to take rank from the 19th of September, 1863 ROSECRANS had been removed from the command of the Army at Chattanooga and Gen GRANT appointed to his place.

Gen GARFIELD was now called to a new field of duty. In October of the year previous, while the Forty-Second was retreating from Cumberland Gap, the people of the Nineteenth Congressional District of Ohio had elected him as their representative to the Thirty-Eighth Congress

He was a Major-General, young, popular in the army, and in high favor at Washington ; he was poor and his army pay was double the slender salary of a Congressman, but he had been chosen by the people of his District as their representative under circumstances which in his judgment would not permit him to decline the trust. Gen THOMAS offered him the command of a corps, but LINCOLN urged him to resign his commission and come to Congress. The President was strenuous and his advice prevailed. There was no want of Major-Generals, but there was need of all the zeal, courage and ability that could be assembled in Congress. So his friends argued, and the sequel proved the wisdom of their demand upon him. Yielding to this, he resigned his commission on the 5th of December, 1863, having served in the army more than a year after his election to Congress, and took his seat on the same day in the House of Representatives, where he has been in continuous service since that day.

The influence of Gen GARFIELD upon the Forty-Second Regiment was unbounded. As Colonel, not less than as Professor and Principal of a Collegiate School, he evinced a rare and extraordinary power in controlling, interesting and inspiring young men. It was due largely to his enthusiastic efforts that the Regiment was made up of some of the best material that Ohio sent into the field. The careful, laborious education, the discipline, the quickening of individual self-respect that the Regiment underwent at his hands while in Camp Chase, were never lost upon its men. Long after he had gone to other duties the recollection of his words was a source of inspiration to the men, and as they went into their first fight at Middle Creek against overwhelming numbers with serene confidence because their trusted Colonel had sent them, so afterwards they fought and marched as though conscious that the eye of their first commander was still upon them.

LIONEL A. SHELDON,

The first Lieutenant-Colonel of the Forty-Second, but during more than two years and a half its highest officer, was born in Worcester, Otsego County, N. Y., August 3d, 1830. He was the eighth in a family of eleven children. His immediate ancestors on both sides were of Revolutionary stock, and Col. SHELDON's excellent military career only continued a family record that had begun as far back as the capture of Andre. While he was quite young his parents brought him to Ohio and settled in Lorain County, where LIONEL attended district school until his services were needed on the farm. Thenceforward he worked at home during the Summer seasons, attending school during the Winters until his eighteenth year, when he had by working out at $8.00 per month earned enough to enable him to study for two consecutive terms at a select school. After this he taught district school during the Winter and in the Spring, Summer and Fall studied at Oberlin. Three months after his twenty-first birthday he was elected Justice of the Peace, which office he held for a year and a half, working hard all the time at his legal studies under the supervision of Messrs. CLARKE and BURKE, then a leading legal firm of Elyria. In the Spring of 1853, young SHELDON went to Poughkeepsie, studied two terms in the law school there, returned home in the Fall of the same year, and opened a law office on his own account. From that time his progress as an attorney was rapid and substantial, and the year 1861 found him one of the leading citizens of Elyria. Three years before the outbreak of the War he had been elected Brigadier-General of the Militia of Lorain County, and commissioned as such by Governor CHASE. It was natural, therefore, that when the State Government began to call upon that County in 1861 for men to resist the Rebellion, it should have called early upon Col. SHELDON. He responded promptly, made speeches to rouse the people, and under special authority of Governor DENNISON, raised five companies in six days for the three months service. He was at that time busy with a large and growing legal practice, was married to a charming wife, and surrounded by various cares and pleasures that made it difficult for him to leave everything behind and enter the army. He declined to do this for the three months service, but promised that if the revolt proved formidable and troops for a longer period were needed, he would go

The call for three years regiments soon came. Col SHELDON laid aside his civil pursuits and gave himself up to the work of strengthening the army. He assisted in raising six companies for various regiments, and when the Wade and Hutchins Cavalry was authorized he organized a squadron for that command. A dispute arose between the members of the squadron about officers SHELDON accepted the Captaincy himself to prevent the men from disbanding, as they had not yet been mustered in and could not be held to service against their will. He took the company to Camp Chase, was mustered in, and made Major of the third battalion. Being wholly inexperienced in military matters, and the Wade and Hutchins Regiment being nearly ready to take the field, Major SHELDON felt somewhat unprepared for his new and responsible trust While ready to do his utmost for the cause, he felt that a place in an infantry regiment, which would give him more time for study and preparation, would be better, both for himself and the good of the service He had a natural and creditable feeling of unwillingness to wear the uniform of an office which he could not from the first moment of taking the field, competently fill

Talking these matters over in a friendly way with Governor DENNISON, he was told that if he preferred infantry he could have the Lieutenant-Colonelcy of the Thirty-First Regiment, then nearly ready to leave camp, or of the Forty-Second, then only a paper organization, the Colonelcy of which the Governor had determined to give to State Senator GARFIELD. SHELDON and GARFIELD were introduced to each other by State Senator MONROE, who knew both intimately and was sure that they would supplement each other admirably in the organization and command of a regiment. Hon. HERMAN CANFIELD was at the same time in Columbus urging for a field position Mr DON A PARDEE, a graduate of the Naval Academy at Annapolis. The three were mutually pleased with each other, and the commissions were made out appointing Col GARFIELD, Lieut Col SHELDON and Major PARDEE, and assigning them to the Forty Second Infantry.

Col SHELDON returned at once to Lorain County and recruited a company, which came down with CHAS. H HOWE as Captain, GEO F BRADY as 1st Lieutenant and MELVILLE I BENHAM as 2d Lieutenant. The organization became Company "E" of the Forty-Second, one of the finest drilled infantry companies in the service. It won the first prize of the Army of the Mississippi in 1863, against the crack veteran regiments of all the Western States.

Returning to Camp Chase, Col. SHELDON gave himself up to the study of military tactics and the duties of his new position. He was from the first an admirable administrative officer, and became immediately popular. When the Forty-Second left Cincinnati for its first campaign, Col. GARFIELD was in command of a brigade and Col. SHELDON commanded the Regiment. He had been sent in advance to Cincinnati to secure transportation to the mouth of the Big Sandy, and as the regiment passed through that city Col. GARFIELD was ordered to Louisville for instructions. Col SHELDON then took his place at the head of the Forty-Second, a place which he held, except while commanding brigade or disabled by sickness, during the remaining time of the Regiment's service. Col SHELDON's qualities as a commander in camp were remarkable. While at Camp Chase and during the first two years of service in the field, his "officers' school" was kept up. Each afternoon the line officers not on actual duty assembled at the Colonel's to recite, discuss and learn their duty in all situations incident to service. Officers of other regiments dropped in at times to listen to these interesting recitations and said as they went away, "No wonder those Forty-Second men know how to soldier." His firm and exact justice between the men and officers of different companies, his equable administration of penalties for petty offences, and his active sympathy and concern for every man in the Regiment, down to the humblest teamster, made Col SHELDON a model administrative officer. He was one of the perhaps half-dozen Colonels in the entire Union Army who knew by name every member of his Regiment.

While at Memphis in December, 1862, Col SHELDON was detached and placed in command of a brigade of new troops, which included the Sixty-Ninth Indiana, the One Hundred and Eighteenth Illinois and the One Hundred and Twentieth Ohio. With the consent of Lieut.-Col PARDEE he detailed Adjutant W. H. CLAPP of the Forty-Second as his Assistant Adjutant-General The brigade behaved admirably in the four days fighting at Chickasaw Bayou, charging across the first bayou on the 28th, and winning from the enemy the ground over which BLAIR's brigade made its assault on the 29th In the dispositions for attack on the 29th it had been arranged that the brigade of which SHELDON was commander should cross by a pontoon bridge, to be laid across the creek early in the morning Every effort was made to lay the bridge, under a heavy fire from the enemy's artillery and sharp-shooters, but the boats were heavy, the enemy's shells soon sunk two of them, and the bridge would not span the bayou By this accident, which a competent pontoon train would have obviated, this brigade was kept out of the attack Col SHELDON stood and watched with aching heart the Forty-Second, his own Regiment, eight hundred strong, moving forward in DECOURCY's

Brigade to an assault which he knew must be a useless sacrifice of brave men, and he watched with a feeling of pride its return from the fiery ordeal in perfect order, covering the retreat as handsomely as though the evolutions had been made on parade.

At Arkansas Post, Col SHELDON's Brigade held the extreme left of the Federal line, resting on the river below the fort. He pushed two of his regiments so close up to the ditch that by lying on the ground ready to fire at the first enemy that appeared, they practically silenced the Rebel fire along that part of the works. When finally the assault was ordered, DeCourcy's Brigade came up in column, the Forty-Second in front, and Col SHELDON, who knew the ground, was asked by DeCourcy to include the Forty-Second Ohio and the Twenty-Second Kentucky in his command. He did so, but the immediate surrender which followed obviated the necessity of an assault.

In the re-organization of the Army at Young's Point in February, 1863, the three brigades in MORGAN's Corps were consolidated into two and constituted a division, commanded by Brig.-Gen. P. J. OSTERHAUS. Col SHELDON commanded the Second Brigade, made up of the Sixteenth, Forty Second and One Hundred and Fourteenth Ohio, the Twenty-Second Kentucky and Fifty-Fourth Indiana Regiments. He commanded the brigade during the advance down the river and led it into the battle at Thompson's Hill near Port Gibson.

During the early part of that action he received a peculiar and painful, though not dangerous wound. While advancing the brigade up the hill under heavy fire, Col SHELDON grasped a small shrub for support in climbing. At that moment a musket ball struck and shattered the trunk, driving his hand full of splinters and giving it a sharp, sudden shock. He remained in command during the day, however, and led the brigade in two gallant charges upon the enemy's position. While in camp at Fourteen

Mile Creek a few days afterward, his wound became so painful as to keep Col. SHELDON from duty and even threatened the loss of his hand. He remained an unwilling inmate of the ambulance during the memorable swoop of GRANT'S Army through Raymond, Jackson and Black River Bridge to the rear of Vicksburgh. On the 24th of May, the beginning of the siege, he returned to the command of the Forty-Second, Col. LINDSEY of the Twenty-Second Kentucky, the ranking Colonel of the brigade, having returned from leave of absence and taken command of it while the corps lay at Fourteen Mile Creek. He commanded the Regiment through the siege and on its sudden march to Black River Bridge to meet JOHNSTON's apprehended attack. While there, on the 5th of July, Col SHELDON was taken seriously ill with typho-malarial fever, terminating in ague. His illness continued for fifty days, and it was not until the 29th of August that he rejoined the Regiment at New Orleans, still shaking with the ague.

On the 6th of September he again took command of the old brigade and was ordered to Plaquemine, on the Mississippi river 110 miles North of New Orleans, where the brigade spent the Winter, guarding the river and adjacent country from the raids of WALKER, who commanded a force of six thousand men stationed thirty miles inland. The brigade built a fort during the Winter, and made several expeditions into the surrounding country, during which between forty and fifty prisoners were captured. Early in April the command was ordered to Baton Rouge, and Col. SHELDON commanded that department until the 15th of July, when the Forty-Second was ordered to the mouth of White River. On the expiration of the Regiment's term of service in September Col. SHELDON repaired to New Orleans, where he resigned his commission late in November and returned to civil life. In March, 1865, he was brevetted Brigadier-General of Volunteers in an order recognizing his services during his military career. It

was a well earned honor, worthily bestowed. He decided to locate in New Orleans, where he soon took a high position as a lawyer. In 1868 he was elected to Congress, and was re-elected in 1870 and '72, leading his ticket in the last election by about three thousand votes. His services in Congress were of great value to Louisiana, and he is still an honored and useful citizen of that State.

DON A. PARDEE.

Don Albert Pardee, first Major, and subsequently Lieutenant-Colonel of the Forty-Second, was born in Wadsworth, Medina County, Ohio, in March, 1837. His father, a native of Onondaga County, New York, emigrated to Ohio at the age of sixteen, and became one of the most worthy and influential citizens of Medina County.

Col. Pardee's early years were passed in work upon his father's farm, and attending the neighboring district school where the foundation of his education was laid. In his fifteenth year he began teaching school, but soon after the close of his first term received the appointment of acting midshipman in the United States Navy and reported for duty at the Naval Academy at Annapolis. Up to this time he had never been more than fifty miles from home, and the transfer to Annapolis formed an interesting and important epoch in his life.

He passed the preliminary examinations easily and at once took a high position in his class, ranking number two at the end of the first year, and number one thereafter, but in 1857 he resigned his appointment voluntarily to follow a civil life. While at the Academy he maintained his standing by his proficiency in mathematics, infantry, artillery and naval tactics, gunnery and the languages. He made two cruises at sea on the United States sloop of war, *Preble*—once coasting along the United States from Eastport, Maine. South to the Carolinas, and once visiting the Azores Islands. On resigning from the Naval Academy, the profession of the law as a livelihood was immediately determined upon, and Col. PARDEE entered the office of his father for reading and study. His father was a lawyer of ability, with a large general practice, and the opportunity thus afforded to the son was timely and valuable.

At the age of twenty-two he was admitted to the bar at the Fall term of the District Court sitting at Medina, and soon after removed there to commence practice. Almost immediately he formed a partnership with the Hon. HERMAN CANFIELD, an able lawyer just returned from the Ohio State Senate. This partnership was a prosperous one, and continued until both partners entered the volunteer service—CANFIELD joining the 72d Ohio Volunteers and PARDEE the Forty-Second. Col. PARDEE married in February, 1861, an old school-mate, Miss JULIA HARD of Wadsworth, Ohio. When the first volunteers were called for in 1861, he was offered a captaincy in a volunteer regiment and also a reinstatement in his own class in the navy; but although anxious to go, the health of his wife, then suffering under a dangerous and lingering illness, made it impossible for him to leave home, and both these advantageous offers were declined. But when the first battle of Bull Run left it doubtful whether the Northern men were cowards, there could be no longer delay, and his wife's health having somewhat improved, he applied for a commission in the army. Through Senator CANFIELD he was soon commissioned Major of the 44th Ohio. In September, 1861, Messrs. GARFIELD and SHELDON were organizing the Forty-Second, and the scholarship and ability of the young men then flocking to their standard required talents of no common order in their superiors. Col.

GARFIELD, seeing in the young Major a natural aptness for command and also that he possessed a valuable knowledge of infantry tactics, determined to secure him, and with PARDEE's consent he was transferred to the Forty Second. He soon reported for duty at Camp Chase, and became at once a valuable officer in the management of military affairs in camp, being able to drill regiments or companies, and having what was of even greater importance, correct ideas of discipline. Captain, afterwards Major, W H WILLIAMS having recruited a fine body of men in Medina County, Major PARDEE secured that Company which became the Company "B" of the Regiment. With Col GARFIELD he also raised large numbers of men in Medina County for Companies "G" and "K"

At Camp Chase the Major was distinguished for his healthy and correct discipline, the necessity of which volunteers could not then understand. Determined and cool, he could always enforce discipline when occasion required. A company of recruits, a few days after entering camp, procured liquor, and became noisy and turbulent. The Major sent a corporal and three men to arrest the rioters. The corporal and guard soon returned with information that the entire company resisted interference, and as they had fire-arms which they threatened to use, arrest would be dangerous. The Major with the same guard proceeded to the scene of disturbance, coolly disarmed and arrested the noisy men and marched them to the guard house.

In the Sandy Valley campaign Major PARDEE rendered conspicuous service. On the arrival of the Forty-Second at Cattlettsburg, Ky, it was found that the 14th Kentucky had retreated down the river without being sure whether HUMPHREY MARSHALL had advanced with five thousand or five hundred men, and the refugees who followed after could give no reliable information. The senior officers who had been in command in that region seemed disposed to credit the most extravagant rumors as to the force occupying Louisa Court House. The Major obtained permission to take forty men and find out something definite concerning the strength of the enemy. In company with Captains F. A. WILLIAMS and W. H. WILLIAMS and forty picked men, mounted on quartermaster's horses, he started with a guide about dusk, and captured the town of Louisa before daylight the next morning from the 4th Virginia Union Cavalry, which had occupied the town since the preceding evening. That the expedition was not dangerous it is easy to see now; at the time it was well calculated to test the nerve of both officers and men. The Major assisted in pushing the column up the river, and his voice was always for a forward movement.

In the battle of Middle Creek his bravery, together with the gallant conduct of Capt. F. A. WILLIAMS, enabled Col. GARFIELD to defeat MARSHALL's overwhelming numbers on the chosen ground of the enemy. He also commanded the Forty Second at the capture of Pound Gap, heading his Regiment in the laborious ascent of the mountains to gain the ridge and flank the enemy.

In the Cumberland Gap campaign the Major, then Lieutenant-Colonel, commanded by special selection the force of six picked companies sent in the night to capture Roger's Gap, preparatory to the army's crossing the mountains to attack Cumberland Gap from the rear. This movement was faithfully and discreetly executed by a rapid, forced march, and the Gap held until the army came up. The mountains were climbed by Col. PARDEE and his force in the night by a steep, winding path, unknown to a single man of the command, and with a single guide, whose fidelity was seriously doubted, and the force holding the pass above unknown. It tried the nerve and discipline of every man in the expedition, and the commander and his men—three companies from each of the Forty Second and Sixteenth Ohio—were well selected. Gen. MORGAN was pleased to say that it was a most hazardous and dangerous movement, and none but brave men could have accomplished it successfully

In Col DeCourcy's expedition to Tazewell, Tenn, Col PARDEE commanded the four hundred selected men from the Forty Second At Big Springs, beyond Tazewell, he was left with one hundred and ninety men to hold the road to Bean Station, while DECOURCY with the train and two regiments went several miles Westward for forage Being instructed to hold the road until sunset, he was attacked about noon by a brigade of infantry, a squadron of cavalry and a battery of artillery, forming the advance of that large Rebel army which afterwards overran Kentucky to the Ohio river, defeating the Union forces at Richmond, isolating MORGAN's army of the Gap and threatening Cincinnati Instead of retreating as many a brave man might have done, PARDEE deployed his entire force as skirmishers, and so managed to deceive the enemy that the requisite time was gained, and in the language of Gen MORGAN "A train of two hundred wagons loaded with forage was saved, and Col DECOURCY's entire command saved from being flanked and cut off from the Gap" Both Col. PARDEE and the Regiment were complimented in Division and Brigade General Orders for their conduct on this occasion.

In the Kanawha Valley campaign in the Fall of 1862, after reaching Charleston, Col. PARDEE was detailed as Provost Marshal of that place, which post he held until his division was ordered down the river At Memphis, Col. SHELDON being detached to command a brigade, Col. PARDEE commanded the Regiment in the Sherman expedition against Vicksburgh, in December, 1862, and also in the expedition against Arkansas Post in the following January.

At Chickasaw Bayou during the week of constant fighting and exposure, Col. PARDEE was constantly with his regiment, leading his men in several gallant charges, and finally, on the day of the disastrous assault on the enemy's works, led the Forty Second in the attack, and out of nine regiments assaulting together, the Forty-Second was the only regiment that came off the field with unbroken ranks When the order was given to retreat Col PARDEE, with his Regiment under heavy fire, gave his orders almost as on parade *Forty-Second Regiment, Halt ! Face by the Rear Rank. About Face ! Forward, Guide Center, March !* His rigid discipline, that had been arduous to many, was always appreciated after that day, and "OLD PARDEE," as the young Lieutenant-Colonel was sometimes called, became from that time a pet name of endearment and affection with the men. The exposure at Chickasaw, and the malaria of the swamps, brought on an attack of fever and dysentery which at last put Col PARDEE on the sick list As soon as the re-embarkation of the troops was effected, and for a few days, the doctors comforted him with the assurance that he would probably die. Not having recovered so as to be on duty when the expedition arrived at Arkansas Post, he knew nothing until he heard the guns opening the fight. He immediately left his bed, dressed and mounted "Charley" to take command of his Regiment Coming up with Surgeon POMERLNE, that excellent physician peremptorily commanded his immediate return to boat, none to soon, for on reaching the boat he fainted and was carried from his horse, back to bed The next day, however, he was out again, and, although two months were spent in recovering, he persisted in doing duty.

On reaching Young's Point, Col. SHELDON returned to the Regiment and Col. PARDEE was detailed as Provost Marshal of the 13th Army Corps. He held this position until the forward movement below Vicksburgh was commenced, when at the special request of Gen OSTERHAUS, Division Commander, he was returned to his Regiment to take command, Col SHELDON being again in command of the Brigade At Perkins' Plantation the sick, lame and convalescent were left behind and the Forty-Second crossed the Mississippi with over six hundred and ninety men, every man able and willing to march his forty miles and carry three days rations and sixty rounds

At Grand Gulf the Forty-Second was selected to lead the assault on the enemy's works as soon as the gunboats should succeed in silencing the batteries The Regiment was held in readiness on a transport with steam up, and enjoyed a fine view of the evolutions and firing of the gunboats

At Port Gibson, Col. PARDEE handled the Regiment as skilfully as the work given him to do would allow, and twice went where the danger was such that he would send no man. Two of the charges ordered were known by the Colonel to be useless, but they were made with the same enthusiasm and determined bravery as though the fate of the army had depended upon them The seventy-five brave men killed and wounded attested the exposure of the Regiment For his conduct in this engagement Col PARDEE was highly complimented by Gen OSTERHAUS and recommended for promotion. During one of the lulls in the battle, although the enemy were firing briskly, the men of the Forty-Second were amused by observing Col PARDEE and a General of a Division, who were sitting near each other in an exposed place When a ball whistled by, the one paid no attention whatever, while the other invariably dodged.

Just after this engagement Col. LINDSEY resumed command of the Brigade, Col SHELDON returned to the Regiment, and Col PARDEE was detailed as Inspector-General of the 13th Army Corps. He served in this capacity, performing all kinds of staff service as well as his own particular duty, until the latter part of June, when his eyes from granulated lids became so weak and painful that both had to be kept closed and covered

While on staff service he was present at all the engagements up to the investment of Vicksburgh. In the assault of the 22d of May, he was, at the special request of Gen. OSTERHAUS, as well as his own, temporarily relieved from staff duty to take command of the Regiment.

He found in the ranks two hundred and sixty-seven of the six hundred and ninety able-bodied men who left Perkins' Plantation but a few weeks before. Col. SHELDON was disabled with a wounded hand, Major WILLIAMS was sick, and Col. PARDEE'S return was welcomed with enthusiastic cheers. Under his inspiring influence every man cheered up, and once more gallantly charged or assaulted where every man knew there could be no result but danger and repulse. The next day he returned to his staff duties and was almost continually in the saddle among heat and dust until his eyes both failed and he was given sick leave. During his journey from Vicksburgh to his home the ice was not removed from his eyes except to change the bandages.

In the following August, although not recovered, he rejoined his Regiment at Carrollton, La. The Division being about to move out to Brashear and the Teche country, he was assigned to the command of the convalescent camp of the 13th Corps

He remained at this post until the camp was broken up, when he and Lieut. HENRY were assigned to duty in the Provost Marshal's Department and ordered at once to Baton Rouge. There, for nearly one year, the responsible and delicate duties of Provost Marshal and Provost Judge were performed by Col. PARDEE and his assistant, Lieut. HENRY, in such a faithful and intelligent manner as to win the approval and confidence of both the Government and the people.

Relieved from duty as Provost Marshal in September, 1863, Col PARDEE rejoined his Regiment at Morganza, La, and thence proceeded to White River, Ark., and finally to Duvall's Bluff, at all of which places the duty performed was mainly post duty, and furnished no opportunity for action.

Gen PARDEE entered the service as Major, September 5th, 1861, was promoted to Lieutenant-Colonel, March 14th, 1862, and was mustered out November 25th, 1864. He was brevetted Colonel and Brigadier-General for faithful, gallant and meritorious services, to date from March 13th, 1865.

He is now serving his second term as District Judge of the Second Judicial District of Louisiana. He resides at Carrollton, La., and is highly respected throughout the State.

WILLIAM H. WILLIAMS

WILLIAM H. WILLIAMS, the original Captain of Company "B," and for two years and a half Major of the Forty-Second, was born in Lafayette Township, Medina County, Ohio, in May, 1836, his parents being among the earliest settlers of that district. He was reared to the usual life of a farmer's son, working during the Spring, Summer and Autumn months, and attending school during the Winters.

At the outbreak of the War in the Spring of 1861, Mr. WILLIAMS, who had been married during the year previous, at once sought to enlist, but the supply of Volunteers at that time far exceeded the demand, and, failing to find an immediate opportunity to enter the service, he was persuaded by the strong opposition of his family and the demands of his business affairs to wait a few weeks until it should be demonstrated whether the War was really a serious matter and would need all the men that were willing to go. During the Summer, however, he took an active part in organizing an independent company of militia, and, having a natural military taste, was made Captain of the organization. When after the disaster at Bull Run the call for three years troops was issued Capt. WILLIAMS assembled his Company, made the men a brief address setting forth the needs of the Government and asked all in the ranks who were willing to enter the service for three years or the War to step to the front. A number of the men stepped forward, and with these Capt. WILLIAMS went to the nearest recruiting station and enlisted. On the 3d of September he received a recruiting commission and proceeded to fill up his Company with the intention of joining the Forty-First Ohio under Col. HAZEN. About the middle of September, Capt. WILLIAMS met Major PARDEE, who had been appointed and assigned to the Forty-Second, and accepted his invitation to join that Regiment. On the 23d, the Volunteers assembled at Lafayette and proceeded by wagons to Grafton, where they took the cars for Columbus. The little squad was joined by a number of stalwart young men from the county, who had not yet enlisted but said they were going into the Army. Capt WILLIAMS procured transportation to Columbus for all who came, and on arrival there drew up his command, counted the men off and found that he had nearly a hundred volunteers, eighty-three of whom were accepted and sworn into service. These were just enough to organize a minimum Company. The new Company held an election and Mr. WILLIAMS, hitherto an enlisted man, was unanimously elected Captain and at once received his commission. The Company marched to Camp Chase and was assigned to the left flank of the Forty-Second as Company "B." It began the regular routine of drill and camp life, Capt WILLIAMS returning to Medina County on recruiting service, where he enlisted men enough to fill his own Company to the maximum, besides a number of others, who were assigned to Companies " G " and " K."

From the transfer of the Forty-Second to the field of active duty in December, 1861, until its final discharge from service, Capt WILLIAMS was constantly with it, often commanding the Regiment for weeks at a time during the absence of the other field officers upon other duty. He was commissioned Major in July, 1862, while the Regiment was in Southern Kentucky in the Division of Gen MORGAN. Col. GARFIELD had before this time been appointed Brigadier-General and transferred to another army. His place as Colonel was filled by the promotion of Lieut.-Col. SHELDON, who was succeeded as Lieutenant-Colonel by Major PARDEE. Both these officers were accomplished and able men, and were subject to frequent requisitions for detached duty. Col SHELDON was for several months at different times in command of the Brigade, and Lieut.-Col PARDEE was likewise frequently called, much against his will, to staff duty and other detached service. This gave Major WILLIAMS a large share of service in command of the Forty-Second while in camp and on the march, and during the latter part of its career he frequently commanded it in battle.

His first experience of this kind was at Arkansas Post in January, 1863, where after the capture of the works the Forty-Second was assigned to the work of guarding and disarming the six or seven thousand prisoners, a delicate task, as they were Texas troops and desperate under the humiliation of defeat. Major WILLIAMS put his Regiment in line around the prisoners and with Company "B," under Capt. POTTER, entered the enclosure and finally succeeded in gathering up the muskets and side arms of the prisoners.

At Young's Point the Regiment, still under command of Major WILLIAMS, was inspected about the middle of February, and was highly complimented for its excellent condition.

On the 3d of March, he took the Forty-Second down to the Young's Point Canal, opposite Vicksburgh, to perform its allotted task in digging that memorable ditch. The men had a pretty clear suspicion that the canal would prove abortive, and went to their task without much enthusiasm, but once there, they took hold with a will, and the Forty-Second did its proportion of the digging in eighteen hours—less time than any other regiment in the Army.

On the 8th of April, Major WILLIAMS commanded three companies of the Regiment in an important expedition up Roundaway Bayou in quest of cotton. The party went in clumsy flat boats, which the men poled across the submerged country, against currents, through forests and over fences, and finally, after severe labor returned with their boats laden, completely successful.

In the engagement at Thompson's Hill on the 1st of May, '63, Major WILLIAMS performed meritorious service, and came off the field at night unhurt, but with four bullet holes through his clothing. He had been sent during the afternoon with Company "B" to cover as skirmishers an important movement of the Brigade, and became hotly engaged with a greatly superior force. The troops were moved rapidly, and when the enemy had been driven back the detachment found itself separated from the Regiment. It found the Forty-Second in camp, long after dark, and learned that Company "B" had been given up as lost.

Immediately after the battle, in which Col. SHELDON had been wounded, Lieut.-Col. PARDEE was detailed for duty upon the Division Staff, and Major WILLIAMS was left in command of the Forty-Second. He led the Regiment through the exciting and important series of movements which preceded the siege of Vicksburgh. The battle of Champion Hills and the brilliant assault of the Rebel works at Black River Bridge, were included in this episode. At Champion Hills the Forty-Second was temporarily assigned to the Brigade of Gen. GARRETT in CARR'S Division, and ordered to move forward through a dense thicket, known to be strongly occupied by the enemy. Keeping in line with the regiments on either side, Major WILLIAMS pushed his men forward and soon became enveloped and concealed by the thick timber. Suddenly the Forty-Second came upon a heavy line of the enemy, who rose up out of the bushes and fired. The Ohioans replied at a distance of not more than a dozen paces. At that moment a general officer arrived to tell Major WILLIAMS that his supports on either wing had fallen behind and that he was in danger of capture. This was immediately apparent. The enemy were on three sides of the Forty-Second, and were trying to close round on its flanks. There was nothing to do but retire, which the Forty-Second did in good order, the men who had been in the brush coming back in obedience to orders without knowing any reason for the movement. The line was re-formed and again moved forward, driving the enemy through the woods and aiding in the rout and pursuit of PEMBERTON's army from that bloody field.

Major WILLIAMS remained in command of the Regiment during the brief but brilliant engagement at Black River Bridge, and after the victory assisted in bridging the stream. The Forty-Second was put at the head of the army and, crossing the river, skirmished up the hills and took possession of the heights beyond, the last defensive position, which had it been properly utilized, might have enabled PEMBERTON to resist the march of the column by the Jackson road to Vicksburgh. Continuing in the advance, the Forty-Second was one of the first regiments to reach the enemy's strong line of entrenchments outside the city, and during the 19th and 20th it performed some hazardous and important duty on the front line of the attack.

Preparations were at once made for the grand assault on the 22d. Officers and men detached from their regiments and companies were returned to their commands, and every organization strengthened to the utmost. Lieut.-Col. PARDEE returned to the command of the Forty-Second, and Major WILLIAMS, who had been for several days suffering from sickness, was relieved from duty for a few days, but did not leave the regimental camp.

On the 18th of June he was placed on duty in command of the picket lines in front of CARR's and SMITH's Divisions, an exceedingly delicate and responsible task, as the Federal trenches were rapidly advancing upon the hostile works and the enemy was using every means to drive the beseigers from their task

During the year of service on the lower Mississippi, after the fall of Vicksburgh and the capture of Jackson, Major WILLIAMS was often in command of the Regiment for weeks at a time, and until the last day of its service, maintained his reputation as a brave, faithful and deserving officer.

CHAPTER II.

ORIGIN AND ORGANIZATION OF REGIMENT—ITS ASSEMBLY AT CAMP CHASE—THE TRANSFORMATION FROM CITIZENS TO SOLDIERS

The Forty-Second Regiment of Ohio Volunteers was one of the products of that deep and earnest awakening of patriotism which followed the disaster at Bull Run. It was recruited and organized after the first feverish excitement which followed the attack on Sumter had passed, when the hopeful dream of a mere ninety days struggle had been dispelled by the pouring of a routed and disorganized Union Army into Washington, and when men of calm, clear judgment saw that the struggle was in reality one which would bury whole armies of men and tax to the farthest limit the resources of the loyal States. Its members assembled in camp and put on the garb of war at a time when it was yet an almost open question whether the men of the North were cowards in battle, as inferior in war to the hot blooded sons of the South as they were superior to them in the energy and intelligence which make a people prosperous and progressive. The men of the Forty-Second were not drawn into service by the glamour and romance which surrounded the earlier events of the War, when volunteers went forth to thirty days or three months service laden with flowers and blessings and chanted as heroes by their friends at home, but when it had become clear that the men who were to save the Government must give up the plans and pursuits of civil life, settle down to the work of becoming soldiers in deadly earnest and be thankful if at the end of the struggle they were left alive. "For three years or during the War," was a serious and comprehensive proposition to the farmer boy who had left his field, the student who had abandoned his unfinished course of study, and to the father who had left wife and babes dependent for support upon his meagre pittance as a soldier. There was no longer any romance or poetry in the life of the volunteer. The war that the country had expected to see decided by a single battle had gone from bad to worse. The terror of Bull Run had been succeeded by mortification and disaster at Ball's Bluff. It was evident that the Union Armies were in the hands of incompetents, and the volunteer as he signed the enlistment roll took the chances of being led by a blundering amateur general to useless slaughter. But it was no time to consider men's lives, and amid the depression and gloom that pervaded the Summer of 1861, the keel of the Forty-Second Regiment was laid.

Much of its earlier inspiration came from the "Eclectic Institute" at Hiram, of which Hon. J. A. GARFIELD, then a leading member of the Ohio Senate, was President. During the term which ended about the 1st of July the students had been reading the news from Virginia, studying Zouave tactics and practising the simpler evolutions of infantry by squads and companies on the College green. A few, unable to withstand the excitement, left school and entered three months regiments, but by the majority it was determined that if after Commencement the exigencies of the struggle demanded enlistments for a longer period, and President GARFIELD thought advisable, they would enlist for the War. It therefore happened that when late in August a meeting was called at the village church in Hiram, at which President GARFIELD spoke, not less than sixty names were signed to the enlistment roll within an hour. It was vacation, all but the resident students had dispersed, but hearing of the meeting many came back and enlisted during that evening. Others flocked to Ravenna where the headquarters of the company were removed, and within a week the student company was full and on its way to Columbus. From Medina came another splendid company of men under Capt W. H. WILLLIAMS, another from Ashland under Capt T C BUSHNELL, a fourth under Capt. J H RIGGS from Mount Ephraim, and the four companies already assigned to the Forty-Second Infantry were mustered into the service on the 25th of September. The students took the right of the line as Company "A," Capt. WILLIAMS' men were placed on the left as Company "B," Capt. BUSHNELL took the colors at the center as Company "C," and Capt RIGGS' men became Company "D."

The four hundred novices went into the rusty, white-washed barracks of Camp Chase, and without arms or uniforms began studying the mysteries of squad and company drill. Bacon and hard bread, coffee in tin cups without milk, beds on hard boards without sheets or mattresses, and the apparently aimless barbarism of turning out for roll call at six o'clock *reveille*, were rapidly mastered and patiently submitted to, and when on the 30th of October, Capt HOWE arrived from Elyria with Company "E," the four earlier Companies were quite content to be regarded as veterans. On the 2d of October they had been uniformed in dark blue trowsers, the course, ungainly blouse of the period, and fatigue caps, which not only had the peculiarity of changing to a light olive brown with exposure to the weather, but warped and shrank until they covered only the extreme top of the wearer's head. They had also performed their share of the monotonous guard duty of the camp, walking up and down their beats in the long line that encircled the barracks and parade ground, and learning the details of guard mounting and relief. There was already a strong feeling of emulation between the Companies, and before the men were provided with weapons they hewed out rough wooden muskets and began to practice the manual of arms Col GARFIELD, Lieut.-Col SHELDON and Major PARDEE had already been appointed and assigned to the Regiment, but at least two of them were for the first two months absent on recruiting duty, while the third remained in charge of the Companies thus far assembled. There were in camp at that time the Fortieth Infantry, already nearly complete in its organization, and the First Ohio Cavalry, the latter uniformed, armed and mounted

Company "F" arrived and was mustered into service on the 12th of November, and on the 26th Companies "G," "H," "I" and "K," were filled and the regimental organization thereby made complete The supply of clothing and all material for the fitting out of troops was at that time very limited and imperfect, and it was not until the 20th of November, long after snow and frost had come, that the men began to receive overcoats. Two days after that the knapsacks were issued, and on the 27th muskets and accoutrements. High hopes had been entertained that they might be armed with Harper's Ferry or Enfield rifles, the fear of being sent to the front with only smooth bore muskets having been the chief of all their troubles, imaginary or real, up to that time. The new muskets were neither smooth bores nor Enfields, but long, heavy rifles of Belgian manufacture, ponderous weapons to carry, but of great range and accuracy. Instead of the showy and formidable looking sabre bayonets for which the men had hoped, the new rifles had only the ordinary lance bayonet, so that their arms were on the whole a dissappointment.

During the latter part of November a fine military band of twenty-two pieces, enlisted by Lieut.-Col. SHELDON, arrived in camp and was attached to the Regiment, under the regulations existing at that time. The band was from its arrival in a fine state of efficiency, and by its services at guard mounting, battalion drill and dress parade, did much to promote the martial spirit of the men.

Rev J H Jones, a Disciple clergyman from Northern Ohio, a man of earnest, enthusiastic temperament and strong, vigorous eloquence, had from the first taken great interest in the Regiment and had consented to become its Chaplain He arrived in camp soon after the first four Companies, and during the pleasant Autumn weather held frequent and regular religious services on the parade ground, at which the Regiment and the troops of friends who came to visit it were regularly in attendance. Chaplain Jones remained with the Forty-Second until the re-organization of Gen. Grants Army at Young's Point in the Spring of 1863, sharing the exposure and sufferings of the men and exerting a strong and wholesome moral influence.

By the 1st of December the equipment of the Regiment was complete, and the men began to chafe and worry for fear that they might be compelled to remain in Winter quarters at Camp Chase This distress was however brief Early in the month the three regiments in camp held a grand brigade drill and review under command of Brig.-Gen. Hill, who was in charge of the camp The troops received three rounds of blank cartridges and a sham battle was undertaken, with the usual result, the eager volunteers firing without orders at the command "Ready," and instead of the sharp, simultaneous volley that Gen. Hill had designed, delivering a long, sputtering broadside that did not die away until those whose muskets had missed fire had recapped their pieces, shaken the powder down into the nipple and tried again Upon the day of this review, the 4th, the announcement was semi-officially made that the Forty-Second would soon be ordered to the field. The spirits of the Regiment rose from that day, and great anticipations of a stirring Winter campaign were thenceforward indulged. As usual in those days of callow soldiery, nearly every volunteer had come to camp with a revolver in his belt, the gift of a liberal parent or an admiring constituency Word had come from the front that the Rebels were armed with long and villanous home-made knives, with which to hew and disembowel the invaders at close quarters, and the revolvers were thought to be a necessary provision against dire results But while in Camp Chase these same pistols had in careless hands killed and disabled from one to three men in each company of the Forty-Second, and in the midst of the packing of linen sheets and other unsoldiery property the order came forbidding enlisted men to carry side-arms. It was a grievous affliction, but discipline prevailed, and the pistols were shipped home with the other impedimenta which could not be carried.

The period of expectation was brief On the 14th of December the Regiment was ordered to prepare to move the next morning. After a busy day and night the men were astir at daybreak of the 15th, and by nine o'clock the Regiment, nine hundred and ninety strong, marched out of camp and took the road to Columbus. It was a bright, beautiful Sunday, and the music of the band as it marched through the streets to the depot attracted a large crowd. Those were days in which citizens generally took a personal interest in the Army, and during its stay at Camp Chase the Forty-Second had made many warm friends among the generous, patriotic people of Columbus. They left their churches as the splendid legion came marching through the city, and congregated on a common near the depot where the Regiment, drawn up in a hollow square, was to receive its battle flag from the hands of Governor DENNISON. The colors were presented by the Governor in an earnest and patriotic address, which was responded to by Col GARFIELD, and without further delay, the Regiment took the train and, amid cheers and good wishes, started toward Cincinnati, where it arrived at eight o'clock in the evening The period of preparation over, the real work of the Forty-Second was now about to begin.

CHAPTER III.

THE SANDY VALLEY CAMPAIGN—FIRST WINTER IN THE FIELD—
BAD WEATHER AND DIFFICULT ROADS—THE ADVANCE TO LOUISA
AND PAINTVILLE—BATTLE OF MIDDLE CREEK— PIKETON—THE
CAPTURE OF POUND GAP—FLOOD IN THE BIG SANDY RIVER—
OUT OF THE WILDERNESS

From the Miami depot at Cincinnati the Regiment marched promptly to the river landing at the foot of Broadway There it found tied to the shore two small, dirty steamers taking on board wagons, mules and company stores These steamers, we were told, had been detailed to transport us to the enemy's country. and those disjointed wagons and untamed mules that were being put on board were to constitute the supply train of the Forty-Second For some reason it was not deemed advisable to embark the Regiment at once So it was drawn up on the levee and waited until midnight, when the right wing went on board the steamer " Lady Jackson," the left embarking upon the " Izetta "

When once on board, the ardent soldiers who had left Camp Chase in such high feather that morning, began to dimly suspect that they had left behind more comforts than they were likely to find. The boats were marvels of dreariness and discomfort. There were berths only for the officers , the men lay down in their overcoats and boots on the upper deck, on the guards and the uncarpeted cabin floor. It was regarded a happy and judicious squad which laid some boards over the boilers and crawled up into that noisy but comfortable atmosphere where warmth if not sleep was possible. It was a wearying, sleepless night, trifling in its hardships compared with very many nights which came afterward, but to the unseasoned volunteers of the Forty Second it seemed the last extreme of dismal sacrifice. The mules brayed and quarreled, the clatter of loading freight and the hoarse whistle of other steamers all about made sleep impossible, and many of the soldiers, discouraged at last, wandered up into the city and strolled about until daylight About eight in the morning the preparations were completed, the lines were cast off, and the two steamers bearing the Regiment and its fortunes backed out and headed up the stream Where were we going? No one knew, and the want of that knowledge made every one unhappy We had not yet learned that first rudiment of the soldier's education, to look only to his haversack and musket and to go where he is sent without wondering or asking questions There was no want of ingenious conjecture as to the destination of the expedition. Some said West Virginia—the Kanawha Valley perhaps—other thought it might be Harper's Ferry, still others were sure that the Regiment had been ordered to the Army of the Potomac. The debate then turned upon what Corps we had been assigned to and what sort of quarters we would probably find Here it was gloomily suggested that our "quarters," in the form of one small wedge tent to every ten men, were boxed up down in the hold, and that part of the discussion ended. All that day, all night and until nearly noon of the 17th, the two steamers struggled against the current of the muddy Ohio

When we awoke next morning the thickly settled, highly cultivated region had been passed, and the cold gray hills on either side of the river looked wild and desolate. We had not supposed that within so short a distance of home there was any such wilderness as this. How little we, even then, knew or imagined of the primeval barbarism that lay before us in Eastern Kentucky! Shortly before noon the "Lady Jackson" sprang a leak, and all hands were ordered below to tumble the ammunition and beans up out of the hold. Before this was finished the boats had neared a small, straggling town at the mouth of a muddy looking river, and the Captain of the leaking steamer, with a recklessness which would have chilled the marrow of a seafaring man, turned his prow to the shore and beached her, head on high and dry, in the oozy sand. There was no further danger of sinking, and the boys, leaving the beans and cartridges, sprang ashore and took a long breath of the atmosphere of rebellion. The sun had by this time dispelled the fog and warmed the atmosphere and the situation brightened rapidly. This then was the end of our voyage—Cattlettsburgh at the mouth of the Big Sandy, the dividing line between Kentucky and Virginia. But wherefore? Why had we come there? Where was the enemy? Half a dozen slovenly looking soldiers straggled out of a tavern on the shore and made a faint effort at three cheers, and to them the inquisitive warriors of the Forty-Second applied for the points of the military situation. They proved to be members of the 14th Kentucky Infantry, the farthest-frightened ragged fringe of the stragglers who had fled down the valley before the victorious advance of HUMPHREY MARSHALL. They had come on foot, some had lost their muskets, all were frightened, and the blood-curdling accounts which they gave were sufficient to perceptibly check the hilarity of the Forty-Second for that day. Innocent patriots! they had not learned the emptiness of camp rumors about the enemy.

Something had to be done, however, or the Rebellion could never be suppressed, and as there was no battle to fight that afternoon, the

Regiment began its campaign by getting the mules ashore. Does any veteran of the Forty-Second live to read this simple narrative, who has forgotten that afternoon with the mules? There were a hundred and fifty in all, an untutored, unmanageable herd. Few had ever felt the restraint of a halter or bridle—if there was one among them which had ever worn a harness we failed to find him. It was first supposed that the animals, hungry and weary from their long confinement on board, would eagerly spring ashore at the first opportunity, and preparations were made to drive the herd down the gang plank into a corral made by piling the disjointed wagons in a small circle on the sandy shore. Alas! how utterly the volunteers of that early day failed to comprehend the moral obliquity of the mule. It was found upon trial that not an animal of the herd had the slightest inclination to go ashore. Individually and in solid phalanx they resisted every effort to persuade or drive them out of the narrow and noisome pen wherein they had kicked and trampled each other for the past fifty hours. It finally became an issue of mere physical force against brute obstinacy. The obliging deck hands brought forth a hawser. A corporal from Company "F," skilled in the art of the *lariat*, threw the noose over each long-eared head, a squad of men with set teeth, and hands and shins ready to be skinned in defense of the Union, held the long end of the rope and gaily dragged the resisting mule to the edge of the boat. That point reached the beast usually changed his tactics and leaped down the gang way as though fired from a mortar, dragging the squad at the other end of the rope through the water and sand as a struck whale would tow a whale boat. There was fun in all this as well as some hard knocks; and, as the boys with skinned hands and bruised limbs retired, their places were eagerly filled by volunteers. By repeating the process a hundred and fifty times the mules were finally landed.

Then came the intricate task of harnessing and breaking them.

The harnesses were in the hold of the steamer, piecemeal as they came from the ordnance warehouse, here a case of bitts, there a box of hame straps, then another box with trace chains and so on to the end. To assemble these *disjecta membra* was the afternoons work of a patient squad on the bluff above. Another party put the wagons together, and still another undertook to harness the mules. This was the crowning difficulty of the day. All previous difficulties paled before the task of buckling those stiff and untried straps around those tawny creatures to whom the pressure of a girth or the rattle of a trace chain was the signal for war. There are doubtless living survivors of that day who can tell how by lifting the harness on the end of poles, by throwing the mules and holding them down until the girths could be fastened, the teams that were so soon to stand between us and starvation were finally equipped and geared to the lumbering wagons. Before mid-afternoon half a dozen of those vehicles drawn by six mules each, bestrode by a happy volunteer, were rattling through the town, to the peril of all fences and pedestrians within municipal limits.

Meantime, details from several companies had been sent out to some fields in the rear of the town to establish a camp. The little wedge tents were brought up and staked down, with much discussion as to how the different sticks and ropes should be used and whether ten men could live under such a mushroom. To our ardent minds, filled with visions of Sibley tents and stately baggage trains, those narrow wedge-shaped bags of canvass were a disappointment too deep for words. The shelter tent had not then been invented, and the Forty-Second men, who hoped that this War might be over before another Autumn, did not realize that before their three years were over a muslin napkin slung over the soldier's knapsack would be the utmost luxury of habitation permitted by the the logistics of war. With all disappointments, however, there was a novelty in first being under canvass and on the enemy's soil, that made every one forgetful of the vanishing luxuries of barrack life. The inflammable rail was lifted from the adjacent fence and kindled into a cheerful blaze beneath the camp kettle, the savory ham, the aromatic coffee and the seductive hard bread were brought forth, and with a valiant picket guard posted on the Valley road to look for the coming foe, the Forty-Second lay down to the first of its many nights on the ground This was the 16th of December. The 17th and 18th were devoted to the mules and practicing the rudiments of camp life. A deserted church near the camp was the rendezvous of the letter writers, and the correspondence dated within those two days from that bleak, unpainted barn of frontier Christianity would fill a volume. These preliminaries were brief

On the evening of the 17th a strong detachment of Companies "A" and "F" was detailed for a reconnoissance to Louisa, thirty miles up the Big Sandy. It was first intended that the party should go as mounted infantry, but as only twenty-five horses could be procured that number were mounted and started overland under command of Major PARDEE on the afternoon of the 18th. The remainder of the detachment, numbering a hundred, was sent to make the journey by water, a small screw steamer being detailed for the purpose The first day's experience was memorable as our first introduction to the uncertainties of Sandy River navigation After bumping along for several hours, running aground two or three times in the course of a mile, the crazy old scow ran hopelessly into the mud, broke her rudder and stuck fast The troops on board therefore clambered ashore, shouldered their knapsacks and set out to march to Louisa Eight miles of tugging and toiling over the hills consumed the remainder of the day, and at night the detachment encamped comfortably in a barn. Early the next morning the march was resumed, and about noon, the party, footsore and weary, reached Louisa. The mounted party had arrived soon after the midnight previous and had taken quiet possession of the town. Here was our first experience of the decayed and sluggish village life that prevailed through the Southern towns during the War. Louisa was at best a straggling, unpainted hamlet, but the hostilities of six months had greatly increased its thriftless, untidy aspect. The men were nearly all in the army on one side or the other; the court house had been used as a barrack by the half barbarous volunteers of the mountain region, and a shabby brick tavern with its kitchen dismantled and its windows broken, still struggled against extinction as a public house by keeping a red nosed ex-hostler and a jug of new apple-jack behind the bar. Early in the War, as it then was, Louisa had been occupied and re-occupied by Federals and Confederates until its women no longer stared at the passing soldier as an object of interest, but charged him fifty cents for a dried peach pie, and as promptly besought the commanding officers to post sentries around their potato mounds and hen roosts, as though taught by the campaigns of a dozen years.

Shortly before noon of the 20th, as before related, the remainder of Companies "A" and "F" arrived, having marched the last twenty miles from where their boat lay hopelessly stranded on a shoal of the river. The troops took possession of the tavern and a picket was posted on the road leading up the river to watch for JENKINS' Cavalry, a small Confederate force that had been prowling in the vicinity. During the night a batallion of Cavalry numbering perhaps two hundred, arrived and joined the command. They were Virginia troops and had seen several months of service in the Kanawha Valley.

During the morning following the remaining ten companies of the Forty-Second began arriving in squads of from two to twenty. The men were footsore, weary and hungry. They had not supposed that thirty miles of travel could involve so much hard work and deep wading. The Winter rains had fully set in and the roads, at best, hardly more than mere bridle paths, were at their worst. The country which the expedition had traversed was a constant succession of hills and valleys, and as bridge building and road making had not been even thought of in that barbarous region, the wagon trains of Col. GARFIELD's command had only to follow the rude paths that wound along the valleys, and at intervals of a few miles crossed some rugged hill or "divide" into a new gorge. Travel over such a road in the rainy season involves the frequent crossing of swollen streams, and the march of the Forty-Second with its wagon train from Cattlettsburgh to Louisa was little better than a thirty mile wade through mud and water. In crossing some of the hills the roads were found so steep and uneven that men were detailed to walk beside the wagons to hold them from capsizing, and slowly as the main body of the Regiment had marched, it reached Louisa many hours in advance of the train. Early in the march it became necessary to relieve the wagons of every possible pound of burthen, and the road was strewn with the *debris* of luxurious mess chests which the men had hoped to keep with them through the War. It may be doubted whether any regiment was seasoned to the hard work and discomfort of campaigning more abruptly than the Forty-Second. In five days they had come from the comfort of barrack life to the hardships of a Winter campaign in a wilderness.

As the remainder of the Regiment continued to arrive at Louisa, preparations were made for a temporary camp. Companies "A," "F" and "K" were sent out in a Southwesterly direction and encamped on the hills, a mile and a half from the town, in a position commanding the junction of two roads leading Eastward from the interior of Kentucky. It was here that the first formal essay was made in the high art of foraging. The boats from the mouth of the river had been detained by shoal water, the rations brought overland in the wagon train had grown scant, and the virgin warriors of the Forty Second, convinced that the Confederacy owed them a living, then and there first turned upon the lean poultry and the spectral swine of the mountaineers. Fragrant and tempting rises in memory the fumes of those earliest fruits of the chase, the slab-sided pigs shot down in their quest for acorns on the hills and the veteran rooster lifted from his roost in the dead of night to fill the maw of the invader.

For two whole days and nights—the 21st and 22d—the rain fell incessantly. Gen. GARFIELD had arrived meantime, and notwithstanding the unfavorable weather, the work of organization went on. On the night of the 22d, the rain turned to snow, and the morning of the 23d brought an icy wind from the North which froze the mud in the roads and made the hills slippery with ice. The night had been so cold that the men could not sleep, but had crawled out of their tents and sat until morning, huddled around their fires.

On the morning of the 23d, marching orders were issued, and by noon the Regiment, preceded by the Cavalry, was on the way to Paintville, a small town on Paint Creek, a mile from the junction of the latter with the Big Sandy, and thirty-three miles from Louisa. Paintville was at that time the advanced post of HUMPHREY MARSHALL, commanding a force from two to four thousand Rebel cavalry, infantry and artillery, who had came over into the Sandy Valley from Virginia to spend the Winter and make the most of the opportunity offered for strengthening his numbers, by recruits from the interior of Kentucky. MARSHALL had descended the Valley as far as Paintville, and, as our scouts assured us, had commenced permanent fortifications at that point. It was against this force that Gen. GARFIELD had been sent, with orders to dislodge MARSHALL and drive him from the State. The force placed at his command for this purpose, consisted of the Fortieth and Forty-Second Ohio Infantry, both new Regiments, the remnant of the Fourteenth Kentucky, a wild, half organized Regiment, which had been driven before MARSHALL as he descended the Valley, and the batallion of Virginia Cavalry already mentioned This command was designated the Eighteenth Brigade, Army of the Ohio The advanced and exposed position of MARSHALL offered at that time one of the few opportunities open to the Union Army to strike a direct and effective blow, and Gen. BUELL, who had accomplished little or nothing, since taking command of the Department, attached no small importance to the favorable result of the expedition up the Big Sandy.

It was important that the Rebel communication between Virginia and Kentucky should be cut off and the drain of men and supplies from the latter State stopped, but it was still more essential that somewhere along the line from Chesapeake Bay to the Mississippi a Federal force should win a victory to encourage enlistments at home and show that the right cause could sometimes win. Just at the moment of MARSHALL'S irruption into Eastern Kentucky, the Fortieth and Forty-Second Ohio Regiments had been reported to Gen. BUELL for assignment to duty, and acting upon a suggestion of Col HAZEN, of the Forty-First Ohio, BUELL made the two Regiments the nucleus of a Brigade, placed Col. GARFIELD in command, and sent the untried commander with his untried men to conduct an independent campaign From Cincinnati, Col. GARFIELD had been summoned to Louisisville for more definite instructions, but he had overtaken his command at Louisa, and as already described, had put it *en route* on the 23d of December from Louisa to Paintville. The first day's march accomplished but ten miles, and ended after nightfall at the Stone House Farm, where amid the dreary discomfort of a cold, Wintry rain the men encamped, wet and hungry, in a muddy cornfield The road over which the march had been made was wretched beyond description, one stream having been forded by the column not less than twenty-six times within a distance of five miles The wagons were left far behind and the camp in the freezing mud of the cornfield was without tents or other equipage, but the necessities of the case outweighed all scruples, and the poultry, pigs and fences of the Stone House Farm passed away like a vision Before starting the next morning Col GARFIELD ordered the troops into line and gave them a brief lecture on the sin of confiscation, then paid the disconsolate farmer for his losses out of his own pocket.

After a march of several miles the column reached the Big Sandy at the mouth of George's Creek, which point had been fixed as a rendezvous for men and supplies. To this place several boat loads of provisions had been sent under escort of a detachment of the Forty-Second, and as the different detachments were reunited, with plenty to eat and tents to shelter them, the situation seemed visibly improved The weather, which for a week past had been cold and rainy, became bright and warm, and under the brightening skies the daily routine of drill and rigorous camp discipline were resumed Arms were inspected, ammunition issued, and everything put in complete readiness for actual service. The Forty Second and the Cavalry remained at George's Creek something more than a week, busied with preparations and waiting for the arrival of the Fortieth Ohio, which had left Camp Chase some days after us, and had not yet joined the Brigade During the week a detachment of Cavalry and Infantry, two hundred and fifty strong, had been sent on a scout in the direction of Paintville and returned with the intelligence that the Rebels had abandoned the town, moved some four miles farther South, and had begun fortifying a strong position commanding the junction of the main Valley road with a branch road leading westward.

On the 27th, a member of MARSHALL's command was captured

a few miles from camp while home on a furlough. He reported MARSHALL's headquarters with his main force at Prestonburgh, fifteen miles beyond Paintville, and on the Eastern shore of the river. These and other reports made it apparent that there was no time to be lost. If the enemy were retreating he should be promptly followed ; if he were fortifying it was important to strike him before his preparations were complete

On the morning of the 31st of December, therefore, without awaiting further reinforcements, the command broke camp and moved up the valley of George's Creek in a Southwesterly direction, nearly at right angles with the Big Sandy. The road was comparatively good for that country, and under the influence of a bright day and the prospect of a fight the column moved forward so gaily that by four in the afternoon it had reached the foot of Brown's hill, across which the road led into another valley. Here at the foot of the mountain the column went into camp, and by way of waiting for supplies to come forward, spent the following day (New Years) in various forms of drill and camp exercises. Skirmishers were deployed up the side of the mountain, and the entire battalion practised field evolutions in a broad meadow in the valley below During the day the teams returned to the mouth of George's Creek and came back at night laden with supplies

On the following morning a small squad of our Cavalry, scouting in the direction of Paintville, encountered a detachment of the enemy, and after a slight skirmish, retired with the loss of three troopers and a citizen guide who were captured. Part of the squad had left their horses in the road and had gone into a house for breakfast. The Rebels came suddenly upon them, drove off those waiting outside and captured those in the house. The news of this little affair set the camp in commotion. A squadron of Cavalry was sent after the marauders, but returned unsuccessful.

Shortly after noon the tents were struck, and the column, crossing the hill, descended into a valley running obliquely toward the Big Sandy and in a Southeasterly direction. But the teams found the hill almost impracticable, and after marching three miles the column was halted and detachments were sent back to help the wagons out of their difficulties. It was long after dark before this was even partially accomplished, and the command bivouacked barely three miles from the camp of the previous night.

The next day it rained incessantly, and the Regiment, many of whose tents had not arrived, spent a cheerless, uncomfortable day, fighting the water which ran through the tents and soaked those without shelter to the skin.

On the following day, the 4th, Company "F" was sent forward as an advance guard and encountered a picket of the enemy on the crest of a hill, two miles from camp. There was a momentary skirmish and the Rebels retired. Company "A" was sent forward to reinforce the advance, and so prepared for emergencies, but none came, and the two Companies in front spent a comfortable night in a barn. The next morning Company "A" returned to camp, and the day was devoted to foraging and getting forward the wagon train. Parties of the enemy were hovering round and several skirmishes occurred between them and our pickets. In one of these little encounters a detachment of the Fourteenth Kentucky killed one rebel cavalry-man and captured another. The latter was brought to camp and on being questioned, described the party to which he belonged as part of a reconnoitering force sent out by MARSHALL to gain some idea of the strength and purposes of the invaders. He also gave an exaggerated account of MARSHALL's strength and represented him as preparing to take the offensive.

From the point at which Col. GARFIELD's column was now established three roads led to Paintville. The one on the left followed down Muddy Branch to its confluence with the Big Sandy, thence up the river a mile to the mouth of Paint Creek; so on, a mile up the Creek to the town. The right hand road bore across the hills in a Southwesterly direction to the ford at the mouth of Jenny's Creek and a mile to the right of Paintville. From the ford a road led down the North bank of Paint Creek to the town. The third road ran directly from Col. GARFIELD's position to the village, accross a succession of ridges so high and broken that the road was impassable for wheels. On all these three roads the enemy had posted strong pickets, three-quarters of a mile from town, supported by an infantry regiment and a battery, who were held in reserve in the village ready to move to the support of whichever picket should be threatened in force. In those days of amateur generalship, it had not occured to Gen MARSHALL that his enemy might turn the uncertainty of the Confederate position to his own advantage.

This, however, was just what the Ohio Colonel did. By dividing his Cavalry, moving it rapidly and supporting it with small detachments of infantry, he managed to strike the three pickets, one after the other in such a way as to entirely mask his own intentions and give MARSHALL the impression that a mighty army was bearing down upon him from three directions. The regiment and battery were hurried frantically from one road to another, as the point of attack seemed to be changed, and in the midst of the panic the straggling troops in the town retreated across the river. The pickets which had been drawn in on the center road came in pell mell, and finding the town deserted, likewise escaped across Paint Creek. The regiment and battery were at this time at the ford opposite Jenny's Creek, and they likewise retreated to the entrenched position three miles South of the town, and Col. GARFIELD's forces, marching by the Muddy Branch and river road, occupied Paintville without firing a shot.

Having learned from the inhabitants the size of the Confederate force and the direction of its retreat, Col. GARFIELD determined to immediately cross Paint Creek and continue the pursuit. The heavy rains of the previous fortnight had filled the streams, and Paint Creek, whose waters were backed up by a mill dam, was impassable. Near the dam stood a saw mill and around this were saw logs To roll them into the stream, lash them together and lay a roadway across was the work of an hour, and by five in the afternoon a thousand picked infantry were across the river and heading Southward in pursuit of whatever enemy had been occupying Paintville A mile further up Paint Creek, at the mouth of Jenny's Creek was a ford passable for horses. From this ford a road led Southward, parallel with the one which the infantry was following.

During the halt in the valley near Tom's Mountain, four or five days before, there had arrived in Camp a detachment of the Second Virginia Cavalry, under command of Lieut.-Col BOLLES. This force belonged to the Military Department of the Kanawha, commanded by Brig.-Gen. J D Cox, a personal friend of Col. GARFIELD, and who, apparently from mere good will, had sent Col. BOLLES with three hundred men to give us a lift in our first campaign. They were armed with sabres and a curious sort of horse-pistol, rigged with an adjustible butt or stock, so as to serve as carbines. They were, besides, well mounted, had seen service and learned to obey orders without wondering what the ultimate purpose was or feeling any individual responsibility in the result.

On the afternoon of the 6th, Col. GARFIELD, having completed the bridge across Paint Creek and crossed fifteen hundred picked infantry, sent Col. BOLLES up to the ford at Jenny's Creek, to attack the cavalry out-post there. If he should drive the enemy, it would be in a Southerly direction, parallel to the advance of the infantry, and the two detachments could co-operate

The infantry started at about five o'clock in the afternoon and before it was well out of sight of the town the short, dark Winter day was spent We were marching along the base of some high wooded hills, from whose crests a cloud of dense fog rolled down into the valley below, and as night closed in, made the darkness almost impenetrable. The column was guided by a trusty native, and pressed wearily on four or five miles, taking a very tedious route, and crossing a high hill, which as we afterwards discovered might have been avoided. We were marching to attack a large earthwork, about whose size and strength dire stories had been told us by prisoners captured from MARSHALL's command. It was said to include acres of ground, to be armed with cannon and in general to be prepared to resist assault or siege.

Splashing along through the muddy path, we came, soon after dark, upon evidences of an enemy's camp. The road had been cut and furrowed by the hauling of heavy timber, and the offal of slaughtered beeves was strewn along the valley amid log huts and rude railings where horses had been picketed. Everything so far as we could see indicated the presence of a considerable force, and notwithstanding the theoretical eagerness of the ardent patriots from Ohio to get a chance at the Nation's enemies, there was a discreet and becoming silence as they marched to their first night-attack upon a fortified position.

At the forks of a small creek which we were ascending, was a large, straggling log house which had been used as headquarters by the commandant of the post. From the women in this house it was learned that the garrison and working force had numbered about nine hundred men, and that they had decamped less than an hour before. At this intelligence the men were permitted to sit down for a few minutes rest, while a detail of volunteers clambered up the hill to inspect the earthwork. This proved to be a heavy redoubt with an area of perhaps two acres, crowning a hill three or four hundred feet high, between the two branches of the creek already described. The parapet was heavily revetted with logs and hewn timber, and traverses for several guns had been partly finished. The excavation was nearly complete, but no guns were in position and no buildings erected within the redoubt. To our uneducated eyes, the place seemed a very Gibaraltar of strength. It commanded the road for a mile down the main valley and for a nearly equal distance up the left fork of the stream which came down from the West at right-angles with its subsequent course.

Viewed by the light of later experience the whole plan of " Fort Marshall," for such was its name, was crazy and absurd. It was built to guard a road which could easily have been dispensed with by taking the parallel one three miles to the right, upon Jenny's Creek. It was built upon ground so high that an attacking force anywhere within half a mile from the foot of the hill would have been protected by the impossibility of depressing the guns of the redoubt so as to bring them to bear. High as it was, Fort Marshall was surrounded by wooded hills still higher, up which, guns might have been dragged and the reboubt easily made untenable. Later in the War, an officer seeking to defend that point would have planted a battery at the base of the hill, with rifle trenches at the flanks and a few rods further up to protect it.

While the detachment was inspecting the earthwork, others of the men invaded the abandoned huts of the Rebel soldiers, where they found every indication of sudden and precipitate retreat. Meat and bread were found cooking before the fire and everything in confusion. From the women at the house it was learned that the Rebels had spies watching the movements of the Federals in the village, and when the column had begun to cross the pontoon bridge, had fled to the fort, giving the alarm which had resulted in a hasty stampede. The enemy had retreated by the road leading

West and intersecting the Jenny's Creek road at a point three miles distant and four miles from Jenny's Creek ford where the road crossed Paint Creek and where Col Bolles had been sent to attack the cavalry of the enemy. To pursue the retreating infantry at least as far as the Jenny's Creek road was the obvious thing to be done, and Col. Garfield put his little force immediately in motion. This was about ten o'clock at night. If a quick march could be made we might overtake a few stragglers, or occupy the Jenny's Creek road in time to catch some of the cavalry between our force and that of Col. Bolles. The road, though muddy and wet, was fair for that country, and the little column marched rapidly It reached the Jenny's Creek road in an hour and found signs that the cavalry had escaped. The road, a mere winding path through the valley, crossing the swollen creek at frequent intervals, was cut and scored by the fresh tracks of rapidly ridden horses. The bank was still wet where it had been splashed by the horses struggling through the creek. An old man in a hut near by reported a great stampede, with firing of guns an hour before, but he was too frightened to know any thing about causes or results

It was useless of course to pursue the retreating enemy, for their numbers were superior to ours, they had a long start, and we had less than half a days rations, the supply boats not having reached Paintville before our departure. It only remained to return to Paintville, and this Col Garfield determined to do, by way of the Jenny's Creek road. Turning Northward he soon found it necessary to build a rail bridge upon which to cross the swollen stream. This done, the column pushed on, and soon came upon the body of a dead Confederate, killed by Col. Bolles' men in their headlong pursuit. It was the first dead enemy that the men of the Forty-Second had seen, and with an eager curiosity that overcame cold and fatigue, they gathered round the poor fellow as he lay there in the frosty night. He was the commonest kind of a backswood bushwacker, clad in the coarse, dirty gray of the mountaineer, but to us he was the first dead Rebel of the War, and the picture of his pallid face as he lay in the flickering torchlight, his frowzy, yellow hair, and his whitened hands raised by his stiffened arms as if in appeal to the cavalrymen who had gone galloping over him, left an impression on our minds that not all the carnage of the succeeding two years could efface.

Wearily the little column pushed on, climbing along steep banks to avoid building a bridge wherever the road crossed the tortuous stream The night had grown intensely cold, and the men, weary and hungry, with wet feet and clothing sodden with the rains of the previous week, began to suffer terribly. Jenny's Creek ford was reached soon after midnight, but nothing was found except signs of a hasty stampede of the Rebel cavalry upon Col BOLLFS' approach. As Paint Creek was impassable, it was necessary to return to Paintville across the hills South of the stream. There was no road, but the guide had been over the ground and thought he could find the way. First it was necessary to bridge Jenny's Creek, which cost an hour of hard labor, Col GARFIELD himself standing in the mud and placing the rails for the frail structure which with the greatest care could hardly be anchored against the rushing current Safely across at last, the column began a weary, straggling march across the hills toward Paintville, which was reached just as day began to dawn. When near the town the advance was fired upon by our own pickets posted on a hill near the river, but the firing was wild and no one was hurt The men reached camp nearly exhausted, and in their condition even the forlorn and shabby little town seemed to offer them a grateful welcome home. The supply boats had arrived, the tents were brought up from the river and pitched on a common near the court house, and partial comfort was soon restored.

During the day there arrived from the interior of Kentucky the

Fortieth Ohio Infantry, our old neighbors at Camp Chase, and six companies of the First Kentucky Cavalry, under Lieut.-Col. LETCHER—the whole commanded by Col. CRANOR of the Fortieth. These troops, previously stationed at Paris and Mount Sterling, had been assigned to Col GARFIELD's Brigade and ordered to march through the mountains and join his command at Prestonburgh, twenty-five miles above Paintville on the Big Sandy As they approached the river they heard of HUMPHREY MARSHALL's forces at and about Paintville, and turning Northward had left Prestonburgh to their right and joined Col GARFIELD's command at Paintville on the 7th of January.

While in Camp Chase, there had been more or less petty hostility between the Fortieth and the Forty-Second Regiments, and when the latter had marched to the front a month before, there were mutual congratulations that the two regiments had seen their last of each other. A month in Kentucky, however, had tamed all this camp hostility, and when the Fortieth appeared at Paintville the Forty-Second turned out to welcome the reinforcements with cheers and congratulations over a happy re-union

Meanwhile, Col BOLLES' command had returned and reported having chased the enemy ten miles up Jenny's Creek, killed several and captured a number of horses. As his orders would not permit him to remain longer Col BOLLES, with the thanks of Col GARFIELD for his timely and excellent service, returned to the department of the Kanawha.

The arrival of the Fortieth Regiment, the Cavalry and the supply boats and teams from below, put the Brigade into condition for an aggressive movement, and giving his men barely a day to rest and make preparations, Col GARFIELD on the morning of the 9th set out with fifteen hundred picked men in pursuit of MARSHALL's retreating force Two days rations were taken in haversacks and further supplies were ordered to be pushed up in boats to

Prestonburgh The remainder of the Brigade was left in command of Col. CRANOR, with orders to follow Col. GARFIELD's column as soon as sufficient provisions arrived to furnish three days rations in addition to those already sent forward.

The advance column marched all day, but the roads were so wretched that it was night before it had reached the foot of a high hill, North of the mouth of Abbott's Creek, three miles below Prestonburgh and on the West side of the Big Sandy. Ascending this hill soon after dark, Col GARFIELD's advance encountered at the summit a cavalry picket, which fired a volley and retreated. Being evidently in the immediate presence of a large force of the enemy, Col GARFIELD brought his command to the top of the hill and with strong guards thrown out to the front and rear, rested until morning It was a bitter January night. The rain which had fallen all day turned to sleet, and a keen, biting gale from the North whistled through the mountain pines and stiffened the wet clothing of the soldiers with ice No fire could be permitted in such a situation, and the men shivered and waited through the long dreary night as best they could. When morning dawned they found themselves on a high hill from which the road descended by a steep, zig-zag course to the valley of Abbott's Creek.

Immediately after encountering the cavalry the evening before Col. GARFIELD had sent back a message directing Col CRANOR to put all of the available men at Paintville in motion at once and march to his support The order reached CRANOR before daylight, and within an hour twelve hundred men made up from all the regiments in the Brigade were on the march.

The advance column meanwhile descended early on the morning of the 10th, to the valley of Abbott's Creek, and found that the enemy had retired up the stream and across the dividing ridge into the valley of Middle Creek, which comes down from the mountains parallel with Abbott's Creek and flows into the Big Sandy about a mile farther up than the mouth of the latter

THE BATTLE OF MIDDLE CREEK.

It was at once apparent that Col GARFIELD was in the immediate presence of MARSHALL'S entire force, and that the latter was disposed to fight MARSHALL was known to have about thirty-five hundred men of all arms—infantry, cavalry and artillery, and had come into the Sandy Valley to spend the Winter and, by occupying the country, promote enlistments into the Confederate service. This purpose he could not of course relinquish without a fight, and he chose his ground for the encounter deliberately and well.

Proceeding cautiously and deliberately in order to allow the reinforcements under Lieut.-Col. SHELDON to come up, Col. GARFIELD passed up the valley of Abbott's Creek, forded the stream, crossed the ridge and descended into the valley of Middle Creek Here he found MARSHALL'S cavalry drawn up in line across the valley, but a few shots from the advance drove them back. One cavalry-man was cut off from the main body and in attempting to swim the creek was captured, the first prisoner of war taken by the Forty-Second on a battle-field A heavy line of skirmishers was thrown across the valley and the advance began. The enemy's cavalry made a formidable show in the broad meadows but kept at a discreet distance. Once they formed behind a small spur of hill that ran out into the valley and from behind that cover charged down upon the advancing column Throwing his troops into a hollow square, Col GARFIELD awaited the attack and when the cavalry came within range sent them a volley which broke and turned them back. The skirmish line under command of Adjutant OLDS advanced again and drove the cavalry from a spur behind which it was attempting to rally.

This little spur of high ground upon which stood a log church, surrounded by a few graves, was then occupied by the Federal force as a base from which to attack or defend as circumstances might require. Drawing up his little force on the slope, Col. GARFIELD saw that MARSHALL had come to a stand. Across the valley half a mile distant was the Confederate cavalry, and on the same line near the foot of the hills, to the right of the creek, a battery was in position, which, as the skirmishers advanced, opened fire and gave the line a momentary check. A few shells were also fired at the main force on Graveyard Point, but the guns were badly trained and the shells buried themselves harmlessly in the mud. The enemy's cavalry and artillery being thus accounted for, it remained for Col GARFIELD to discover the location of his infantry. On the South side of the creek to the right of the battery rose a high hill, heavily timbered and crowned with a ledge of rock Around the foot of the hill wound the creek and close beside this, but on the opposite side of the stream, lay the road. It was at once conjectured that MARSHALL's infantry had occupied the hill and that the Federal column, if it advanced round the curve, would be caught by an ambushed fire from the opposite bank. To verify this theory GARFIELD sent his escort, a handful of Kentucky cavalry, to charge up the road and draw the fire of the main body. The ruse was boldly performed and was completely successful As the little group of horsemen galloped up the creek and round the curve in the road, the battery fired harmlessly over their heads, and the whole infantry force, with the trepidation of new troops, opened fire at long range, and completely unmasked their position They occupied the wooded hill from its base half way to its summit It was now time for real work

About four hundred men of the Fortieth and Forty-Second Ohio were sent to ford the creek, climb the mountain and attack the Rebel position in front. Major PARDEE of the Forty-Second, who

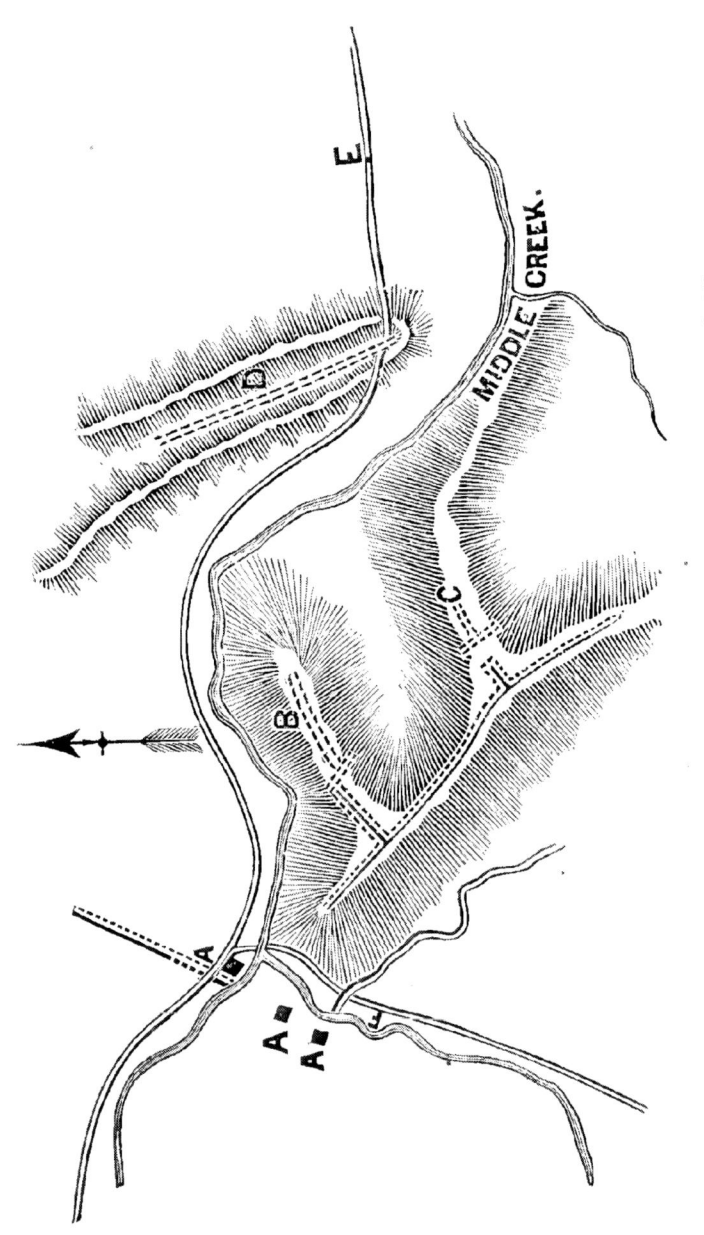

BATTLE-FIELD OF MIDDLE CREEK.

A—Rebel Artillery, 6 and 12 pounders. C—Ridge taken by the Kentuckians under Monroe. E—Approach of reinforcements under Col. Sheldon.
B—Ridge taken by the Ohio boys. D—Garfield's reserve. F—Road by which the enemy retreated.

.... Federal lines.   .... Rebel lines.

was practically in command of the fighting in that part of the field, threw forward as skirmishers his detachments of Companies "A" and "F" of the Forty Second and Company 'A" of the Fortieth and began the ascent. The skirmish line was in command of Capt F. A. WILLIAMS who, like Major PARDEE, seemed to take naturally to the business of fighting. Two companies of the Fourteenth Kentucky, under Lieut.-Col. MONROE of that regiment, were sent to cross the creek lower down, gain a narrow ledge or crest of a ridge that ran up to the main hill, and by advancing along that ridge attack the enemy in the flank and save WILLIAMS' little force from being overpowered. As WILLIAMS' line advanced up the hill it soon encountered heavy opposition. A sharp fire came from behind the trees, logs and rocks, and the Rebels swarmed down the hill, shouting and firing as they came. Half of the remaining reserve on Graveyard Point was sent to PARDEE's support and, thus strengthened, he pushed forward.

The firing now became as hot as a thousand men on one side and three thousand on the other could make it. Had the casualties been proportionate to the amount of powder burned, the Union force at least would have been annihilated. But the Rebels fired unaccountably wild. They were fighting down a steep hill, and, as is usual with raw troops in such a position, they overshot their mark and their bullets for the most part merely barked and scarred the trees over their enemies heads. They were moreover armed to a large extent with smooth-bore muskets and squirrel rifles of small calibre, and fought like a mob, without plan or unity of action.

The Federal line on the other hand advanced steadily, kept well under cover, fired deliberately, and, as the result proved, with excellent effect. The Rebels were so numerous that the trees and logs were insufficient to cover them. Four or five frequently sought behind one tree. Instead of rushing down upon WILLIAMS' line and profiting by the weight of superior force, MARSHALL'S men stood and skirmished with an enemy whose very disparity of numbers, by enabling every man to keep well under cover, became almost a positive advantage. Firing up hill with their heavy, long range Belgian rifles, the Ohio men delivered a steady and effective fire Gradually they pushed the enemy up the hill. Reinforcements came up over the crest and down to the Rebel line, which seemed to be preparing for a charge down the slope, when at the opportune moment, Col. MONROE'S Kentuckians appeared on the ridge to the left and from the rocks on the flank and rear of the enemy's line opened an enfilading fire.

At the moment of Col. MONROE'S appearance in the fight, Lieut.-Col. SHELDON, who, with twelve hundred men, had left Paintville that morning and marched through mud and water nearly twenty miles, appeared round a curve in the road, a few hundred yards in the rear of GARFIELD'S little reserve on Graveyard Point. The advancing column sent up a cheer of encouragement, which was caught and repeated by the reserves and re-echoed by their comrades fighting on the hill.

Dr. POMERENE, the kind-hearted, enthusiastic Surgeon of the Forty-Second, who had grown anxious with the sight of this maiden battle. had discovered MONROE'S line streaming over the hill and fancied that Major PARDEE'S force was being surrounded. The Twenty-Second Kentucky men were uniformed in sky blue, the first we had seen, and through the foggy afternoon the good doctor mistook their clothing for gray. Mounting a horse, hatless and distressed, he came splashing through the mud to hurry up the reinforcements. Coming within hail of Col. SHELDON he begged him for God's sake to hurry, "or the boys on the other side would be captured." The men gave another cheer, tried hard to double-quick through the mud, and promptly formed a line across the road in the rear of the log church, where the ground was so soft that some of the men mired and the line was moved up on Graveyard Point. The effect of this new show of force was decisive, if indeed there were needed any thing more to decide the victory of that day

Marshall, though far outnumbering his assailants, had been out-fought from the first, and his line, pressed hard by Pardee, began to retreat up the hill Inspired by the cheers of their comrades from below, the gallant Ohioans —to whom that day's business was the first baptism of war—pushed stubbornly forward, driving the Rebels into the ledge of broken rocks at the summit of the hill, which position they held until the already gathering night closed the fight

Col Sheldon promptly upon his arrival forded the creek and began to climb the hill, but before Major Pardee's position could be reached, darkness had settled down upon the combatants and the battle was over.

The position not being one that could be safely or advantageously held during the night, orders were sent directing Monroe and Pardee to retire They came down the hill, carrying their wounded, crossed the creek, and the whole of Col. Garfield's force was reunited for the night on Graveyard Point Strong pickets were posted up the road and beyond the creek, and notwithstanding the belief that a still harder struggle would come on the morrow, the little army slept proudly upon its first victory.

Shortly after dark a brilliant light blazed up from behind the hill upon which the fighting had taken place during the afternoon. What it meant could only be guessed until the next morning, when a reconnoisance at daylight showed the hill abandoned and the enemy gone. The illumination of the night before had come from the funeral pile upon which Marshall had sacrificed his wagons and baggage— every thing that could impede his retreat through the mountains to Pound Gap, the gateway of the Cumberlands into Southwestern Virginia Pursuit was, of course, useless. With ten hours start, a perfect knowledge of the country and a competent rear guard of cavalry, the now unencumbered enemy could have safely retreated from any pursuers however formidable.

Col. GARFIELD's little force was weary and short of food. It had started with but two days rations, the country afforded nothing and it was necessary to return to the river, from which supplies could be received It remained only, therefore, to look over the field of yesterday's fight, bury the dead and carry the wounded as carefully as possible to the river A careful survey of the ground upon which the fight had taken place showed a remarkable disparity in losses. On the Federal side the entire loss was but one killed and eleven wounded—eight of the latter being members of the Forty-Second, viz.

DAVID HALL,	Private, Company		"A."
SHERMAN M LEACH,	"	"	"A"
HENRY FORNEY,	"	"	"C"
FREDERICK H COFFIN, (mortally),	"	"	"F"
CHARLES CARLTON,	"	"	"F"
WILLIAM GARDINER, (mortally),	Corporal,	"	"G"
JACOB JAMES,	Private,	"	"G."
JACOB GRIFFITH,	"	"	"H."

The enemy suffered far more severely. Nineteen dead were found on the hill-side up which MARSHALL's men had been driven by WILLIAM's men, and among the rocks at the summit of the hill. The heartless way in which the Rebels disposed of their dead made a strong impression upon the not yet callous-hearted boys from Ohio. At one place eleven of the Confederate dead had been tumbled down into a large fissure in the rocks They were taken out by the reconnoitering party next day and decently buried A squad of the Fourteenth Kentucky still further violated the decencies of war by stripping the corpses of their buttons and trifling valuables. There was abundant evidence that the Confederate loss was by no means limited to the nineteen dead soldiers found on the hill. Seven graves were found at the foot of the mountain near where the baggage had been burned. A native whose hut was near the scene of the burning, professed to have filled the graves during the night and said that they contained the bodies of officers. From his account not less than fifty wounded had been carried away in wagons by the retreating enemy.

The remarkable disparity in losses is explained by the facts already stated. The Federals had the better weapons, they fired up hill from behind trees, and fought from first to last with remarkable coolness and skill The scars made by their bullets on the trees were mainly less than five feet from the ground The bullet marks of the Rebels on the other hand were wild, being often ten and twenty feet above the ground

On the Federal side the battle of Middle Creek was fought by less than a thousand men The principal fighting detachment was led by Capt FREDERICK A WILLIAMS of Company "A," Forty-Second Ohio, who six months before had been a student at Hiram. If there was a single man in his command who had ever before been under fire, that fact was not known then and is not known to day. Col. GARFIELD accepted battle from an enemy whom he knew to out number his own force by at least three to one, and the fight was won by simply attacking the foe promptly in his own position, making intelligent use of whatever advantages the ground offered and fighting with steady courage and skill as long as daylight lasted.

The Forty-Second Regiment was engaged in many bloodier and more renowned battles during its three years of service, but it may be fairly questioned whether the Regiment even performed a days duty of more timely and permanent value to the country The battle of Middle Creek, skirmish though it may be considered in comparison with later contests, was the first substantial victory won for the Union cause. At Big Bethel, Bull Run, in Missouri, and at various points at which the Union and Confederate forces had come in contact, the latter had been uniformly victorious The people of the North, giving freely of their men and their substance in response to each successive call of the Government, had long and anxiously watched and waited for a little gleam of victory to show that Northern valor was a match for Southern impetuosity in the field. They had waited in vain since the disaster at Bull Run during the previous Summer, and hope had almost yielded to despair ! The story of GARFIELD'S success at Middle Creek came, therefore, like a benediction to the Union cause Though won at a trifling cost, it was decisive so far as concerned the purposes of that immediate campaign. MARSHALL'S force was driven from Kentucky and made no further attempt to occupy the Sandy Valley. The important victories at Mill Spring, Forts Donelson and Henry, and the repulse at Shiloh followed The victory at Middle Creek proved the first wave of a returning tide.

It was now the 11th of January. It had frozen on the night after the engagement and Col GARFIELD'S little army marched down the Middle Creek valley on nearly solid ground The dead Kentuckian was buried in the little graveyard on the Point and the wounded carried with all possible care and tenderness. Shortly before, noon the troops reached the bank of the Big Sandy, opposite Prestonburgh, and during the afternoon were ferried over on the two or three small steamboats which had come up the river with supplies.

Prestonburgh was found to be a village which, at its best estate, might have had a thousand inhabitants, but as the place had been occupied and re-occupied alternately by Union and Confederate troops, most of the people had been driven away. The court house, a large brick building, stood vacant on the bluff bank of the river, and into this and the deserted houses of the village the weary and weather-worn soldiers swarmed with thankful hearts The wounded were placed in an improvised hospital and received every attention, but in spite of Surgeon POMERENE's most assiduous efforts, their condition was far from comfortable. WILLIAM GARDINER of Company "G," wounded in the shoulder, died on the 12th

Col GARFIELD remained at Prestonburgh three days, when, learning through his scouts that MARSHALL had crossed the mountains into Virginia, he began preparations for returning his troops to Paintville. His only avenue of supply in that barren and roadless country was the river, and between Prestonburgh and Paintville there were shoals and bars which made navigation at all times difficult and at low stages of water, impossible. Paintville was the head of reliable navigation on the river, and at that point the Brigade was to be assembled for Winter quarters The return from Prestonburgh began on the 13th, the third day after the battle Ten men of those least able to travel were selected from each company to return with the wounded by boat and the remainder marched by the river road, reaching Paintville on the night of the 13th

On the way down the river, FREDERICK C COFFIN of Company "C," died from his wounds received on the 10th His remains, together with those of GARDINER, who had died at Prestonburgh, were brought to Paintville and buried on a hill near the village with military honors They were the first men of the Forty-Second who had fallen in battle.

The Brigade encamped for a few days in the valley below the town, but the mid-winter rains set in and continued with such persistence that the cornfield in which the camp had been established became a miry swamp. Before the end of a week the

Forty-Second removed to a hill North of the town, and the men set cheerfully to work to erect comfortable dwellings for the Winter. They had a cherished ideal as to the meaning of Winter quarters, and had not yet learned how uncertain is the soldier's tenure upon his hut in time of war. Pine logs were cut on the crest of the ridge, rolled down the hill and built into huts, which were chinked with billets of wood and plastered with mud. Volunteer details of men went several miles up Paint Creek, rafted down lumber and carried it up the hill to make roofs and furniture for the new cabins. It is on record that several of these buildings were completed about the 29th of January. The weather continued to alternate between bright, warm days, and heavy, persistent rains. Supplies had become abundant, but the wet and discomfort of the camps and the severe exposure incident to guard or fatigue duty told on the health of the men, and the hospitals and graveyard at Paintville filled rapidly.

It was during the brief season of rest and preparation at Paintville that an incident occurred which is worthy of record, because it illustrates perfectly the quality of Col. GARFIELD's energy, and the kind of pluck that was demanded to ensure success in the Sandy Valley. The river was bank full, the current swift, and the troops at Paintville were living upon less than half rations. Col. GARFIELD went down to the mouth of the Big Sandy to see what made the supply steamers so slow and uncertain. He found there the "Sandy Valley," a small, rickety, stern-wheel steamer, tied up to the wharf at Cattlettsburgh. He ordered her to take on a load of supplies, and start up the river. The Captain said the water was too high, and the trip impossible. Efforts to get other steamers having failed, GARFIELD took command. had the vessel loaded, stationed an army officer on deck to keep the Captain to his duty, and himself took the wheel. His canal-boating experience stood him in good stead now, and notwithstanding the protests of the Captain that no boat could stem such a current, the wheezing craft crept slowly up the stream. There were sixty feet of water in the channel, the trees along the bank, submerged nearly to their tops, rocked and swayed in the rushing current, and the rickety steamer, doing her utmost, could only make three miles an hour Night came, and the Captain insisted that the boat must be tied up. To continue such a voyage as that by night was, as he said, simple madness But the man at the wheel was Captain then, and he had come from a country where boats did not usually tie up at night He ordered the fires freshened, and still kept the bow up the stream. Finally, in rounding an abrupt bend in the river, the boat was caught by the current and swung round, hard and heavy, on a bar of quicksand. Every effort to back and spar her off failed. Tools were brought and excavations dug around the embedded bow, but in vain "Get a line to the opposite shore!" ordered GARFIELD. The boatmen protested, and swore that it could not be done. The Colonel himself leaped into the yawl and steered it across. The current swept them down, but finally they reached the shore, made fast a line, twisted it with a grail until the strain drew the steamer from her bed in the mud, and once more she headed up the river.

All Saturday afternoon and night, Sunday and Sunday night, Col GARFIELD kept his place at the wheel, with only a brief interval on Sunday, when the Captain, throughly conquered, could be trusted to run the boat. At nine o'clock Monday morning the "Sandy Valley" reached Paintville and the hungry brigade was fed

The river was still at a stage which made it easily navigable to Piketon, fifty miles farther up and practically the head of navigation, as it was of civilization, on the Big Sandy. In and beyond Piketon there was a numerous population still devoted to the Union cause. Upon these people raiding parties from Virginia and Pound Gap were perpetrating constant outrages. The people appealed to GARFIELD for protection, and their demands could not be ignored. For the better protection of the Valley, Gen. GARFIELD, (whose commission as Brigadier had been issued, to date from the day of his victory at Middle Creek,) determined to transfer his entire force to Piketon, and the movement began by boat on the 9th of February. The Forty-Second arrived on the 10th, and encamped on a sandy knoll above the town and near the river. Excavations were made under the tents, rude fireplaces constructed, with chimneys of empty bread barrels, and the Regiment congratulated itself upon the change from the dreariness and discomfort of Paintville. The stay of the Brigade at Piketon lasted until the 28th of March, and was marked by three incidents—an expedition up the river in pursuit of guerrillas, a flood in the Big Sandy, and a raid to Pound Gap.

The first of these was occasioned by a report brought to camp by a frightened woman, riding without saddle a very lean horse. She arrived after midnight, and reported that rebel marauders from Pound Gap were raiding through the valleys above, murdering Union men, and driving off horses and cattle. The only road to the scene of the outrage was a mountain path, impracticable except for foot soldiers and for horses reared in the country and accustomed to climb. A small volunteer party was therefore organized, including ten men from the Forty-Second Regiment, and the party, some thirty in number, under command of Major WILLIAM JONES of the Fortieth Ohio, set out across the hills, in a Southeasterly direction, following the general direction of the river. After twelve hours of laborious marching, the party came suddenly upon the body of a man hanging suspended from a tree over a small creek. A quarter of a mile up the valley was found the house of the murdered man. The evening before, a party of guerrillas had suddenly surrounded the house and demanded an interview with the husband of the weeping and terrified woman who now related the story. The man went out, and was told that the visitors had come to conscript him for service in the Confederate army. He replied that he was a Union man, and refused to go. After a momentary dispute, they seized him and declared their purpose to take him by force. This being overheard from the house, the father of the prisoner—an old, infirm man—shut and barricaded the door. The Rebels fired through the door, dangerously wounding the old man in the side, and when Major JONES' party arrived, the day afterwards, he was lying on the bed in a dying condition They cut down the body of the son, brought it to the house, and gave it decent burial. There were indications of a desperate struggle at the scene of the hanging, and the execution was, either from awkwardness or design, so clumsily performed that the death of the poor victim must have been one of protracted and terrible suffering The patient, hopeless grief of the poor widow, left alone and destitute with two helpless children and a dying father in that dreary wilderness, was pitiful in the extreme. The incident was a page from a chapter in the history of the War which the Northern people, to this day, very imperfectly understand—the desperate, malignant struggle between the poor Union men of the mountains and their Confederate neighbors and foes.

Leaving the desolate scene, the little expedition pushed on, and before noon came upon a force of bushwhackers who fired down upon them from the hills. A rambling, irregular fight was kept up until night, the Union soldiers gradually driving the bushwhackers before them, but without gaining any material advantage The next day, Major JONES, the commander of the party, was severely wounded in the head by a shot fired down from above, and the expedition abandoned all other purposes but the one of bringing the wounded officer back to camp. A litter was made and the sufferer carefully placed upon it; but he was delirious and wild, and the labor of carrying him over the steep and narrow paths was toilsome and difficult. After two days' effort they reached the river, and set about constructing a raft upon which to float the wounded man to Piketon. The raft proved unmanageable in the swift, broken current, and came near drowning those who ventured upon it. Finally, after nearly a week of extraordinary labor and privation, the party reached camp, having accomplished practically nothing.

Meanwhile, the rains had continued, and on the 23d of February reached a climax. For twenty-four hours the rain-fall had been heavy and incessant. During the afternoon the river began to rise with extraordinary rapidity. The channel at that point is deep, and notwithstanding the heavy rain, it was not apprehended that the river would escape its banks. The oldest native could recall but one instance in which the town had been submerged, and with this assurance the troops felt secure. But soon after midnight the water overflowed the banks of the river above the town, and came pouring down over the plateau on which the Brigade was encamped. The Fortieth Ohio was literally washed out of its camp, losing most of its tents and miscellaneous property. The Forty-Second was awakened by the water creeping up into its tents, rising at the rate of a foot per hour. The men were called out, gathered up their blankets, and retreated to the crest of a small ridge, along the sloping side of which the tents had been pitched. There they stood until morning, cracking dreary jokes and counting the chances of a swim across the muddy lagoon to the hills behind the town. When morning dawned, a curious scene presented itself. The entire site of the town was submerged, the water being four feet deep upon the ground-floors of the houses. Gen GARFIELD's head quarters were in the midst of a lake, and communication was kept up with the Regiments by means of rude boats hastily improvised from troughs and boxes. The Fortieth Ohio Regiment, tentless and forlorn, was bivouacked along the hillside. Nearly the whole of the large supply of stores which Quartermaster Stubbs and Commissary Heaton had collected with such pains and labor, had been swept away. Large quantities of bacon, bread and forage had been rolled to the top of the bank during the night, but the flood had overtaken everything, and the food that the troops so badly needed was gone. The river was filled with drift-wood, stacks of hay, cattle, sheep, fences and other property. Occasionally a log house intact came floating by

Finally, after having risen sixty-eight feet in thirty hours, the waters came to a stand, and began falling as rapidly as they had risen It was just in time to save the Forty-Second from a perilous swim, for the water had huddled the Regiment on the crest of a knoll where a rise of two feet more would have left no dry ground for a human foot. The waters receded rapidly, the steamboats, which had come boldly up into the main street and moored to the fences and horse-posts, slipped back into the river, and the town was left to dry itself out of the thick stratum of slimy mud that the flood had left behind. The loss of the stores was a serious misfortune, and from that time the health of the troops became visibly worse.

Meanwhile, the aggressions of the enemy from the vicinity of Pound Gap continued, and Gen GARFIELD determined to strike a blow in that direction From the best information that could be gained the Gap was garrisoned by a small brigade under command of a Colonel. The position was naturally strong, and had been still further strengthened by abatis, trenches and a few pieces of cannon.

Gen. GARFIELD was confident of his ability to capture the place even with a greatly inferior force, and on the 15th of March he set out with a party of six hundred infantry and one hundred cavalry—the latter commanded by Major MCLAUGHLIN, to attack the Gap. The distance to be marched was about twenty-five miles, and in order to facilitate progress over the execrable roads the expedition was divided into two detachments, the cavalry and part of the infantry following a route along the river — the remainder of the infantry taking a path more direct, but rugged and difficult beyond all our previous experience It was in fact a simple mountain bridle path, following the valleys of small streams and at intervals crossing the rugged hills or "divides" which separate one creek system from another. Much of the distance the road was simply the bed of the creek itself, and to follow it required constant wading. Travel, upon such a road in the rainy season of the year, was of course a process which put the endurance of men and horses to the severest test. Still, bad as the roads were, there were no better, and Gen. GARFIELD's two detachments splashed cheerfully along, each eager to be the first at the Gap.

Pound Gap, or "Sounding Gap" as it is known in some of the earlier maps of that region, is simply a notch in the Cumberland mountains, some three or four hundred feet lower than the crest of the range on either side From the earliest settlement of the country it had been a gateway of communication between Virginia and Kentucky, and on the Virginia side State enterprise had graded the road and provided bridges where necessary. On the Kentucky side the descent, though practicable, was much more abrupt, and at the time of Gen. GARFIELD's attack the road down the Western slope had been thoroughly blockaded with logs, brush and fallen trees At the foot of the mountains ran a road parallel with the range, and on this road, at a point three miles North of the Gap, Gen. GARFIELD's two detachments were united about eight o'clock on the morning of the 15th The morning was heavy and dark, a thick mist veiling the mountain and a drizzling rain falling, which, as was subsequently discovered, was frozen to snow on the mountain top.

The plan of attack was ingenious, and the thick weather, which obscured every movement, was highly favorable to its successful execution. The cavalry under Major McLaughlin was to proceed along the road to the foot of the Gap, then march boldly up, and make a show of attack in front, keeping at sufficient distance to avoid serious losses, but pressing the attack with enough vigor to keep the enemy busy and interested. The infantry, under lead of Gen Garfield himself, was to climb at once to the crest of the mountains, along which there was a rude path to the Gap. By approaching in this way the place would be attacked in flank and rear, and if the cavalry could succeed in drawing the enemy part way down on the Kentucky side the chance seemed good that the infantry might capture a portion of the garrison.

At nine in the morning the ascent began. From the foot to the top of the range was more than two miles, and up this slope, over rocks and logs, through dense thickets of laurel and vines, the six hundred climbed. The top was reached in an hour, and along the crest the soldiers followed, in single file, a narrow path which led to the Gap. A furious snow storm was falling, so dense as to shut out from sight everything beyond the distance of a few yards. Before the column had gone a mile along the mountain top the firing was heard, which showed that the cavalry had arrived and begun its work. The infantry hurried forward, a small advance guard under Capt. Bushnell leading the way. When within less than half a mile of the Gap, the column hurrying through the storm ran suddenly upon a picket of three men who had been aroused to special watchfulness by the firing in their rear. The pickets fired upon the advance, then dropping their guns ran toward the Gap. The dozen or fifteen soldiers in the advance of

GARFIELD'S column returned the fire, and then the whole force started in pursuit, deploying down the Eastern slope of the mountain, as it advanced, so as to present a line of battle-front to the enemy. But the frightened sentinels were too swift, and enabled the garrison to escape. They knew the ground, while the Union force had to pick its way over a rugged and unknown path, through a blinding storm. Rushing through the village of log huts that formed the post, the three fugitives shouted to the garrison that it was surrounded, the mountain was black with Yankees, and to run, run for life—which every warrior of them did with such promptness and success that when, a few minutes later, the eager Federals came sweeping down into the Gap they found only a flying and demoralized rabble to fight. A sharp fire was immediately opened upon them, but it was like shooting birds on the wing. Three of the enemy were killed, four wounded, and four or five captured; the rest escaped. The detachment that was fighting the cavalry was cut off, but escaped along the mountain side, and eventually rejoined the main force. The surprise and stampede had been complete. Sixty permanent and comfortable log huts, including a quartermaster's and commissary department, magazine and hospital, were abandoned in a few moments. Food was left cooking before the fires, dinners left unfinished, and guns, clothing and other property abandoned in terrified haste and confusion. After some delay the cavalry worked up past the obstructions, crossed through the Gap and pursued the retreating enemy six miles into Virginia, but without result.

The soldiers explored the place, thoroughly loaded themselves with clothing, guns, knives and other plunder, feasted royally upon the corn-bread and bacon which the Rebels had left behind, and then by order burned every hut and building to the ground.

Great quantities of correspondence, mainly love-letters, was found in the abandoned quarters, and from these it was learned that the sweet-hearts of those mountain warriors, though wildly reckless of grammar and spelling book, and in general disgusted with the War, still hoped that their cavaliers would each slay a Yankee or two before he sheathed his sword. Particularly interesting, also, were the scores of great, villainous-looking knives, made from scythes and old files, with which the defenders of the Gap had hoped to carve the invaders of the South. Many of these weapons were nearly or quite two feet in length, with strong wooden handles, rough leather scabbards, and heavy as cleavers. They were common among Southern soldiers during the first year of the War, and represented the blood-thirsty craving of the poor white of the South for side-arms, something with which his quarrel with the Northern Yankee could be fought out on a personal basis.

Having completed the work of destruction, the expedition set out to return, following the two roads by which the advance had been made, and reaching Piketon during the afternoon of the 17th. From muster rolls captured at the Gap it appeared that the garrison was a batallion of nine hundred men, commanded by Major J. B. Thompson, and was part of the special force recruited under Gen Zollicoffer, in Kentucky, for the defense of the mountain passes. From the letters found in the camp it appeared that there was at least one company from Memphis. The expedition, though it failed to capture or destroy as many of the enemy as was hoped, completely broke up the military post at Pound Gap, and it was never afterwards permanently reoccupied by the Rebels during the War. The raid, which occupied four days and involved a march of between seventy-five and eighty miles, was the severest trial of endurance that the men of the Forty-Second had yet undergone. They returned to camp wet, weary and foot-sore, but with the consciousness of having rendered an important service.

An incident growing out of the Pound Gap expedition may be

here related, as illustrative of the utter degradation and ignorance of the poor whites of that remote region. On the evening of the day after the victory at the Gap, two enlisted men of Company "A," Forty-Second, left the road by which the column was marching, and ascended a little valley to the distance of a mile in quest of food They found a double log-house inhabited by a family named BLANE. The cabin stood in the midst of a cleared space, of perhaps fifty acres, the produce of which, with what game the father and sons could kill in the woods, constituted the sole reliance of the household for food and clothing The family included the father, mother and twenty-one children, the eldest, a daughter, being twenty-six years of age. The three oldest sons were in the Confederate army, and the three oldest daughters, mothers without marriage, contributed their progeny to the unrecorded census of that prolific race. Every head was a shock of tow-white hair, every form was clad in a monotony of coarse gray home-spun cloth, and among the children under fifteen years of age there was no peculiarity of hair, dress or face by which sex could be distinguished. The father, sixty years of age, had never been farther from home than Piketon (sixteen miles distant), and the mother had never been out of the little valley in which she then lived and was born. The father had twice seen a steamboat, but not one of the family ever had heard of a railway, or had the vaguest conception what it was. There was but one book in the house, an old, yellow, mouse-eaten copy of the Bible, brought from North Carolina by the grandmother sixty years before, and which had laid undisturbed on a beam since her death, many years ago. Not one of the family could read, or had ever been inside of a church. The smaller children stared in amazement at a common pocket-knife that could be opened and shut. Their language was a dialect of back-woods slang, interlarded with harmless, because unconscious, profanity. As a degradation of the English tongue, it was even more rude than the *patois* of the plantation negroes of the Gulf States

The chief fact of importance, outside of the family residence, seemed to be the existence of a sorghum distillery two miles down the valley, the proprietor of which—a Lothario named HANKS—was the reputed father of the grandchildren in that easy-going family. Neither daughters nor parents seemed conscious of any shame or impropriety in their unwedded polygamy. As to the causes and chances of the war, only the vaguest notions prevailed. The Rebel recruiting sergeant who had taken the the sons away, had told them that the Yankees were coming to take away the negroes and murder the whites. Who, or what the Yankees were, they had no idea. They had heard that Washington and Lincoln were in the war, but upon which side they could not tell. And thus were native white people living in the very center of a nation which sends missionaries to reclaim the happy barbarians of the Pacific isles.

The work of Gen. GARFIELD and his Brigade, in Sandy Valley, was now done. No enemy was left within reach; the whole of Eastern Kentucky was protected and tranquil. Spring had come, important movements were in preparation in Central Kentucky and along the Mississippi, and the Forty-Second, weary of life in that rude country, hoped that it might be needed in a more important field. That hope was soon realized. On the 24th of March, orders were issued to prepare for removal. Boats were to arrive within a day or two to transfer the Forty-Second to Louisville. The orders on which this movement was based were issued at Washington on the 14th, and directed Gen. GARFIELD to post the Fortieth Ohio and the Fourteenth Kentucky, with McLAUGHLIN's Cavalry Squadron, at Prestonburgh, leaving Col CRANOR, of the Fortieth, in command of the post, and to proceed with the remainder of his command, by way of the Ohio river, to Somerset, Kentucky, a point near the head-waters of the Cumberland river, and about one hundred miles south of Lexington

After waiting impatiently two or three days for the boats, an order was issued for Company "A," of the Forty-Second, to construct a raft upon which to float down the river. The task was begun with alacrity, but before the raft was completed the steamers arrived, and at two o'clock the following morning the Regiment embarked, the band playing, as it marched to the landing. "Oh, ain't I glad to get out of the wilderness!"

Notwithstanding the last few days of the stay at Piketon were brightened by pleasant weather, the health of the troops had steadily deteriorated. The tremendous exertions, and the constant exposure to which the Brigade was subject, during the months of January, February, and the early part of March, had proved too severe for the endurance of many, and nearly a third of the entire command was on the sick list, or in hospital at Ashland. A steamer, laden with sick, had been sent to Ashland when the Brigade had left Paintville for Piketon on the 9th of February, and almost every supply steamer that afterward went down the Big Sandy brought a reinforcement to the little army of sufferers from pneumonia, measles and fevers. Among the sick, at the time of the Regiment's removal from Piketon, was Capt F. A WILLIAMS, of Company "A," the young officer who had so conspicuously distinguished himself in the engagement at Middle Creek About the first of March he had been taken ill with pneumonia, and, although attended with the utmost care, his disease made such progress that, at the time of the Regiment's removal, grave fears were entertained for the result. He was tenderly carried on board the steamer and brought with his company to Cincinnati, whence, after a few weeks' careful nursing at the house of a friend, he was sent to his home in Ravenna. While there, notwithstanding he had apparently weathered the crisis of his disease, a relapse occurred, and Capt. WILLIAMS died on the 25th of July, 1862. He had been promoted to Major on the 14th of March, the date at which Lieut.-Col SHELDON had been raised to the Colonelcy, left vacant by the promotion of Col. GARFIELD, and Major PARDEE had become Lieutenant-Colonel. In the death of Major WILLIAMS, the Forty-Second lost one of its bravest and most accomplished officers. To Company "A" the bereavement was one of no ordinary character. The company was made up of students from Hiram College, and the choice of Capt. WILLIAMS as its leader was based upon long and intimate acquaintance as classmates and friends. It was a sad day in the Regiment that brought the news of his death.

The passage of the Forty-Second from Piketon to the Ohio river, and thence to Louisville, was one protracted season of rejoicing over its escape from the dreary, uninteresting region in which it had spent the Winter. The Regiment was upon two small Sandy River steamboats, which made fair progress during the day, but tied up to the bank at night, not daring to risk collision during the darkness with the overhanging trees. During the afternoon of the second day, the leading boat reached Cattlettsburgh, where five companies of the Regiment were transferred to the side-wheel steamer "Bostona," and proceeded, with only a brief stop at Cincinnati, to Louisville, where the boat arrived late in the evening of the 30th of March. The next morning, the battalion marched out through the city, and encamped in a beautiful grove near Cave Hill Cemetery, known as Preston's Woods. On the 2d of April, the remaining five companies arrived on the steamer "Ben Franklin," and the Regiment, reunited and overjoyed with its return to civilized surroundings, gave itself up to the work of preparing pay-rolls, and restoring its clothing and equipage to the proper standard. Convalescents were brought from the rear,

Sibley tents issued, and on the 16th of April two months' pay was received. Two weeks amid the alternate rain and sunshine of the early Southern Spring, passed like a happy dream.

Gen. GARFIELD, on the 3d of April, had been ordered to report in person to Gen. BUELL, commanding the Army of the Ohio, and then *en route* to Nashville. The Forty-Second had been, at the same time, assigned to the Seventh Division, commanded by Gen GEORGE W. MORGAN, then operating in the neighborhood of Cumberland Ford, in the Southeastern part of Kentucky. It was a bitter trial for the Regiment to realize that it might have to serve thenceforth under another brigade commander than Gen. GARFIELD, and, for a fortnight after his departure for Nashville. we anxiously hoped that each day would bring an order assigning us to his command in the army of Gen BUELL. But no such order came; and when, on Sunday, the 13th of April, the Regiment broke camp and took the cars for Lexington, it felt instinctively what proved true, that the beloved commander who had created the Forty-Second and led it to its first victory, was lost to it, and that as a Regiment it would see him no more.

CHAPTER IV.

THE CUMBERLAND GAP CAMPAIGN—CAPTURE OF THE GAP AND A HARD SUMMER'S WORK IN ITS DEFENSE—FORTIFYING AND FORAGING—THE RETREAT OF MORGAN'S DIVISION TO OHIO.

The defeat of HUMPHREY MARSHALL in the Sandy Valley, and that of Gen. ZOLLICOFFER by Gen THOMAS at Mill Spring, left the Army of Gen. BUELL at liberty, after the capture of Forts Henry and Donaldson, to proceed Southward, capture Nashville and attack that important artery of Southern communication, the Memphis and Charleston railroad. This could be done without danger of a flank movement upon BUELL's rear from Southeastern Kentucky, provided that the Confederate force at Cumberland Gap could be held in check, or better still, the Gap itself captured and the gateway closed from Eastern Tennessee into Kentucky. For this important service a special command was organized under orders of Gen BUELL, and designated as the Seventh Division, Army of the Ohio. The order for the assembling of this Division was issued on the 28th of March, and when the Forty-Second left Louisville for Somerset on the 13th of April, Brig.-Gen. GEORGE W. MORGAN of Ohio, to whose command the new Division had been assigned, was already at Cumberland Ford, where the road from Tennessee through Cumberland Gap to Lexington crossed the Cumberland river. The ford was but twelve miles from the Gap, and under the disposition of hostile forces then existing, was a point of considerable strategic importance. The ford had been occupied since early in the previous Winter by a brigade consisting of six regiments of infantry, a battalion of cavalry and the Ninth Ohio Battery, the whole commanded by Brig.-Gen. L. P. CARTER This brigade was to be the nucleus of the new Division, and Cumberland Ford was selected as the point of assembly. Thither, the Forty-Second was ordered to proceed without delay, and when it arrived in Lexington, on the afternoon of the 13th of April, it tarried only long enough to dispose of such sick and convalescents as would not be able to endure the march, and set out on the morning of the 16th for Camp Dick Robinson, near which point the road Southward crossed the Kentucky river.

Camp Dick Robinson was reached on the evening of the second day from Lexington, and on the 21st the Regiment passed the end of the turnpike, three miles South of Crab Orchard It had rained heavily every day during the previous week, and the rude, unimproved road, into which the men and teams now plunged, was a dismal reminder of their experiences in the valley of the Big Sandy.

The 20th was Sunday, and services were held in an old church, while the troops waited for the rain to slacken. During the next four days the Regiment with its wagon train waded through mud from six inches to two feet in depth, making from seven to ten miles per day, and encamping at night in the most favorable spots that could be selected in that drenched and sodden region. Such were the demoralizing influences of the march, that on Sunday the 27th, by which time the Regiment had reached Laurel Creek, Chaplain JONES felt impelled to deliver a special sermon on the sins of stealing and swearing.

Finally, on the evening of the 29th, the Forty-Second reached the Cumberland river, six miles below the ford, and went into a pleasant and briefly permanent camp. Here it remained during the organization of the Division which was completed as follows:

SEVENTH DIVISION ARMY OF THE OHIO,

Brigadier-General GEORGE W. MORGAN, Commanding.

FIRST BRIGADE,

Brigadier-General L. P. CARTER, Commanding

First Tennessee Infantry,	Col. Q. K. BYRD.
Second Tennessee Infantry,	Col. J. P. T. CARTER.
Third Kentucky Infantry,	Col. T. T. GARRARD.

SECOND BRIGADE,

Brigadier-General J. G. SPEARS, Commanding

Third Tennessee Infantry,	Col. L. C. HOUCK.
Fourth Tennessee Infantry,	Col. ROBT. JOHNSON.
Fifth Tennessee Infantry,	Col. JAS. T. SHELLEY.
Sixth Tennessee Infantry,	Col. JAS. G. COOPER

THIRD BRIGADE,

Col. JOHN F. DECOURCY, Commanding

Forty-Second Ohio Infantry,	Col. L. A. SHELDON
Twenty-Second Kentucky Infantry,	Col. D. W. LINDSAY.
Sixteenth Ohio Infantry,	Lt.-Col. G. W. BAILEY.

FOURTH BRIGADE,

Brigadier-General A. BAIRD, Commanding

Thirty-Third Indiana Infantry,	Col. JNO. A. COBURN.
Nineteenth Kentucky Infantry,	Col. W. J. LANDRUM
Fourteenth Kentucky Infantry,	Col. J. C. COCHRAN.

ARTILLERY.

First Wisconsin Battery,	Capt. J. T. FOSTER.
Seventh Michigan Battery,	Capt. C. H. LANPHERE
Nineteenth Ohio Battery,	Capt. WETMORE.

There was besides a Battalion of Kentucky Cavalry under Col. MUNDY, and a Company of Mounted Pioneers commanded by Capt. WM. PATTERSON.

The maintainance of such a force at that season of the year in a totally unproductive country, eighty miles from the nearest base of supply, and connected therewith by a road so difficult that a ton of freight was a sufficient load for a six mule team, was naturally a work of no ordinary risk and difficulty. It was necessary, however, in order to organize the Division for the work in hand. The road to Crab Orchard was repaired as well as possible, the means of transportation largely increased, and though compelled to subsist on short rations, the troops maintained their position and progressed steadily in the work of discipline and organization. The regiments drilled six hours daily, reviews were held on the river plain, and a siege battery organized by assembling a detail of one man from each company in the Division.

Cumberland Gap was in plain view, twelve miles distant, and occupied by a garrison variously reported at from ten to seventeen thousand men. On the 6th of May, intelligence was received, through a captured prisoner, that heavy reinforcements had been received at the Gap from Chattanooga.

East Tennessee was at that time a Confederate department, under command of Maj.-Gen. E. Kirby Smith. It was the avenue of communication between Virginia and the Central and Southwestern States of the Confederacy. It was fertile, rich in supplies, easily defended, and, with its important railroad from Richmond to Chattanooga, was a district of great importance to the Confederacy. To this stronghold there was but one approach from the North practicable for an army, viz, through Cumberland Gap. But Cumberland Gap was strongly garrisoned and fortified, and was believed by the Confederate authorities to be impregnable, as it would have been if properly defended.

Gen. Morgan, while waiting for the Spring floods to subside and while seasoning his little army for its work, was carefully studying the strength of the Gap and the best plan for an attack.

Two formal reconnoisances were made—one open and in force, the other secret. Engineers were sent to various points on the foot-hills in the neighborhood of the Gap to make careful drawings of the position, with the location of batteries, camps, trenches, etc. From the knowledge thus gained, Gen. MORGAN plainly saw the impossibility of carrying the Gap by assault from the front. He accordingly began to look about for means to capture it by a flank or rear approach. The Confederates relied upon the impossibility of such an approach and continued to strengthen their position in front

Pound Gap, ninety miles to the Northeast, was the only point in that direction at which a column with artillery could pass the mountains. This would have required a march of two hundred miles from Cumberland Ford, and when arrived there the enemy would have had time to concentrate a large force to meet the Union troops in the mountain passes on the South side before Powell's Valley could be gained. Four miles to the West of Cumberland Gap on the North side and eight miles on the South is Baptist Gap, a rugged pass which was already strongly blockaded by the Rebels, and was moreover under the immediate eye of its fortified neighbor.

Nineteen miles West of the latter is what is called Rogers' Gap, where the mountain range is not less high but less rugged and precipitous From the statement of the mountaineers it appeared that lightly laden wagons sometimes passed the mountains at that point Fifteen miles still further West is Big Creek Gap, a deep gash in the mountains opening vertically from the bed of the creek to the mountain crest. The road leading through this defile was heavily blockaded for a distance of eighteen miles Northward.

MORGAN determined to pass the mountains at these points and thus threaten the enemy's base of supplies at Clinton, as well as Knoxville, the heart of that region, and the rear of Cumberland

Gap. Secrecy and rapidity were essential to success, as serious obstacles had to be overcome. The Seventh Division had, on the 20th of April, about seven thousand bayonets for duty, with twenty-two guns and a battalion of cavalry, while the Confederate force under KIRBY SMITH was understood to be from eighteen to twenty thousand strong.

Four miles South of Cumberland Ford on the State road leading to Cumberland Gap, and ten miles from the latter place, stood a farm building known as the Moss House. From this point diverges a lane leading towards Lambdin's farm, nearly equidistant from Big Creek and Rogers' Gap. DECOURCY's Brigade was sent forward to effect a mask at the Moss House, and as a ruse MORGAN caused an earthwork to be constructed at that point. In the meantime another brigade was pushed forward towards Lambdin's. Never before had wagons attempted to pass that road, over what is known as the Bushey Mountain, and men and horses frequently toiled at the same ropes in dragging the guns up the steep ascents. As soon as one brigade had passed, the masking brigade was sent forward under cover of night and another brigade took its place, a new battery being placed in the position whence the other battery had been withdrawn. In this manner the entire Division was removed from Cumberland Ford.

The difficult duty of opening the blockade leading to Big Creek Gap had been assigned to Gen. SPEARS' Brigade some weeks before. While engaged in this duty KIRBY SMITH made an attempt to cut him off. Mrs. EDWARDS, a patriotic woman residing at Clinton, passed the mountains in the night and gave timely warning of his approach with a force three times as great as that of SPEARS, who was ordered to fall back. SMITH, cheated of his prey, returned to Knoxville, and SPEARS went back to work at the blockade.

DECOURCY's Brigade had remained at the Moss House, building

defenses, partly for show and partly with the expectation that they might be needed, from the 22d of May until the 8th of June. The position was in plain view of Cumberland Gap and the Brigade was in constant apprehension of an attack. Whole companies were kept on picket duty, and the entire Brigade slept on its arms, ready for immediate duty at any hour of the night. Bodies of Confederate cavalry frequently came down and skirmished with the Federal pickets, but as DeCourcy's orders were to hold the position with as little loss as possible, the fighting was unimportant.

Finally, the time came for a general movement. Spears' Brigade had cleared the road to Big Creek Gap, and Rogers' Gap had been explored by scouts and found barely practicable for wheels. On the evening of the 7th of June, orders were read on parade, announcing that everything was in readiness, the loyal people of East Tennessee were waiting anxiously for relief from the North, and that at four o'clock on the morrow the movement would begin. Promptly at the hour named the column moved, DeCourcy's Brigade leading, with the Forty-Second in advance. The weather was fine, the climate bracing and healthy, and though there was known to be hard work and possibly hard fighting ahead, the troops marched gaily as though going to a review. The first days march was ten miles. The next morning the journey was resumed, the column coming within sight of Wilson's Gap shortly after leaving camp. Fifteen miles on that day brought DeCourcy to within two miles of the Tennessee line, and when at eight o'clock the next morning the line was crossed, the troops sent up cheer after cheer, while the bands played "Dixie," a Northern greeting to Rebel-ridden and suffering Tennessee

That evening the column encamped at the foot of the mountain range. Companies "A" and "B" of each regiment in DeCourcy's Brigade were detailed as a special detachment to push forward that night and occupy Wilson's Gap, five miles away, and two miles nearer than Rogers' Gap, where the main column was to cross. With four days rations the six companies, under command of Lieut.-Col. PARDEE, set out at dusk, marched the five miles in two hours, and, piloted by a trusty guide, began to ascend the pass. The road was a mere bridle path, very steep and rugged, but the moonlight was clear and bright, and the ascent was silently and rapidly effected. At eleven o'clock the detachment reached the summit, posted a picket a few rods down on the further side and lay down beside their loaded muskets to sleep. At dawn the next morning they were roused, and as the sun rose beyond the distant hills, a panorama of exquisite beauty was opened before them. Away to the East, a blue line on the sunlit horizon, lay the mountains of North Carolina. Under their feet and stretching away to the Northeast and Southwest, were the Cumberlands, with clustering foot-hills at their bases on either side ; behind them lay the hill region of Kentucky lit up by the morning sun into long billows of gold and azure ; and before them, stretched along the foot of the mountains, as far as the eye could reach, lay Powell's Valley, green and luxuriant with the verdure of early Summer.

While lost for a moment in admiration of the scene, and forgetful of the rude business which brought them thither, the little battalion was startled by four or five rifle shots fired in quick succession, a few rods down the Southern slope. In a moment the men were in line, and moving down the path toward the scene of disturbance. The alarm was soon explained. In the early dawn a small squad of Rebel cavalry had left the camp in Powell's Valley and rode up to the summit of the Gap, where they had been accustomed to keep guard during the day. As they approached the top they were fired upon by the picket thrown out by Col. PARDEE on his arrival the night before. Three of the cavalry-men rolled off from their horses and scrambled into the bushes, leaving their horses, their hats and their weapons, which were captured. Two of the five, who were riding some distance in the rear, escaped and reported in the camp below that they had encountered a few Kentucky bushwhackers on the mountain. Even then there was no suspicion among the Confederates in Powell's Valley that MORGAN's army had left its position at Cumberland Ford and was seeking to force a passage into Tennessee.

Toward noon another squad of cavalry from Powell's Valley was seen slowly coming up the pass. Twenty or thirty men were posted in the bushes near the path, a few rods below the summit, while the main body lay in wait behind the crest of the hill. The plan was to draw the horsemen into a trap and capture the entire party. They came cautiously along and the game seemed likely to succeed, when, just as they were passing the squad concealed in the bushes, Private SHATTUCK of Company "A," Forty-Second Ohio, seeing a good chance for a shot, fired without orders, and unmasked the trap. The cavalry-men wheeled, lay close to their horses, and spurred headlong down the hill A volley was sent after them, killing one horse and wounding three men, but all managed to escape, and from that time they kept carefully out of range of Wilson's Gap

By this time DeCourcy's and Baird's Brigades had reached the foot of Rogers' Gap, two miles further to the West, and the laborious ascent began. It may fairly be doubted whether there was in the whole War a more brilliant achievement of its kind than the crossing of those two Brigades, with thirty pieces of cannon, over that difficult pass The ascent was two miles in length, with a sheer altitude of a thousand feet. Twelve horses were attached to each gun or caisson, and in places even this was insufficient. Prolonges were spliced and manned by regiments, and the guns dragged by main force up declivities which the horses could hardly climb. In other places the road had to be cleared and graded anew, but the pluck and zeal of the men were superior to all difficulties, and before evening of the second day DeCourcy's Brigade, with the Ninth Ohio Battery, had crossed the mountain into Powell's Valley. Baird's Brigade, with the First Wisconsin and Seventh Michigan Batteries, were close behind and crossed during that night and the following day. The detachment at Wilson's Gap remained in possession of that pass until the crossing was complete, when it marched along the crest of the mountain to Rogers' Gap, descended on the Southern side, and re-joined the column in Powell's Valley.

The first great step of the movement was now effected; it was necessary for Baird and DeCourcy to wait for the Brigades of Spears and Carter, which without artillery were crossing the mountain at Big Creek Gap, fifteen miles further to the Westward.

The Rebel cavalry was still visible, galloping about the valley, two or three miles distant on the road to Cumberland Gap, and the Forty-Second was sent out to look after it. Lieut.-Col. Pardee, who was in command, conceived a plan to trap some of them. Approaching as nearly as possible to their camp, he posted Company "A" in the road behind a small hill, and pushed the remainder of the Regiment forward among the bushes beside the road. After waiting in ambush several hours, eight mounted Confederates came leisurely down the way. At some distance behind them came a larger body, and, while waiting for the main force to come into the trap, the eight in advance saw something to arouse their suspicions, and in an instant they wheeled and fled across the valley. Two or three companies which were within range fired after them, killing two and wounding three. Several horses were captured, but the result fell so far short of Col. Pardee's hopes that his usually serene face was clouded for the rest of that day.

Toward evening word came from the rear that the whole Division had been ordered to re-cross the mountain to Williamsburgh, Ky This was incomprehensible and disheartening. After all the waiting and preparation of the past two months, after all the hard work of crossing the mountain, Gen Morgan's little army, when within striking distance of the enemy's rear, was now to be turned back empty-handed and without striking a blow! Officers and soldiers were alike disappointed and dismayed. The messenger who brought the order reported that Gen. MORGAN almost shed tears as he dictated the despatch, and from this it was rightly conjectured that the order to turn back was from outside authority, from Gen BUELL, perhaps, who in ignorance of the real situation, had formed new plans, not knowing that MORGAN was already in the enemy's rear. This conjecture, as was subsequently ascertained, was correct. Gen. BUELL had failed in his movement toward Chattanooga, and his failure had set free Gen. KIRBY SMITH and his entire force at Knoxville, to reinforce Cumberland Gap and invade Kentucky. The thing to be done, as Gen. BUELL thought, was to relinquish the attempt to capture Cumberland Gap and throw MORGAN's force back upon the Cumberland river to oppose the march of the Confederate army into Kentucky. It was expected that the order would reach MORGAN before he could cross the Cumberlands into Tennessee, but his celerity distanced the expectations of his superior, and the summons to return caught him in the very moment of success.

But it was not in the hard fortune of war that a movement so adroitly planned and so boldly executed should be shorn of its fruit. During the day that the Brigades of DECOURCY and BAIRD lay resting in Powell's Valley awaiting the removal of the heavy artillery back across the mountain, a soldier named REYNOLDS, of the First Tennessee Infantry, had crept along the mountain tops and cautiously approached Cumberland Gap. To his amazement he discovered the whole Confederate garrison in confusion, destroying its tents and gun carriages, and preparing for precipitate retreat. The evacuation had indeed begun, and long columns of men were seen filing down the Gap and taking the road toward Knoxville. Hurrying back along the dizzy path, the intrepid mountaineer reached Rogers' Gap at mid-night, just as the head of DeCourcy's Brigade had reached the summit, on its unwilling retreat. He told his story. DeCourcy, "taking the bits in his teeth," ordered a halt, and dispatched a courier to Gen. Morgan, fifteen miles away, at Lambdin's farm. Morgan in turn, hearing the news, assumed the responsibility, faced the Division about and marched for the rear of Cumberland Gap.

Baird's Brigade, weary and disgusted, had just reached Lambdin's and Carter's troops were on the way, but the order to countermarch and re-cross the mountain was received with cheers. As rapidly as possible the four Brigades were again concentrated in Powell's Valley, near the foot of Rogers' Gap. Gen. Morgan arrived at the rendezvous on the 14th, and on the following day Baird's Brigade arrived, marching down the mountain to the air of "Dixie," played by the band of the Thirty-Third Indiana.

During the night, Gen. Spears captured a letter written by the the Adjutant of the commanding officer at Cumberland Gap. The letter showed that the enemy was restless and uneasy, alarmed by enormously exaggerated reports of Morgan's strength, and in a condition to be terrified by a bold display of the little force. The letter also spoke of troops moving to attack Morgan in Powell's Valley, and heavy reinforcements coming from Knoxville.

Carter's and Spears' Brigades arrived utterly worn out, and a day of rest was imperative before offering battle. The enemy was reported in force at Thomas' farm, eight miles distant, on the road to the Gap, and it seemed inevitable that though the citadel had already been partially abandoned, the battle for its possession would have to be fought in the Valley.

With this expectation the Division, having sent back its provision train and all other incumbrances, started at three o'clock on the morning of the 18th, marching by two parallel roads so as to make a strong display of force and at the same time keep the two columns within supporting distance. At nine in the morning, DeCourcy's Brigade, leading the right hand column, passed through the abandonded camps of at least a Division of the enemy. They had not made a stand where Morgan had expected. The column was now within sight of the Gap, and moving on rapidly, reached the road at the foot of the Southern slope at noon. Not an enemy was there, and DeCourcy's Brigade, the Forty-Second leading, marched up and took possession of the citadel, Company "C" raising the Regimental flag on the main parapet of the fortifications, while Lanphere's Battery fired a triumphant salute. Cumberland Gap had been taken without the loss of a man. The other Brigades followed rapidly up the pass, and long before night the troops were posted behind the Rebel works, batteries in position, and Morgan prepared to defend the place against any army that the Confederates could send. He had come just in the nick of time, for the enemy's rear guard had not left until ten that morning. A day later, Morgan's weakness would have been discovered and the evacuation countermanded.

From the late headquarters of the Confederate commander, Gen. Morgan sent to Gen. Buell his congratulations and regrets for having been impelled by circumstances to disregard an implied order from superior authority. That the offence was promptly forgiven was shown by the following order issued by Gen. Buell from his headquarters in Alabama:

Headquarters Army of the Ohio,
Huntsville, Ala., July 11th, 1862.
General Order No. 29.

The General commanding the Army of the Ohio, takes pleasure in announcing the success of an arduous and hazardous campaign by the Seventh

Divison, Brig.-Gen GEO W MORGAN commanding, by which the enemy's fortified position at Cumberland Gap was turned and his forces compelled to retreat, as our troops advanced to attack. The General commanding thanks Gen. MORGAN and the troops of the Seventh Division for the ability displayed in the operations against this important stronghold, and for the energy, fortitude and cheerfulness which they exhibited in their struggle with difficulties of the most formidable magnitude for an army.

By command of Major-General BUELL.

JAS. B. FRY,
Colonel and Chief of Staff

To this was added the following letter, embodying the thanks of the President and War Department:

WASHINGTON, June 22d, 1862.

Brigadier-General GEO W. MORGAN:

This Department has been highly gratified with your successful occupation of Cumberland Gap, and commend the gallant conduct of your officers and troops, to whom you will express the thanks of the President and the Department. With thanks for your diligence and activity,

I remain, Yours truly,

E. M. STANTON,
Secretary of War.

In analyzing the means by which this important though bloodless victory was won, it is impossible not to ascribe great credit to Gen. MORGAN for the masterly way in which he managed to move his little army of seven thousand men adroitly and rapidly, in spite of overwhelming difficulties, and to make it seem like a large and formidable force when occasion required By the ruse of throwing up entrenchments at the Moss House, and replacing each night the one brigade and battery originally posted there with another, while the first was moved away under cover of darkness towards Rogers' and Big Creek Gaps, he managed to get his whole Division thirty miles on its way before the commandant of the Gap discovered that it had left Cumberland Ford. Having by splendid exertion and perseverance crossed his troops with their provision train and artillery over into Powell's Valley, he spread out his force so as to make the most formidable appearance possible The fact of his crossing the mountains in two points gave the impression that a large army was invading Tennessee from Kentucky. The Rebel cavalry in Powell's Valley, which kept the commandant at the Gap informed of the Federal movements in that quarter, reported Wilson's, Rogers' and Big Creek Gaps all simultaneously occupied, and three heavy columns of troops pouring into Tennessee. Gen KIRBY SMITH jumped to the conclusion that MORGAN'S Division formed one of these three columns, and that the others were probably two corps from BUELL'S army advancing upon Knoxville. He, therefore, in order to save his headquarters at Knoxville, and the all-important railroad, ordered the Gap abandoned and its garrison to reinforce his own army at Clinton The Confederate army of fourteen thousand men at the Gap spiked its guns, destroyed its tents, strewed its provisions over the ground, and retired Southward to Tazewell, twelve miles distant.

It turned out afterwards that Gen. KIRBY SMITH, hearing on the morning of the 18th more reliable accounts of the real size of MORGAN'S force, saw his mistake, and ordered the Gap to be re-occupied, and its late garrison even started from Tazewell, posthaste to obey that order, but the Yankees had been too quick for them, and when SMITH'S advance arrived at dusk within sight of the citadel, it saw the Federal camp fires gleaming along the hills and knew that the golden opportunity was gone. Nothing but a siege could recover what they had abandoned the night before.

THE OCCUPATION.

Cumberland Gap is situated at the point of junction between Tennessee, Kentucky and Virginia. Standing upon the peak that overhangs the notch from the East, the spectator looks down upon three States, and sees in the blue distance the mountains of

North Carolina. The Gap is merely a natural notch or opening in the top of the Cumberland range which for more than a hundred miles forms the boundary between Virginia and Kentucky. The pass is about a thousand feet above the valleys at either base of the range, and is overhung on the East by a peak nine hundred feet higher. To the Westward the ridge rises less abruptly to a height of seven hundred feet. The South face of the mountain is precipitous and impracticable, even for infantry, except by way of the road, which was built through the Gap many years ago, at State expense, and with considerable engineering skill. In a country where practicable roads are so rare, the military value of such a gateway will be obvious. The place is described by Gen. BRAGG in an official report as "the gateway to the heart of the Confederacy."

In June, 1862, when Gen. MORGAN captured it, the advance of BUELL Southeast of Nashville seemed to be checked; and it seemed likely that the main advance into the vitals of the Confederacy, failing at Chattanooga, would have to be made through Cumberland Gap to Knoxville, taking Chattanooga in the rear and opening a way into Georgia. Under instructions from Washington MORGAN immediately prepared to render Cumberland Gap an impregnable base of operations against East Tennessee. His troops were disposed to the best advantage in and about the pass, and the partially destroyed earthworks of the Confederates were repaired and armed with the artillery that he had brought across the mountains. Rifle trenches and covered ways were cut, and when, at the end of a few weeks, Lieut. W. P. CRAIGHILL of the U. S. Corps of Engineers arrived from Washington to superintend the fortifications, a large force of men was put under his direction, which in two months made the Gap simply impregnable against assault from its Southern front. Meanwhile, the road to Lexington, hardened and settled by the dry weather of Summer, was graded and repaired, and heavy trains of wagons were employed bringing supplies. An arsenal was built and stored with four thousand stand of small arms. Four thirty pounder Parrott guns on seige carriages were brought and mounted in advantageous positions. The four sixty-eight-pounder smooth-bores and two seacoast howitzers, spiked and left by the enemy, were left where they lay, there being no amunition for them, and they being so inferior to the rifled ordnance of our own service. A large magazine was built in the side of the mountain and stored with ammunition sufficient to withstand a long siege. Commissary and Quartermaster's depots were built large enough to contain six months supplies for twenty thousand men. Had those buildings been filled when KIRBY SMITH entered Kentucky in August the story of MORGAN'S Division during the next six months would have been different from the one that the historian is now constrained to write.

In all the work of fortifying and guarding the Gap during the months of June and July, the Forty-Second, which was always ready and always kept in advance, did its full share of watching and work. It first encamped at the summit of the pass, and then moved down into a thicket at the North base of the mountain where a spring of fresh water and clean, level ground offered admirable facilities for a pleasant and permanent camp. Here it remained until the middle of July, when, the Gap being threatened by an attack from the East along the top of the range, the Forty-Second was moved out three miles and encamped on what was known as the Harland road. During the first two months at Cumberland Gap the life of the Forty-Second, though active and in some instances laborious, was serene and pleasant. Heavy details were made for fatigue duty on the permanent fortifications then in progress, and the entire Regiment was often on guard duty at night. Communication with Lexington was constant.

Mails to and from home were regular and frequent; provisions, though not over-abundant, were of excellent quality; the berries which grew in enormous quanties on the foot-hills, contributed variety to the diet of the men, and in that high, bracing mountain air the health of the Regiment was perfect. Convalescents and recruits were brought up from the rear, and on the 1st of July the Forty-Second was numerically as strong for duty as when it marched out of Camp Chase eight months before. It had had, moreover, some active and valuable experience; the men were beginning to comprehend what a serious task the war really was, and to nerve themselves up to the duty of fighting it through. Officers and men had come to know each other, not as civilian companions, but as comrades and allies in the serious business of war, one month of which develops more strength or weakness in a man's character than years of peaceful life. The citizen may be cowardly and mean and yet live for years under a close mask of culture and conventionality without being known for what he is; but one campaign strips off the disguise, and the man, be he generous or selfish, hero or craven, is revealed to those around him.

There was also in the Forty-Second that sentiment of security which comes from mutual reliance between officers and men. When in April, Col. GARFIELD, promoted to a Brigadiership for his successes in the Sandy Valley, had been transferred to another army, a feeling of bitter disappointment had naturally been felt by the Regiment. There might be other officers as brave and even more skillful than he, but he had been from the first the creator and the inspiration of the Forty-Second, and his transfer to the command of a brigade of unknown troops, seemed to the unseasoned sensibilities of his old Regiment an unnecessary defiance of personal preferences. But the men soon learned to regard their bereavement philosophically. Col. SHELDON had developed rapidly into an admirable commanding officer. He was cool, brave, even-tempered, and besides his excellent qualities as a fighter, he was one of the best administrative officers that ever commanded a brigade or regiment. He knew personally every man in the Forty-Second, and his firm, quiet administration of justice in all the details of duty, promoted thorough harmony and confidence.

Lieut.-Col. PARDEE had, from the first time that he was with the Regiment under fire, evinced the qualities of a resolute and impetuous fighter. His military education had made him an iron disciplinarian, but behind and with that was that strength and readiness in emergencies, that tenacity and power of command, which wins from soldiers a respect which no lighter attributes can inspire. In all the hard fighting hours of the Forty-Second, from first to last, the clarion voice of Col PARDEE was its inspiration and guide.

Major WILLIAM H WILLIAMS, promoted to that rank from the Captaincy of Company "B" during the Summer at Cumberland Gap, was, from the first, a brave, popular and efficient officer. It was often his province to command a battalion of two or three companies detailed from the Regiment for a special duty, and on these occasions never failed to acquit himself with excellent credit

Thus officered, and enjoying the special confidence of its Brigade and Division Commanders, the Forty-Second passed at Cumberland Gap, a comparatively pleasant and interesting Summer.

Soon after the occupation of the stronghold by MORGAN's Division, the enemy took up a strong position in the passes of the Clinch Mountains, fifteen or twenty miles to the Southward on the road to Morristown MORGAN was anxious to take the offensive, and, with the Gap as a base, invade East Tennessee. The people of that country were, to a large extent, still loyal to the Union, and only needed an opportunity to rise and aid a Union Army in driving the Confederates beyond their borders. Already in MORGAN's Division were five Tennessee Regiments, made up of men who had fled from their homes to escape conscription or assassination. They had left their families defenceless, and in many cases unprovided for, and they were eager to return as part of an army capable of defending their State and homes. MORGAN repeatedly begged for reinforcements and permission to advance into East Tennessee. He argued that the occupation of that district and the destruction of the Virginia railroad would be a severe blow to LEE, if indeed it did not force the evacuation of Northern Virginia. It would cut off an important foraging ground and destroy an interior communication between the head and body of the Confederacy.

On the 22d of June, being in secure and complete possession of Cumberland Gap, he telegraphed as follows to the Secretary of War and Gen BUELL· "I might as well be without eyes as without cavalry. The enemy is said to have taken up a strong position in the Clinch Mountains in the direction of Morristown. I would advance if authorized, but this place would be threatened from the enemy's present position if I pursued another route. One strong brigade, with five hundred cavalry to act as foragers and scouts, should be left here. I should be strengthened by two brigades of infantry, one battery of artillery, and two regiments of cavalry. With such a force I could sweep East Tennessee of every Rebel soldier."

On the 1st of July he again telegraphed, "I believe that the enemy's force in East Tennessee has been more demoralized by his evacuation of Cumberland Gap than it would have been by an unsuccessful battle. I am certain that with three more brigades I could sweep East Tennessee from Abingdon to Chattanooga." Reinforcements were not sent, and Secretary STANTON directed MORGAN not to advance without orders.

The whole attention of the War Department was concentrated upon Gen. BUELL, who was operating with an immense army

South and East of Nashville, and permitting BRAGG and FORREST to escape through Middle Tennessee into Kentucky. MORGAN was restricted to the simple duty of holding Cumberland Gap.

About the 10th of August KIRBY SMITH moved Northward and invaded Kentucky. SMITH's army marched in two columns—one crossing at Rogers', the other at Big Creek Gap. The Federal magazines and supply depots were captured and MORGAN's sources of supply entirely cut off. His trains were captured and destroyed, and instead of being able to augment his reserve supplies during the season of harvest and plenty, he was obliged to fall back upon the scanty store already accumulated. At no time during MORGAN's occupation of Cumberland Gap did his troops have full rations, and during much of the time they subsisted on less than a third of the prescribed allowance. On the 10th of August, after repeated appeals for more food and forage, he telegraphed to Secretary STANTON "I have only three weeks supplies and these are half rations." That was his last direct communication with Washington. That night JOHN MORGAN's cavalry, the advance of KIRBY SMITH's army, struck the telegraph near Cumberland Ford, and from that time Gen MORGAN and his Division were lost from the records of the War Department until they emerged in October from the wilderness near the mouth of the Big Sandy.

Early in August, as a mask to the Northward movement of Gen. KIRBY SMITH, Cumberland Gap was invested on the South side by Gen C. L. STEPHENSON with an army variously reported at from sixteen to twenty thousand men This was to defend Knoxville against a raid from Cumberland Gap and blockade MORGAN in his citadel, while SMITH invested his rear and made his capture secure. In order to hasten MORGAN's surrender, Gen STEPHENSON drew his lines close around the Gap so as to restrict MORGAN's foraging territory to the small area under range of his guns Before this investiture was made complete, the garrison had displayed great zeal in raking Tennessee within a radius of fifteen or twenty miles, of every pound of food or forage that could be reached. One of these foraging expeditions, made in force early in August, resulted in a sharp encounter with the enemy.

THE TAZEWELL EXPEDITION.

The Federal force engaged included the effective men of three Regiments—the Sixteenth and Forty-Second Ohio and Fourteenth Kentucky Infantry, and a section of FOSTER's Wisconsin Battery, in all about thirteen hundred men. The expedition was under command of Col. DECOURCY of the Sixteenth, and convoyed a train of two hundred wagons, in which to gather and bring back provisions and forage

It started on the morning of Saturday the 2d of August and at four o'clock in the afternoon reached Tazewell, a small village twelve miles South of the Gap The Brigade encamped for the night in the neighborhood of the town, and in the morning proceeded Southward about four miles to a point known as Big Springs, where there was a live stream of water. Near the crossing of this stream was a fork in the road—the right hand branch leading up the valley of the creek in a Westerly direction, the other bearing off to the Southeast across the Clinch Mountains to Bean's Station. A mile or two up the first of these roads from the junction above mentioned, was a mill reported to contain several thousand bushels of corn, which last it was the purpose of the expedition to secure It was therefore necessary to pass the fork of the road with the wagon train and to guard that point from capture so that the train could return. Col. DECOURCY with the Sixteenth and Fourteenth Regiments and half of the Forty-Second, went on with the wagons, leaving Lieut.-Col. PARDEE with Companies "A," "B," "C," "I," and "K," of the Forty-Second, and FOSTER's two guns, to hold the junction of the roads. It was already evident that there were enemies in the vicinity, and Col. PARDEE made his dispositions for defense with great care and judgment. One gun was planted in the road near the junction, in a position to rake the approach from Bean's Station, it being from that direction the attack was expected. The other gun was placed to the right and farther to the rear, on some higher ground, from which it commanded the approach from either direction. Company "C," fifty-four men, under Capt. BUSHNELL, was sent forward a quarter of a mile on the Bean's Station road as an out post. The Company took position on a thickly wooded hill which overlooked the road and commanded a view some distance beyond. Part of Company "A," under Sergeant HENRY, was posted in a cedar thicket in front of and near the junction of the highways; the remainder of the Company, under Capt. OLDS, supported the gun planted in the road. The remainder of the Companies under Col. PARDEE, were posted in squads along a line at right angles with the main road and nearly a mile in length, to give the most exaggerated impression of his defensive strength. In order to improve his opportunities for observation, Col. PARDEE detailed Sergeant O. J. HOPKINS of Company "K," a zealous and clever soldier, to ascend a high hill to the left and front of the main position, and communicate the results of his observations by means of signs previously agreed upon. Certain gestures and attitudes were specified to indicate the approach of infantry, cavalry or artillery. HOPKINS climbed to his perch and mounted watch. This was shortly before noon. About one o'clock, he began to display extraordinary activity. First he made the sign to indicate the approach of cavalry, then infantry was signalled, and finally artillery. All the signals were repeated with great vigor for some minutes, when a column of cavalry appeared, winding down the road to where Company "C" was posted. Capt. BUSHNELL reserved his fire until the horsemen were within easy range, when he gave them a volley which emptied a number of saddles, and wounded and killed several horses. The fire was kept up for several rounds as fast as the men could re load, and the enemy, confused and demoralized by an attack which could not be returned, broke into a precipitate and disorderly retreat. The cavalry was, however, promptly supported by the Confederate infantry, a brigade of which came up in line of battle and evidently prepared for fight. Capt. BUSHNELL reported this to Col. PARDEE, and Company "C" was withdrawn from its exposed position to the main line at the fork of the road. A Rebel battery then came up within perhaps three-fifths of a mile, and taking position, and opened fire upon FOSTER's two guns. These replied promptly, and with their accustomed accuracy, the result being a very picturesque artillery duel which lasted until night with little result on the Federal side beyond that of warning DECOURCY and his force up the valley to return to Tazewell by another road, and thereby avoid re-passing the point at which PARDEE was fighting.

By the most adroit and skillful display of his two hundred men, marching and re-marching them in single rank so as to make companies look like battalions, Col. PARDEE managed to hold in check until nightfall a whole division of Gen. KIRBY SMITH's army, under Gen. STEPHENSON, while the wagons were loaded and returned to Tazewell. It was one of the handsomest manœuvres of its kind in the whole record of the War. STEPHENSON thought that he had encountered the whole of MORGAN's army on its way to attack the Virginia and Tennessee railroad. He accordingly chose a defensive position and awaited attack.

To the rear of Col. PARDEE's position, and between Big Spring and Tazewell, lay a high ridge, across which ran the main road along which the expedition had advanced. Soon after dark, Col. PARDEE retired to this ridge and remained on guard during the night. Enough of the strength of the enemy had been seen during the afternoon to suggest the necessity of strong and alert picket duty at night.

Early in the morning Col. PARDEE and his five Companies were relieved by Company "B" of the Sixteenth Ohio and one Company of the Fourteenth Kentucky. The men thus relieved retired and joined the remainder of the Brigade with the wagons at Tazewell. The two Companies on picket duty stacked their arms and began to regale themselves with berries which grew in great quantities in the woods. While thus engaged, Company "B" of the Sixteenth was surrounded by a regiment of the enemy advancing under cover of the fog, attacked, and Capt. EDGAR, its commanding officer, killed. His men made a gallant effort to rally and recover their muskets, and partly succeeded, but most of the Company was killed, wounded or captured. The survivors, with the Company from the Fourteenth Kentucky, abandoned the ridge and retreated across the valley to the main body near the village STEPHENSON moved up his advance brigade and occupied the position from which the Federal pickets had been driven

A broad, open valley now lay between the hostile forces. It was evident to Col DECOURCY that he was confronted by a vastly superior force, and it became an object with him to make the utmost display of his strength, and thereby keep the Confederates in check until his long train of wagons, now laden with forage, could be got well in motion towards Cumberland Gap.

About nine o'clock in the morning the fog lifted, and a regiment of the enemy was seen to come out of the woods on the hill where the pickets of the Sixteenth had been captured, and advance down into the valley towards the town. At the foot of this slope and at right angles with the advance of the regiment was a lane following the general course of the brook in the valley At the point where this lane debouched into the main road, one of the guns of FOSTER's Battery had been posted the night before, and had not retired when the infantry pickets had retreated in the morning. The gun and its horses were concealed from the view of the advancing regiment by a fringe of bushes which skirted the lane. Sergeant HACKETT, in command of the piece, double-shotted it with canister and trained it so as to rake the lane. On came the Confederates down the slope in line of battle, with colors flying, and, without breaking their line, attempted to cross the lane. At that moment, when the narrow passage was filled with men, HACKETT'S masked gun blazed out of the bushes, sweeping the lane with a hail of canister. How many were killed and wounded is not precisely known, but the slaughter, as related afterwards by members of the Rebel regiment, was enormous. The whole force was thrown into disorder, and, under cover of the momentary panic, the gallant Sergeant limbered up his gun and, with his horses at a gallop, made good his escape to the main body. This daring little exploit had been watched with anxious interest by DeCourcy and his command from the hills above the town, and Sergeant HACKETT and his squad received on their return the congratulations due to their success, and a warning not to take such a risk again.

The enemy now appeared in still increasing force on the farther hill, and it became a matter of doubt whether he could be held in check until night. Col. DeCourcy had learned from scouts and prisoners that the force opposed to this little brigade was a full division of four brigades, and numbering in all not less than seventeen thousand men. The disparity was so great that in the face of such odds he dared not retreat by daylight. Repeating Col PARDEE's tactics of the day before, he spread out his Brigade in single rank, counter-marching companies over exposed points to give the appearance of an army corps taking position for battle. Gen STEPHENSON watched the scene through his glass from his position a mile away, held his division in readiness to meet an attack, and so threw his opportunity away. As darkness settled down over the hills, DeCourcy wheeled his Regiments into the road behind the town, and, marching rapidly, reached Cumberland Gap at three o'clock in the morning, without the loss of a wagon or a man except Capt. EDGAR and those of his Company who were killed, wounded or captured through being surprised while on picket duty. Every wagon was brought back loaded, and a large quantity of supplies was thereby added to the stores of the garrison. The management of the expedition had been so competent and successful, and reflected such credit upon the officers and men engaged, that it was made the subject of a congratulatory order by Gen MORGAN.

THE SIEGE AND EVACUATION OF CUMBERLAND GAP.

DeCourcy had in fact run against the head of an army moving to the invasion of Kentucky. STEPHENSON followed him to within range of the heavy guns on the peaks of Cumberland Gap, and from that time the investiture was complete. Still MORGAN did not give up the effort to eke out his scanty supplies. A few thin cornfields were ripening in Powell's Valley, inside the cordon of the enemy, and these were fought for and gathered acre by acre Twenty-pounder Parrotts were taken out and posted on Poor Valley ridge, a large foot-hill a mile or more South of the Gap, and these drove the enemy back, while a brigade of infantry with wagons could swoop down and gather a few acres of corn. Often a sharp skirmish would be kept up in the edge of a field, while the corn was rapidly harvested in the rear. Movements of this kind were controlled by signals from the Gap, where an officer looking down upon the scene, could see every movement of the enemy, and by flagging frequent messages could keep the Federal force constantly at an advantage The amount of food and forage to be gained in this way was of course limited, and as all communication with the rear was cut off, the supply at the Gap dwindled day by day.

The army of KIRBY SMITH had invaded Kentucky, as already stated, about the 10th of August. His two columns, commanded respectively by Gens CLAIBORNE and CHURCHILL, numbered together twenty-five thousand men. At the same time HUMPHREY MARSHALL, with seven thousand five hundred men, had entered the State from Southwestern Virginia by way of Pound Gap. Gen. SMITH established his headquarters at Barboursville, thirty miles Northwest of Cumberland Gap, and Gen. McCOWN, with two divisions, occupied Cumberland Ford McCOWN soon after his arrival sent a flag of truce to MORGAN with a demand for the surrender of the Gap. He received the reply that if he wanted the place he must come and take it, a task that he did not seem inclined to rashly undertake.

On the 16th of August MORGAN sent a scout through to the Ohio river with this telegram for the Secretary of War. "KIRBY SMITH cannot remain in my rear three weeks, while I can hold this place five weeks with my present command" He held the Gap four weeks and five days after the date of this message

Three days afterward the Federals at Big Hill in Kentucky were defeated and driven back by SMITH's advance. On the 30th he gained another decisive victory over ten thousand raw troops at Richmond, and on the 2d of September occupied Lexington. Frankfort was evacuated, and not a single Union soldier remained between Cumberland Gap and the Ohio river, a distance of two hundred and fifty miles. Gen. HALLECK had promised MORGAN reinforcements, but they never came In order to save the artillery and quartermaster's horses from starvation and at the same time to reinforce the Federal column at Lexington, Col. GARRARD had been some days previously ordered by Gen. MORGAN to mount four hundred of his infantry and, united with

MUNDY'S Cavalry, to proceed to Lexington and report to the General in command at that place. As KIRBY SMITH had advanced toward Lexington he overtook at Loudon and attacked Col. HOUCK, who had occupied that place with a battalion of the Third Tennessee. HOUCK succeeded in escaping to Cumberland Gap. The other battalion of the same regiment did good service at Big Hill, and three battalions of the Seventh Division participated in the action at Richmond.

The question of holding Cumberland Gap was now reduced to one of subsistence only. The fortifications were complete, ammunition was abundant, and no enemy would dare attack it. But how subsist the garrison until the Rebel occupation of Kentucky could be broken? Still continuing his battle for food, MORGAN, on the 8th of September, started DeCOURCY'S Brigade with the Seventh Michigan Battery towards Manchester, thirty-eight miles Northward, and about ten miles East of the main road to Lexington. The Brigade marched at five in the afternoon, leaving all its tents and camp equipage except what the men could carry, but taking in convoy a hundred and nine wagons, of which thirty-nine were loaded with fixed ammunition. The Forty-Second was in advance, and at four o'clock the next morning the Brigade halted and slept in its old quarters at Cumberland Ford. At five p.m., the march was resumed, and on the evening of the 11th the column reached Manchester and camped in a pleasant spot North of the town. The purposes of this movement had been, to reduce by four thousand the number of mouths to be fed at the Gap, secondly, to endeavor to gather and send back food and forage, and, lastly, to have an advance guard and ammunition train thrown out well in advance in case evacuation of the Gap should prove unavoidable. The first and last of these points were gained, the second was lost. The country about Manchester was poor, and it had been already stripped. DECOURCY could find nothing to send back to MORGAN; it was with difficulty that he could subsist his own men and the teams. On leaving the Gap, his Brigade had drawn three biscuits per man, to serve as five days rations, and when corn and sour apples failed they fell back upon paw-paws, the one natural product of that desolate country which could sustain human life. The weather was intensely hot and dry, and JOHN MORGAN'S Cavalry, foraging and recruiting through the country, hovered near enough to keep DECOURCY'S men continually under arms. It was evident that MORGAN knew the position of DECOURCY'S wagon train and was determined to capture it. Nevertheless the defenders maintained a reasonable serenity, and on days when the cavalry was less pressing than usual, the time was improved in brigade and battalion drill

In order to employ the troops at the Gap, Gen. MORGAN, in the hope that KIRBY SMITH would be defeated in Kentucky, had sent detachments to blockade the roads leading to Rogers' and Big Creek Gaps, with the purpose of falling upon the retreating enemy as he was endeavoring to clear away the obstructions. Various other expeditions were made to pick up small detachments and stragglers from SMITH'S army, in the direction of Barboursville and Loudon These little forays, otherwise unimportant, resulted in the killing of one hundred and seventy of the enemy, and the capture of five hundred more, with trifling loss to the Union side

Meanwhile, the suspense at Cumberland Gap was growing serious, unless the enemy were disloged from Central Kentucky and communication re-opened within a few days, the Gap must be surrendered with its garrison or evacuated The first was not to be thought of, the latter would be a desperate alternative MORGAN'S Division was two hundred miles from the Ohio river and the only practicable road thither was held by the enemy.

On the 12th of September the Quartermaster reported to MORGAN that the mules could no longer be fed, and advised that they should be sent to the Ohio river by way of Manchester. To do so would be to give our artillery to the enemy in event of evacuation. The wagons would have to be burned, and the Quartermaster's advice was rejected. For six days the troops had been without bread, and all other supplies were being rapidly exhausted. If MORGAN continued to hold the Gap until compelled by hunger to leave, he would transfer to the enemy thirty-two guns, more than twelve thousand stand of small arms and four hundred wagons. In addition to the Division proper there was a large Quartermaster's force, and a much larger number of East Tennessee refugees who had taken shelter within our lines. All had to be fed.

On the 14th of September a council of war was held. The following are the minutes of the proceedings:

HEADQUARTERS, CUMBERLAND GAP,
September 14th, 1862

A council of war, convened by Brig.-Gen. MORGAN, commanding the forces at Cumberland Gap, assembled at the Headquarters at 11 a.m., to-day. Present—Brig.-Gen MORGAN, commanding, Brig.-Gen SPEARS, Brig,-Gen BAIRD, and Brig.-Gen CARTER. The Brigade of Col DECOURCY absent on detached service. The proceedings were opened by Gen MORGAN stating in detail the information in his possession relating to the position and numbers of the Union and Rebel forces in Virginia, Kentucky and Tennessee, and as to the probabilities of succor, both men and supplies, reaching this post, and of the condition of the troops, as to supplies of food, clothing and ammunition. Gen MORGAN stated that the council was convened to consider the question of remaining at the Gap or evacuating the position, and that he should be governed by the decision of the council as far as that question was concerned After a free interchange of opinion it was agreed unanimously that in view of all the circumstances of the case, the position should be evacuated

Signed by   GEO W. MORGAN, Brigadier-General.
,   J G SPEARS,   "   "
     A BAIRD,   "   "
     S. P. CARTER,   "   "

W P. CRAIGHILL, 1st Lieut. of Engineers, U S A.,
Recorder of the Council.

The following statement shows the total supplies on hand, estimated for twelve thousand men on the day of the evacuation.

STATEMENT OF SUBSISTENCE STORES ON HAND ON THE SEVENTEENTH OF SEPTEMBER, THE DAY OF EVACUATION.

50,384 lbs.	Bacon,	12,000 Men,	5¼	days rations.
336 bushels	Beans,	"	15	"
9,000 lbs.	Rice,	"	7½	"
1,300 "	Sugar,	"	¾	"
19,250 "	Coffee,	"	16	"
11,890 "	Mixed Vegetables	"	17	"
3,631 "	Desicated Potatoes,	"	3½	"
5,650 "	Soap			
75 barrels	Salt			
295 gallons	Vinegar.			

(Signed,) G. M. ADAMS,
Commissary of Subsistence, U S A.

There was but one practicable line of retreat, and that lay through a wilderness destitute of supplies, and sometimes without water for a distance of thirty miles. It was the opinion of Capt. LYONS, who had been the Deputy-Surveyor-General of Kentucky, that that route was impracticable for artillery or a wagon train. There was nothing to do, however, but attempt it. Every instant from the adjournment of the council was devoted to preparation. On the night of the 16th of September a large train was sent towards Manchester, under convoy of the Thirty-Third Indiana Infantry, two companies of the Third Kentucky Infantry, and the Ninth Ohio Battery.

In order to throw the enemy on the Tennessee front off his guard, on the 17th, MORGAN sent Lieut.-Col. GALLUP to the hostile picket line with despatches for Gen. STEPHENSON relative to the exchange of prisoners, and requesting an answer by the next morning. While GALLUP was entertaining the officers of STEPHENSON with gossip and enjoying with them a cigar, some indiscreet bungler set fire to the buildings of the Quartermaster. One mile South of the Gap is the Poor Valley Ridge, which rises abruptly from the plain and extends across the entire valley at the base of the Gap, but leaving two narrow defiles through which run an

East and West as well as a North and South road near the base of the mountain. This ridge forms a complete mask to Cumberland Gap on the South side, but thick smoke from the burning buildings began to curl over its crest and excited the suspicions of the enemy. These were allayed by GALLUP, who ascribed the smoke to the burning of brush on the mountain side After dark the regular pickets were withdrawn, and GALLUP with two hundred picked men undertook the delicate duty of holding the narrow defiles which flanked the Poor Valley Ridge At dark the Brigade of SPEARS with FOSTER's Battery, crossed through the Gap with orders to deploy at the Northern base in line of battle, facing the Westward approach from Baptist Gap, and to hold position until the entire command had passed towards Cumberland Ford

At length the enemy seemed to suspect what was going on, and his pickets pressed forward in the defiles already described They were met by a sharp fire from GALLUP's detachment and fell back CARTER's Brigade then (10 p.m.) passed the Gap, closely followed by BAIRD. The night was dark, and the slow, dangerous and difficult descent was lighted by fires kindled on the mountain side, and by the glare of the now burning buildings The road leading up to the Gap on the South side had been heavily mined, and as soon as the rear of MORGAN's column had gone forward, Capt PATTERSON exploded the mines, and the principal buildings containing quartermaster stores were given to the flames. GALLUP kept out his pickets until nearly morning, when he hurriedly retreated, burned the remaining buildings at the summit of the Gap, and with his own hand fired the train, which with a tremendous explosion that shook the earth for miles, blew up the principal magazine

STEPHENSON, even when he knew the Gap was evacuated, feared to occupy it for several hours, and MORGAN's little army marched away securely, and in as perfect order as though on parade. For more than five miles along the valley road streamed the column of infantry, wagons and ambulances, field and siege artillery, the rear being covered by GALLUP's gallant little force and a small squad of cavalry. As the silent column, lit up by the blazing beacons on the mountain, marched away into the darkness to an uncertain fate, the scene was one which might have inspired a painter or poet.

The march made during the first night was extraordinary for so cumbrous a column. By daylight, the advance had reached Flat Lick, twenty miles from the Gap From that point the division advanced Northeastward by two parallel roads along the valleys of Goose and Stinking Creeks, to the vicinity of Manchester, which point was reached on the night of the 19th. The enemy's cavalry now hovered on our rear and flank, and made a dash at one of our trains, but was repulsed by Col. COOPER. A day's halt was made at Manchester, to more fully prepare for the ugly march before us, and to enable the men to recover from the labor and fatigue which they had undergone.

While there, a sad and unusual episode occurred—the execution of a soldier for murder. A private named STIVERS had the evening before, while intoxicated, quarreled with a comrade, and shot him with his musket. A Court Martial was convened at nine the next morning, at ten the murderer was sentenced to be shot at five in the afternoon The Division was to start at six in the evening, and at the hour appointed for the execution, DE COURCY's Brigade, on drill as usual, formed the sides of a hollow square Just outside the center of the enclosed space was a shallow grave, and to this there came a detachment with the prisoner, followed by an open farm wagon, containing a plain wooden box rudely stained with lampblack. This was placed beside the grave, the death warrant read, and the eyes of the prisoner blindfolded with his handkerchief. He then knelt upon his coffin, the firing squad—

a detail of twelve men from the Sixteenth and Forty-Second Ohio—took their places, and the Lieutenant in command drew his sword

"READY!"—the twelve rifles were raised and cocked;—"AIM!"— they were leveled;—"FIRE!" There was a report as from one musket, and the poor fellow, pierced through the breast and neck by every bullet sprang into the air and fell dead! The band struck up a march, the regiments filed by the flank past the open grave, and the Brigade, without halting, took the road toward the North as rear guard of the Division

With the departure from Manchester began one of the most arduous and perilous marches of the War Thus far the Division had had a reasonably practicable road for its retreat, and it had moved rapidly and without serious obstacle. Thenceforward it had to literally cut and dig its way through nearly two hundred miles of broken, mountainous country, almost wholly barren of supplies, and in many places, for long distances destitute of even water. The interior of Kentucky being occupied by a powerful Confederate army, MORGAN'S only chance of saving his valuable trains and artillery lay in avoiding contact with the enemy, and fighting only what opposition was thrown in his way Two routes to the Ohio lay open to him from Manchester one through Irvine, Jeffersonville and Mount Sterling to Maysville, the other by West Liberty and Grayson to Greenupsburgh, a small town nearly opposite Ironton, Ohio, and twenty miles below the mouth of the Big Sandy. The Maysville route offered the better road, but it would lead to inevitable conflict with a heavy force of infantry and cavalry posted on that route to intercept MORGAN'S retreat and capture his trains The route by West Liberty and Grayson was one of stupendous difficulties It was, in fact, so bad that the Confederates, knowing the country well, considered it impassable and ambushed their heavy force on the road to Maysville. The Grayson route ran Northeasterly across the rugged ridges along the headwaters of a series of small creeks that flow Eastward into the Big Sandy. The few roads that exist in that country run East and West, leading from the interior of the State to the Sandy Valley and Virginia, and following, as is natural, the valleys of the streams which flow in that direction. But MORGAN's route was across the country, through a region so barren and inhospitable that even the mountain corn-cracker and ginseng gatherer had abandoned it to desolation. There was nothing to do, however, but make the effort; and on the night of the 22d of September, as already related, the Division left Manchester for Proctor, on the Kentucky river, at which point the roads to Maysville and Greenupsburgh diverged. The difficulties of the route began immediately. Within sight of the town, the road lay through a deep and narrow defile, just wide enough to admit a wagon. The chasm was filled with large boulders, its slaty bed was so cut and channeled by the stream which ran through it, that there was scarcely sufficient footing for the teams. Strong details of men accompanied the wagons and gun carriages, and held them from capsizing as they were dragged through the gulch. So serious was this first obstacle, that, although the head of MORGAN's column started before sunset, it was midnight before DE COURCY's Brigade, the rear guard, was in motion. Soon after passing this gorge the road forked, and from that point the Division advanced to Proctor in two columns. Capt. ADAMS, the Division Commissary, had been sent forward with a Cavalry escort to seize what supplies could be found at Proctor. He moved rapidly, but the Confederate raider, JOHN MORGAN, was in his front with a brigade of cavalry, intent upon blockading the road and destroying every vestige of subsistence. MORGAN held Proctor until ADAMS approached, when he burned a large flouring mill there, destroying a large quantity of flour, and retreated down the river to Irvine, on the road to Maysville. The main Federal column marched all night of the 22d, all day of the 23d, halted at 9 p m, bivouacked until 2 a m, when the reveille sounded. and the troops again moved forward. Just at dusk on the 23d, a caisson belonging to the Ninth Ohio Battery was capsized into a creek. The shock exploded a percussion shell, which ignited the powder in the chest, tearing the carriage to atoms, wounding four men, and killing a mule.

The Rebel cavalry now appeared in MORGAN's rear in considerable force. One evening a squad made a dash and captured nine men of the Third Kentucky Regiment, who had straggled off in search of something to eat. They came on again, and were handsomely repulsed by the Forty-Second, which was still guarding the rear. After marching all night, SPEARS' and DECOURCY's Brigades, which had taken the hill route, reached Proctor, nearly famished for water. Finding the mill burned and all supplies destroyed, they halted only until noon; then, crossing the river, they took to the hills again, marched all night, and until late in the afternoon of the next day, when they emerged from the hills into a wide, clear, though but partially cultivated valley. They were five miles from Hazel Green. Pushing on, they entered the town at nine o'clock in the evening, capturing a Confederate colonel and captain, who were recruiting in perfect security as they thought—no one for a moment supposing that the Yankees at Cumberland Gap would endeavor to escape through that region. SPEARS and DECOURCY encamped their men in the pleasant meadows about the town, collected and slaughtered the few cattle and sheep that could be found, and awaited the arrival of BAIRD and CARTER, who, with the wagon-trains and the heaviest artillery, were coming from Manchester by the river road, which, though worse cut and destroyed than the road over the hills, afforded an abundance of water. They arrived about noon of the 25th, and the whole Division, reunited in a pleasant spot, rested until the following morning. Hazel Green was a hotbed of secession, there being but five Union men in the county. The Federal troops gave the shiftless inhabitants a novel entertainment by raising the stars and stripes on a hickory pole that stood in the main street, and the band played patriotic airs, which, being neither appreciated nor understood, fell upon stony ground. During the day the valleys about the place were thoroughly searched for cattle, and when the column moved next morning, it had a drove of about sixty head, which were herded and driven in the rear, guarded by the Twenty-Second Kentucky under Lieut.-Col. MONROE. Before the Federal column had been gone from Hazel Green an hour, a company of Confederate cavalry came in, raised sixty recruits in half an hour, and started on to recapture the cattle. They came up with the rear guard just before dusk, caught MONROE'S men in a moment of carelessness, rushed in, killed the herdsmen and stampeded the cattle through the woods. MONROE rallied his men promptly and drove the raiders back with a loss of three killed, but the cattle were scattered, night was at hand, the rest of the column moving rapidly along, and the beef was lost Word was immediately sent forward, and the troops halted and lay down in the road without fire until morning

The Division was now surrounded with foes and had to be prepared to fight at any moment. As before stated, the enemy had counted upon Gen. MORGAN being obliged to retreat toward Maysville. They therefore withdrew from his front at Proctor, and prepared to make a stand at Irvine By pushing his main column and trains to the East of Proctor via Boonville, and sending SPEARS' and DeCOURCY'S Brigades through Proctor, and thence off across the hills to Hazel Green, MORGAN had completely eluded the enemy It only remained to be seen whether the Confederate commander could yet move an infantry force Eastward quickly enough to reach West Liberty or Grayson before MORGAN, and thus intercept his retreat.

The Confederate force was put in motion, and the Rebel JOHN MORGAN sent with his cavalry to blockade the road in front of the Federal column and impede its march He did this zealously but his men were no match in digging and wood-cutting for PATTERSON'S Pioneers In MORGAN's supply train were a number of wagons laden with the axes and shovels which had been used in fortifying Cumberland Gap These were distributed among the men so that the entire command became a force of pioneers, When the enemy's cavalry blockaded the road with rocks and fallen trees, the beleagured column either cut the logs away in a few hours or built a new road round the obstruction. In one case the Rebels had spent nearly a day in filling a rocky gorge nearly two miles in length, with fallen trees They rightly calculated that the logs could not be cut out and the way cleared in less than twenty or thirty hours. But Capt PATTERSON laid out a new path along the side-hill above the blockaded road, the shovels and picks were brought into requisition and in three hours the column marched through. The advance guard came upon and dispersed the blockaders, who, counting upon the inability of MORGAN to get through in less than a day, had gone into camp in a valley beyond

Thus alternately fighting and digging, the Division moved on. The ordinary hours for labor and rest were disregarded. Some part of the column was always in motion. The only rest of the advance brigades was while waiting for the trains and rear guard to pass an obstruction. The only real rest of the rear brigades was while waiting for the advance to dislodge the enemy or clear the blockaded or impassable road. The whole command was reduced to the very verge of famine. The little corn that could be gathered along the way became the only resource of the

Division against absolute starvation. The ears were carefully gathered and if soft, roasted and gnawed from the cob, or if hard, rasped into coarse meal upon rough graters, made by punching holes in tin plates with a bayonet point Each company or mess detailed a man to ride in one of the wagons and grate corn during the march. Each battery had its squad of corn-graters riding on caissons and limber chests, and the monotonous rub, rub of the crackling ear against the perforated tin plate became the only music of the dreary march For days and days together horses were not unharnessed nor cartridge boxes unslung The men slept in their clothing by the roadside, in the woods, wherever the command halt! met them, they rose and fell into their places mechanically when the bugle sounded the advance.

By the evening of the 27th, the head of the column had reached West Liberty. More than two-thirds of the distance from Cumberland Gap to the Ohio had been traversed, and the belief began to grow general that we would somehow get through. Not one in five had any such expectation when the Division left Manchester. From the two recruiting officers captured at Hazel Green, Gen. MORGAN had learned that a strong infantry force was marching to join JOHN MORGAN at West Liberty.

Having now reached that point in advance of the enemy, Gen. MORGAN felt that an important point had been gained. If the enemy came, he would have to fight us on our own ground, while the trains could be sent forward out of danger. Both officers and men were indignant and savage at being obliged to retreat at all. They had been dogged and harrassed by the enemy's cavalry until they were ready and eager for a fight. Gen MORGAN determined to give the force said to be marching from Mount Sterling a chance. Three miles West of West Liberty, on the road from Mount Sterling, is a stream, said to be the only running water in that direction for a distance of more than twenty miles. On reaching Mount Sterling, a brigade was sent out to cross that stream and take up a strong position beyond it. In this position Gen. MORGAN waited two days for his Division to close up, rest, and give the enemy time to arrive. BAIRD and CARTER, with the two rear brigades, arrived in good condition after an exceedingly toilsome march, but the enemy did not appear. Then the report came that the Confederates had turned still further North, and were marching with all speed to head us off at Grayson, fifty miles further on our road. The men had become excessively weary with their long march and hard labor, and in order to lighten their task as much as possible, orders were issued to burn all clothing, blankets and other baggage that could be spared Fires were kindled, and great numbers of overcoats and blankets were burned.

On the afternoon of the 29th, Gen. SPEARS' Brigade moved out six miles, in order to permit the trains to start during the night and overtake the advance by daybreak DECOURCY's Brigade followed, and bivouacked four miles from the town Early next day the whole column started again, but at ten o'clock the advance encountered another heavy blockade, which required several hours to clear away This constant blockading gave color to the theory that the enemy's cavalry was still trying to detain us until a heavier force could reach and occupy the road in our front.

On the evening of the 29th, a foraging party of twenty-one men belonging to SPEARS' Brigade was captured, with some horses and cattle SPEARS sent out a detachment and recaptured the lost cattle, and a number of others which the Rebels were trying to drive away. Next day the Division moved at two o'clock in the morning, but encountered two heavy blockades, one of which was cut away, and the other evaded by cutting a new road nearly a mile in length After twenty-two hours hard work, the troops bivouacked without fire or water and with very little food, having made but eight miles.

The next day was even worse. Starting at two o'clock, after only four hours' rest, the command came before daylight to where the road ran through a deep, rocky gorge, which had been completely obstructed with huge rocks and fallen trees rolled into it from above. Putting a brigade at work upon it, Morgan sent several regiments forward, which soon found other equally serious obstructions. Seven blockades were found and overcome during that memorable day, and a road built round a bridge that had been burned. At this bridge the advance came upon the blockaders and attacked them sharply. Two prisoners were captured, one of whom (a captain) was splendidly mounted and equipped. He was captured by an artillery sergeant and a private of the Forty-Second. In the pockets of his saddle were two pieces of corn-bread. The captured property was divided into two lots—the horse and saddle forming one, the bread the other—and the private was given his choice. So famished was the poor fellow that he chose the bread.

During the day, a captain in a Tennessee regiment was shot through both lungs by a bushwhacker, small gangs of whom had begun to harrass the column night and day. The march was continued without halt or rest until three o'clock next morning, when, having arrived within two miles of Grayson, the column halted while an advance regiment went forward to reconnoiter. It was known that the enemy was in possession of the town, but in what force could not be learned. While the advance proceeded cautiously on its mission, the remainder of the column, staggering with weakness and fatigue, lay down in its tracks and slept. For twenty-five hours the troops had been marching and working, and in that time not one in five of the men had tasted a morsel of food. Even the paw-paws had failed; and as the soldiers marched under oak trees, they picked up the bitter acorns and ate them like famished animals.

At sunrise, after two hours sleep, the bugles again sounded, and the Division marched along the now excellent road into Grayson. The rebels had just gone, driven out at daybreak by our advance. The Division poured forward rapidly, a strong guard was posted on the road leading in from the West, and once more the weary troops were permitted to snatch a few hours' sleep.

The Rubicon was now passed. Grayson was the last point at which an enemy could intercept the retreating column, and that was already in our hands. The tremendous labor of the two preceding days had enabled Gen. MORGAN to pass the blockades in half the time that the enemy calculated, and the Division had reached Grayson two days in advance of their expectations. Those two days purchased safety. The cavalry that we had driven out of Grayson retreated Westward, met a division of Rebel infantry, told the commander that he was too late, the Yankees were already at Grayson, and there the pursuit ended.

It was but fifteen miles further to the Ohio river, and worn out though they were, the troops were eager to be once more on the way. At four in the afternoon, DeCourcy's Brigade, the advance guard, moved out on the Northern road, followed by the trains and the remainder of the Division. Just as the rear of the column was leaving the village, the alarm was given that the enemy was coming by the road on which the Union troops had arrived in the morning. A brigade was quickly thrown into position. Foster's Battery was run out into a field, unlimbered and double-shotted with canister, and for a few moments the troops were on the defensive. The Rebels, however, did not come. They were only a small troop of cavalry, which intended to occcupy the town after the Yankees had left it, but had no idea of hurrying them away.

Four miles from Grayson, the road passes a place known as "The Narrows." At this point the way is cut along the face of a cliff, overhanging the river. The road is just four inches wider than the tracks of an ordinary wagon, and there is a precipice both above and below. To drive four inches out of the way is to throw wagon and team down the steep into the river. Naturally, such a pass as this, several hundred yards in length, was a serious obstacle. Skilful as the drivers of Morgan's Division had become, they were not all equal to the task of passing "The Narrows" safely by night. The first two wagons passed over safely. The third and two others went over the cliff and down into the river. Then the column stopped and waited until daylight, when, with careful and deliberate management, the batteries and the remaining wagons passed over in safety. This was the last trial that beset that memorable march. The weary troops were within ten miles of the Ohio, where food, rest, clothing, and, better than all, news from home awaited them. Their last letters from Ohio had been dated early in August, and it was now the 3d of October. There was no lagging or straggling for nuts and corn that day. Every man was in his place, and the march was rapid and joyous. Shortly after noon, the advance emerged from a rugged gorge into the valley of the Ohio river, and saw before it, half a mile away, the little town of Greenupsburgh, its white walls and spires bright in the October sunshine. The people, as we approached, came out to welcome the lost Army of Cumberland Gap. They had read in the Cincinnati papers of its confinement and probable capture, and when, that morning, a courier sent on ahead announced that the lost Division, with its trains and artillery, was coming, they hurried to prepare food, and came out to welcome us as men resurrected from death. The troops poured into the little town and spread out into the surrounding meadows. The Ohio regiments stacked their arms on the shores of the river, and looked longingly across to the fertile hills of their native State. To those ragged, brown, weary men, Ohio seemed at that moment like an enchanted land. After such a night of sleep as could come only with utter exhaustion, the Division next morning began to cross the Ohio. The batteries were ferried over in large barges, the horses being made to ford and swim. DeCourcy's Brigade, with the Forty-Second, marched six miles down the river, and embarked on three small steamers, which dropped down the river and landed the regiments at Wheelersburgh—on their native heath at last, on loyal ground, amid friends who honored their bravery and pitied their sufferings, among people who cheered their tattered battle-flags and welcomed them to a Union State. It was a bright, warm, Autumn Sunday, and the march of the tattered troops was everywhere an ovation. Congregations assembled at church with great baskets of food, and instead of the ordinary service, they thronged the roadside and fed the soldiers as they passed. Farmers loaded their tables with the best that their land afforded and considered themselves honored by the hungry, ragged and unknown guests who shared their hospitality. It was a day never to be forgotten by any soldier of the Seventh Division.

At Wheelersburgh the troops took trains as fast as they could be provided and were transported to Oak Hill, in Jackson County, where they formed a camp of re-organization and rest. Gen. MORGAN issued an order, congratulating the officers and men of the Division upon the courage, patience and endurance evinced by them during the entire campaign, and for their successful retreat of more than two hundred miles through a mountain wilderness, in the face of enemies and obstacles, dragging through their siege and field artillery and heavy trains laden with valuable Government property.

Major Gen. A. G. WRIGHT, Commanding the Department of the Ohio, forwarded the report of Gen. MORGAN with the following endorsement:

CINCINNATI, October 15th, 1862.

Gen. G W. CALLUM, Chief of Staff,
Headquarters of the Army of the United States

GENERAL,—I have the honor herewith to transmit a copy of the report of Brig.-Gen. GEO. W MORGAN, dated the 12th instant, detailing the circumstances of the withdrawal of his forces from Cumberland Gap. While the evacuation of the Gap is to be regretted, I do not see, with starvation staring him the face, and with no certainty of relief being afforded, how he could have come to any other conclusion than the one arrived at.

The march of Gen MORGAN from Cumberland Gap to the Ohio river was most successfully accomplished, and reflects much credit upon him and his officers for the skill with which it was conducted, and upon the men for the cheerfulness with which they bore the hardships of a toilsome march of some two hundred miles on scanty fare over a country affording little subsistence, and often for long marches without water.

H. G WRIGHT,
Major-General Commanding.

Th evacuation of Cumberland Gap, though variously criticised at the time and censured by Gen. HALLECK, was long ago shown to have been the one course left, by which Gen. MORGAN could save his army, after the occupation of Kentucky by BRAGG and KIRBY SMITH in the Summer of 1862. The testimony of Col VANCE, who commanded a brigade of STEPHENSON's army and wrote to Gen. MORGAN in 1864, describes the plan by which STEPHENSON within forty-eight hours more would have surrounded the Gap, blockaded and occupied all the roads, and made MORGAN's escape with his train and artillery impossible. Col. VANCE says: "It was the opinion of every officer of rank in our army that you moved at exactly the proper time, and with great skill and judgment."

Gen. BRAGG, in his official report of the operations of the Confederate army in Kentucky during the Summer of 1862, gives this interesting and significant testimony:

"Orders had also been given for a close observation of the enemy at Cumberland Gap, and that he should be intercepted in any attempt to escape. On my arrival at Bardstown, I learned from Gen SMITH that the enemy was moving from Cumberland Gap endeavoring to escape by the valley of the Sandy river in Eastern Kentucky, and that he had sent his whole available force in pursuit. A sufficient force to prevent *this escape and compel the enemy's surrender, had been ordered and confidently expected from another quarter* to have followed Gen. SMITH's movements in time for this purpose. Circumstances in the then isolated position, and over which I could not control, had prevented this consumation so confidently relied on, and so necessary to success. The delay resulting from this pursuit of the enemy by Gen. SMITH, prevented a junction of our forces and enabled Gen. BUELL to reach Louisville before the assault could be made upon that city."

CHAPTER V.

IN THE FIELD AGAIN—FROM OHIO TO WESTERN VIRGINIA, AND THE YAZOO RIVER—THE ASSAULT AND REPULSE AT CHICKASAW BLUFFS—THE TRAGIC CLOSE OF A MEMORABLE YEAR.

The brief but welcome period of rest and preparation at Oak Hill, which followed the campaign in Southeastern Kentucky and the arduous retreat from Cumberland Gap, proved an important turning point in the history of the Forty-Second. From that time it may be said that the fortunes of the Regiment underwent an important change. Its previous experiences had been in connection with movements and events of secondary importance in the grand drama of the War. Though doing bravely and well the work set before it, the Regiment had during its first year of service served as part of comparatively small detachments of the Union Army and operated on the margin of the great struggle rather than its center. The close of the Cumberland Gap campaign was to the Forty-Second very nearly the end of that kind of service. From that time it became identified with the great and important movement which closed the war in the Mississippi Valley, and first made the assurance of ultimate victory secure.

Before joining in this important movement, however, there was a brief episode of desultory service, which, though unimportant in its results, yet formed a part of the history of the Regiment. The pleasant period of relaxation and leisure at Oak Hill continued from the 9th to the 23d of October. Though a pleasant contrast to the experiences of the previous ten months, it was by no means the luxurious episode that might have been expected. The Division, nearly naked and destitute of every material and equipment essential to camp life, was turned loose in an upland township, already brown with the sharp frosts of October, to literally shift for itself. There were neither tents, barracks, clothing, blankets, or sufficient food. Only one small railroad was available for bringing supplies, and this was quickly overtaxed. Many articles of Quartermaster's stores could not be supplied in sufficient quantity from Ohio and had to be brought from Eastern departments. Many of the men were wholly without trowsers, and went about wrapped in blankets like Indians. Others had pantaloons but were barefooted. Some made rude, awkward garments from blankets, and others still, sent home for clothing to cover their nakedness. For days at a time the troops were without bread of any kind. In pleasant weather they lived in pens made of rails or under the oak trees; when it rained they took refuge in barns and the neighboring houses. A hundred recruits, bravely dressed and equipped, came to the Forty-Second from Camp Dennison at this time, and the rueful looks of the novices as they looked at the ragged, bare-footed veterans, was the theme of many a joke. Finally, after about ten days of disappointment and grumbling, the supplies began to arrive. They were promptly distributed, the whole Division paid, and nearly the entire Forty-Second began to ask leave of absence, when orders were received to march overland to Gallipolis.

The distance was about forty miles, and the Regiment, newly

shod, clothed and equipped, its muskets polished and its knapsacks heavy with the offerings of liberal homes and the pay day opulence of the Sutler's tent, turned its face Southward and made the journey in joyous spirits on two bright October days. Having reached Gallipolis it was found that the re-organized Seventh Division had been, temporarily at least, assigned to the forces of Gen. J. D. Cox, commanding the Department of West Virginia, with headquarters at Gallipolis, and that the immediate purpose of this reinforcement was to enable Cox to dislodge the Rebel Gen. FLOYD, who, with several thousand men had descended the Great Kanawha, captured Charleston and the important salt works at that place, and threatened, unless resisted, to descend the Kanawha to its mouth and lay an embargo upon the navigation of the Ohio. It was reported that FLOYD was fortifying Charleston and a position some miles below it, and had obviously come to stay. One great need of the Confederacy was salt, and the immediate re-capture of Charleston was therefore an object of importance.

At Gallipolis we found everything in a state of active preparation. Artillery and cavalry were refitting, and supplies were being collected and forwarded to Point Pleasant, the mouth of the Kanawha. The Forty-Second, being already in complete condition, had only to drill and enjoy itself during the few days of its stay at that curious old French town. A review of DeCourcy's Brigade passed off with great *éclat*, the Forty-Second receiving the special commendation of Gen Cox for its fine marching and soldierly bearing.

On the 27th, the Brigade broke camp, marched seven miles up the Ohio, crossed the river upon steamboats at Point Pleasant and began the march up the Kanawha Valley to Charleston, sixty miles distant. The march was for the most part uneventful. The weather was perfect, the road, compared with what we had traversed in Kentucky, was admirable, and although an enemy of unknown strength and purposes was in front, the movement upon Charleston was one of the pleasant episodes of the year.

The fact which most seriously interfered with the happiness of the Forty-Second in those days, was what was then regarded the unnecessarily harsh and irksome discipline enforced in the Brigade by its commander, Col. JOHN F. DeCOURCY. This officer, the Colonel of the Sixteenth Ohio, was a graduate of the British service, a brave but not always judicious soldier of fortune, who had joined the Union Army mainly because it afforded him employment in the line of his profession. He had no personal attachments with any of his subordinates, and he set out to bring the volunteer soldiers of his regiment and brigade under the strict, precise discipline of the British service It was an experience which the Forty-Second, like other volunteer regiments, undoubtedly needed, but it was a trying experience at the time. To the practical volunteer who had gone into the service for the sake of whipping the Confederacy, rather than that of becoming an accomplished soldier, the general result naturally overshadowed all little niceties of method. To such a man, accustomed to do his work in the easiest, most direct and effective way, there was a boundless absurdity in the requirement that a soldier on guard, walking a beat hour after hour, should carry his knapsack with his overcoat and blanket strapped thereon, and his haversack dangling below. Why not set down the knapsack at one end of the beat and march up and down unencumbered? said the soldiers, but DeCOURCY said otherwise, and as he held the rank he carried his point. The slightest infractions of discipline, little irregularities committed in entire innocence, were punished by the most degrading penalties. A favorite device of the austere Colonel was to have the men whose muskets were found spotted with rust, loaded with rails and marched up and down in front of his quarters during the evening. This kind of discipline may have made the men of the Forty-Second better soldiers, but it did not increase their affection for their Brigade commander.

The march to Charleston occupied three days. On the evening of the 30th, our advance neared the town and found the enemy gone and going Gen. FLOYD had been accurately informed of the force coming against him, and as his irregular force was adapted to the duty of raiding rather than fighting, he abandoned his entrenchments on the approach of DECOURCY's column and withdrew across the mountains. A small detachment of cavalry with a section of artillery pursued the retreating enemy as far as Gauley Bridge, but the expedition from first to last was a bloodless one. The infantry, including the Forty Second, encamped on a broad, beautiful meadow below the town and resumed the regular routine of company, battalion and brigade drill. A few articles of clothing and equipage which had failed to reach us at Camp Jackson were brought forward by steamer and the troops were made once more as comfortable in respect to clothing and equipment as the regulations and exigencies of field service would permit.

But this period of rest was brief Important events were in progress, and the Government could spare no such Division as that of Gen. MORGAN to go into Winter quarters in November. On the 9th of that month, orders were received for a return to the Ohio river. On the morning of the 10th camp was broken, and the Brigade set out on what proved a forced march of twenty-five miles per day, to Point Pleasant. As there was no apparent cause for haste, the conclusion was that Col. DECOURCY had pushed the Brigade through on quick time by way of exercise, to see how much the men could stand. However that may have been, it reached the Ohio river on the 13th, and at once went on board the sidewheel steamer "Fannie McBurney," whose officers gave us the first hint of our destination. They were under orders, they said, for Memphis, and it was rightly conjectured from that moment that we were to be transferred to a new Department, and to share in more important campaigns than those of the Big Sandy and Cumberland Gap.

The time had now come for the breaking up of Gen MORGAN's little army, the Seventh Division of the Army of the Ohio. Gen. BAIRD's Brigade was sent to Kentucky, those of SPEARS and CARTER returned to Tennessee, while Gen. MORGAN, with DeCOURCY's Brigade and FOSTER's Battery, were ordered to Memphis to join the army there organizing under Gen SHERMAN for a campaign against Vicksburgh, at that time the grand objective point of military operations in the West.

The embarkation of the Forty-Second at Point Pleasant was the end of its service in the border States and the beginning of a long and interesting voyage. Six months' pay had been received, and a halo of opulence illumined the voyage down the river. November in that latitude corresponds in climate very nearly to the October of the lake region, and the mellow haze and brilliant foliage of Indian Summer still overspread the land. The boats containing the Sixteenth Ohio and Twenty-Second Kentucky, which constituted the remainder of our brigade, kept us close company, and on the 16th the little flotilla reached Cincinnati. It was not deemed consistent with the interests of the service that either officers or soldiers should go ashore, so the "Fanny McBurney" was anchored out in the stream. Finally, however, she was constrained to come up and be moored to a wharf-boat while coal and other supplies were taken on board Then the vast ingenuity of the Forty-Second men was brought into play to devise means for getting ashore. A few of the more adventurous spirits tied up their clothes in their water-proof blankets, harnessed the bundle with a string which they held between their teeth, swam ashore and made a hasty toilet on the bank.

It was a hazardous and uncomfortable method of debarkation, but a few thus made their point and got ashore, and to a soldier, loose in a city like Cincinnati, with money in his pocket, the peril of wet feet and a blue nose had no terrors. The next morning, it was discovered that a numerous delegation of the Forty-Second men had managed to land, and were disporting themselves in the city. A provost guard was at once detailed and sent ashore to gather in the fugitives. As the squad marched up the levee, it suggested an idea to those remaining on board. Within half an hour, two more squads, with neatly polished muskets and shapely knapsacks, marched along the planks and passed the guards unchallenged. Had not an officer seen through the trick and interposed, it is possible that the whole Regiment would have been ashore within an hour, each soldier operating on a plan of his own to surround and bring the remainder of the Regiment on board. Finally, Lieut.-Col. Pardee, who was in command, seemed to think that the fun had gone far enough, and dispatched a new force of provost guards to bring in the previous ones. At the head of one of these squads, Sergeant Flynn, of Company "E," won the only commission ever gained in the Regiment by a single act of meritorious duty, picking up and bringing back under guard every comrade he could find. Sergeant Flynn earned a lieutenancy, and set a valuable example.

There was little comfort or enjoyment to be found under existing orders during our stay at Cincinnati; and there was a very general feeling of relief when, on the morning of the second day, we found the boat again under way and steaming down the Ohio. The voyage to Memphis was pleasant until it became monotonous; after that it was endured like everything else. The river was low, and on dark nights the boats were tied up to the shore to avoid risks. As we passed Cairo, Island No. 10, Fort Wright, and other points of interest, there would be a stir among the men and a marshaling of the curious ones on one side of the boat to see the passing wonder, but at other times, sleeping, card-playing, letter-writing, and patient but hardly successful efforts to cook coffee and bacon at the furnace fires, wore out the lagging but not unpleasant hours.

Finally, on the night of the 26th, the steamer reached Memphis, and the next morning we found our boat anchored out in the river in front of the city. A high, bluff bank rose from the shore, pierced at two or three places with steep roads or paved streets, which ran down to the levee, to which wharf boats were moored as we had seen them at Cincinnati. Two iron-clad gunboats, low, dark, mysterious-looking crafts, were anchored near us, and as they had already become famous through the part which they had played at Fort Donelson and Island No. 10, we surveyed them with great interest During the day, we received the welcome order to make preparations for going ashore. The boat swung up to the wharf, and the Forty-Second, putting its best foot foremost, marched up the levee and through Memphis to a beautiful camping ground a mile or two in the rear of the city. It was the first real city that the Regiment had marched through for many a weary month, and the sight of the handsome buildings, the busy, well-dressed crowds, and the evidences of comforts and luxuries to which we had so long been strangers, made the day's experience a novel and fascinating one. Our camp ground was a beautiful plain, with oak trees scattered here and there, and afforded ample facilities for systematic camp life and drill. It had been formerly a fair ground and race course, then for a long time a Confederate camp of instruction, and before we reached it had been so thoroughly stripped of fences and everything that would burn or aid in the construction of a soldier's hut, that it resembled a city lawn or the carefully-kept meadow of an English farm. With only the vaguest idea of what it had come to Memphis for, the Forty-Second went into camp with the hope that this was to be its home for the winter. Although nearly the first of December, the weather was warm, bright and balmy, like the earlier days of October at home. That we should be permitted, after all our rough service, to have one winter of city duty, seemed too good to be true, and we yet clung to the hope until delusion was no longer possible.

But we could not long deceive ourselves. There was nothing about us to indicate a quiet or settled condition of things. The city was full of soldiers; away to the South of us two divisions of troops were encamped. They had just returned from an expedition to Corinth and Holly Springs and beyond, and their wagons and gun-carriages splashed with mud, their poor, worn horses and travel-stained appearance confirmed the report of hard marching and rough service. They had been under GRANT, they said, and had suddenly been turned back and hurried to Memphis, which, as we could plainly see and feel, was the gathering ground of a powerful expedition.

Meanwhile, the Forty-Second had been put to its work. A small daily detail was made for picket duty on the roads leading out of the city, and the remainder of the Regiment drilled from morning till night. Squad drill, company, battalion and brigade drill, with all their wearying iteration of what we thought we had learned sufficiently in Camp Chase, filled those few busy, but pleasant days.

One of the events of that period was a grand review of our Division by Gen. SHERMAN, in which we had an opportunity to learn something of the strength and organization of the command to which we had been assigned. Our Division was the Third of the Army of Mississippi, and formed the right wing of the Thirteenth Army Corps. It was commanded by Brig.-Gen. GEO. W. MORGAN, and was constituted as follows:

FIRST BRIGADE,
Col L A SHELDON, Commanding.

Sixty-Ninth Indiana Infantry,	Col T. W. BENNFIT
Hundred and Eighteenth Illinois Infantry,	Col J G FONDA
Hundred and Twentieth Ohio Infantry,	Lt.-Col. D. FRENCH.

SECOND BRIGADE,
Col. D W. LINDSAY, Commanding.

Third Kentucky Infantry,	Lt.-Col. D W. RITZELL.
Forty-Ninth Indiana Infantry,	Col JAS. KAIGWIN
Fourteenth Ohio Infantry,	Lt.-Col H B. MAYNARD.

THIRD BRIGADE,
Col JOHN F DECOURCY, Commanding.

Sixteenth Ohio Infantry,	Lt -Col. P KERSHNER.
Forty-Second Ohio Infantry,	Lt -Col. DON A. PARDEE.
Twenty-Second Kentucky Infantry,	Lt.-Col J W MONROE.
Fifty-Fourth Indiana Infantry,	Col. F. MANSFIELD.
First Wisconsin Battery,	Capt JACOB T. FOSTER.
Seventh Michigan Battery,	Capt. C. H LANPHERE

This Corps contained, besides, the Divisions of FRED. STEELE, A. J. SMITH and MORGAN L. SMITH, and had an aggregate strength of thirty thousand men. They were mostly veterans, the flower of the Western Army, collected from various departments for a special duty Organization went on rapidly, ammunition was issued, arms inspected, and every preparation rapidly made complete.

On the 14th of November, marching orders were issued, and on the 19th the Corps, stripped of all but absolutely essential baggage and equipage, broke camp and marched through the city to the river. The Forty-Second embarked on the large side-wheel steamer " Des Moines," and the men quickly adapted themselves to the close quarters, the smells, the noises and other familiar discomforts of shipboard. The Divisions of A. J and M L SMITH, which had been arriving from Holly Springs by regiments and brigades for a fortnight past, were also embarking, and the loading of artillery, wagons, horses, entrenching tools and supplies of every kind went on all day and until eleven o'clock at night, when the fleet got under way, the long line of colored lights streaming down the river for miles.

The bright sunlight of the following morning revealed a magnificent spectacle. The squadron included nearly seventy of the largest steamers on the river. They moved in single file, preceded by two powerful gunboats, the steamers preserving intervals of five or six hundred yards. The water was at a good stage and rising, and as the long line of boats, covered with troops and gaudy with flags and streamers, swept down the broad and winding river, to the music of bands and the battle-songs of regiments, the scene was one of superb color and spirit. It was a glimpse of the "pomp and circumstance of war," the brief, bright holiday before the battle. Last of all came a steamer laden with plain wooden coffins. There was a grim suggestiveness about that particular craft which gave birth to many facetious remarks, but we had seen too many dead men buried without coffins to be much disturbed by that careful provision for the inevitable.

We had left Memphis on Saturday night, stopped at Helena before daybreak for the boats of the rear division to close up, and in the morning resumed the voyage. During the day, the leading boats were fired upon by some guerrillas on the Mississippi shore, whereat the gunboats shelled a small village to which the marauders had retreated. The shells set fire to the town, and as night had come, the fleet was tied up to the bank and remained until morning, the pilots being unwilling to risk the chances of a night attack.

On the afternoon of the 25th, the expedition reached the mouth of the Yazoo, a dark, deep, sluggish stream coming in from the Eastward. The gunboats proceeded up the Yazoo, the transports remained during the night, waiting for something which we could not understand. It was inexplicable, that on the eve of an attack which ought to have been so sudden as to give the enemy no gratuitous opportunity to reinforce and fortify, the whole fleet should be held waiting for a day within sight of Vicksburgh, while our officers held a Court Martial to try a common soldier for vandalism during the voyage down. In fixing the responsibility for the subsequent failure of the expedition, that mysterious delay at the mouth of the Yazoo should be seriously considered.

Gen. BURBRIDGE's Brigade was landed on the West side of the river, and started off rapidly in a Southwesterly direction, its object being, as we afterwards learned, to sieze and destroy the Vicksburgh and Shreveport railroad, by means of which the enemy at Vicksburgh had maintained communication with Western Louisiana and Texas.

THE ATTACK UPON CHICKASAW BLUFFS.

The operations of Gen. SHERMAN's expedition during the five days from the 26th of December, 1862, until the 1st of January following, gave to the history of the War a chapter which has since been the theme of vigorous dispute. It was a desperate assault, bravely and tenaciously made, but it failed, and was rightly regarded in the North a serious and ill-timed disaster to the Union cause. Thirteen years afterward, the commanding officer of that expedition has published a narrative which lays the blame of his failure upon his troops, specifically upon the Brigade of which the Forty-Second Regiment formed a part. Justice to the dead and living, and fidelity to the truth of history, alike require that this account of those terrible five days be carefully and impartially written.

On the morning of the 26th, the fleet of transports carrying Gen. SHERMAN's army steamed up the Yazoo river between ten and twelve miles, and, under protection of the gunboats, which lay still farther up the stream, promptly effected a landing on the Southern or left bank of the river. The fleet was extended two or three miles up and down the shore, and along this front infantry lines were thrown out and advanced several hundred yards back from the river, to cover the ground necessary for disembarking the army and its equipment. DeCourcy's Brigade, which landed at a point known as James' Plantation, was included in this temporary line of defense. It lay on its arms during the greater part of the day, while strong details of men were unloading the artillery and other encumbrances from the boats. Late in the afternoon, the Brigade advanced perhaps two miles along a plantation road leading in the direction of Vicksburgh. Just before night, it encountered a cavalry picket of the enemy, which, after a brief skirmish, was driven in, and DeCourcy's command bivouacked for the night in a cold, dismal rain, which greatly increased the dreariness and discomfort of the situation.

In order to comprehend intelligently the difficulties of the attack upon Chickasaw Bluffs, a clear, specific understanding of the ground is essential. The alluvial plain upon which Gen. Sherman's army had landed is a triangle, some twelve miles long by four or five in breadth. The Northern line of this triangle is the Yazoo river, flowing Westward into the Mississippi, which it intersects at a point nine or ten miles above Vicksburgh. Below the mouth of the Yazoo, the Mississippi bears strongly to the Eastward, forming an acute angle with the line of the Yazoo. Across this acute angle, and forming the third and shortest side of the triangle, runs Chickasaw Bayou, a deep, tortuous, sluggish stream, debouching at one end into the Yazoo, and at the other into the Mississippi. The bayou is in fact the central ditch or channel of a cypress swamp (once no doubt the main bed of the Yazoo), extending from the Yazoo, just below Haines' Bluff across to the Mississippi, a sort of short-cut for the waters of the former stream during the flood season. The triangular island is rich, mellow bottom land, subject to overflow, and about equally divided between heavy timber and open cotton-fields, at that time soft and miry from the late Autumn rains.

East of the bayou, and extending parallel with it in a Northeasterly direction from Vicksburgh to the Yazoo river, is a range of hills At the point where this line of hills intersects the Yazoo it is called Haines' Bluff. Nearer the city the elevation is known as Walnut Hills, but to SHERMAN's army the whole ridge was known from first to last as the Chickasaw Bluffs.

Along this commanding position, behind a series of entrenchments, more or less formidable as the ground required, lay the enemy, already strong in numbers, and being hourly strengthened by the arrival of reinforcements from Jackson, Mobile, and from PEMBERTON's army at Grenada and Holly Springs Haines' Bluff was heavily and permanently fortified on its Yazoo front, and from there along the entire ridge to the parapets of Vicksburgh ran a system of trenches and batteries which made the naturally strong position practically impregnable against attack in front. Had the ground at the foot of the bluff been firm and solid, had no other obstacle than the high ridge, seamed with trenches and manned from end to end by an equal force, confronted SHERMAN's little army, the task of capturing Vicksburgh from that direction would have been a well nigh impossible one. Add to these difficulties the fact that between the Confederates in their trenches on the hills and the Federals on the plain below lay the deep bayou, at some places eighty feet in width, flanked on either side by cypress swamps, the heavy timber of which had been slashed down in confused heaps and windrows of logs and brush, and the difficulties of the assault become still more obvious.

With this brief glance at the battle-field we return to the Forty-Second, bivouacked as advance guard along the road from James'

Plantation to Vicksburgh, and a mile from Yazoo river. The 27th dawned clear, warm and beautiful, and, as usually happens, the favoring weather dispelled the temporary gloom of the situation and put the troops into a more contented and hopeful frame of mind During the forenoon the column moved forward across a wide, open space, and by noon had reached the margin of a heavy wood, along which ran a small creek, flowing in the direction of our march and emptying, as we afterwards discovered, into Chickasaw bayou. As we neared this wood, a line of skirmishers came out to meet us, and as our front was covered with a strong skirmish line a spirited little encounter took place, more showy and picturesque than serious. In this part of the days work the Forty-Second bore a part, Companies "A" and "G" being deployed as skirmishers during the day. The Rebels made no definite stand there but fell back across the creek into the woods, and the column, following the farm road along the stream, soon encountered more serious opposition. About two o'clock in the afternoon, SMITH's Division, advancing perhaps a mile to our right by a parallel route, struck the enemy in force at the edge of the woods which skirted the bayou and swamp. SMITH used his artillery to drive the enemy out of the dense thicket in his front Gen. MORGAN's column halted for a few moments, strengthened its advance guard and again pushed forward to where the road, still following the margin of the little creek, turned into the swampy woods. Here the enemy was encountered in strong force and a hot engagement ensued. FOSTER's Battery, which had been kept well up to the front in support of the skirmish line, unlimbered and began firing over the heads of the skirmishers with percussion shells and afterwards with canister. But the Rebels, strongly posted behind large trees and the shelving bank of the creek, held their ground stubbornly, keeping themselves covered while the Federals were on open ground. At one time the enemy worked round under cover of the thick underbrush, and, firing across the creek, attacked Gen. MORGAN in flank and at very short range. The infantry, which had been marching by the flank, simply faced to the left forming line of battle, and raked the thicket with a volley that drove the enemy's skirmishers out. By this time the short December day was nearly gone. SMITH's Division on our right had been fighting desperately since early in the afternoon. MORGAN threw out a brigade to the right, pushed it forward into the edge of the woods, driving the enemy back into the swamp where the thick undergrowth and the darkness of the gathering night obscured their movements and made further pursuit at that time impracticable. The troops bivouacked in line where they stood at the close of the fighting, and LANPHERE's Battery was brought close up and posted so as to be ready for attack or defense. FOSTER's Battery of twenty-pounder Parrott guns was posted immediately in rear of DECOURCY's Brigade and near the margin of the wood

About nine o'clock in the evening the Forty-Second was stirred up and withdrawn from the front line and set to work to build an earthwork around FOSTER's Battery to serve as a shield for the gunners in case we were hard pressed on the morrow. The men worked briskly, and by two o'clock in the morning the earthwork was finished, and the six Parrotts grinned out through embrasures neatly revetted and ready, if need were, for a serious siege.

The night was too cold for sleep, and as the Fifty-Fourth Indiana had taken the place of the Forty Second in the front line, there was nothing to do but shiver round until morning in that dreary discomfort that pervades a fireless camp on a Winter's night. At dawn small fires were kindled, and the weary men snatched a few moments of comfort and a hasty meal.

As soon as daylight became clear the Sixteenth Ohio moved forward, and, finding the enemy in position just within the margin of the wood, promptly began the attack. LANPHERE'S Battery chimed in immediately, then the Twenty-Second Kentucky, followed by the Fifty-Fourth Indiana, and before sunrise the firing in our front had become a continuous roar. The morning was hazy, the smoke of battle settled thick and heavy over the swamp, and through this mist the rising sun shone red and ominous. We thought of the sun of Austerlitz, and wondered whether the red glow of that morning would prove the harbinger of triumph to us or our enemies.

Until nine o'clock the firing continued fierce and incessant. The Union line had advanced only a few rods and seemed to have met a permanent check. For the last hour the two opposing lines had stood in their tracks, neither advancing nor retreating a step. The losses were becoming serious and nothing important had been gained. Preparations were made for a push forward to drive the enemy through the woods and across the first bayou to the slashed swamp and open fields beyond.

At nine o'clock, the Forty-Second, which had remained at the rear in support of FOSTER'S Battery, was sent to the front. Two sections of the Parrott guns were dragged out of the earthwork and sent forward by hand without caissons. It was too hot a place to take horses into. DECOURCY'S Brigade was quickly deployed— the Twenty-Second Kentucky on the right, then the Fifty-Fourth Indiana, the Forty-Second next, and the Sixteenth Ohio on the left. The line moved promptly forward, and a sharp fight ensued at short range, both sides taking advantage of the heavy timber and uneven ground to keep as well as possible under cover. The swampy valley was cut and seamed with dry ditches and water courses, which afforded strong and numerous lines of defense. From this point to close of that days fighting the work of the Forty-Second is so well described in a published letter written by Capt. OLDS of Company "A," that his spirited account is here inserted in his own words, as a memorial stone in the pages of this history to the memory of a brave officer and a blameless man.

"At twenty minutes past nine," says Capt. OLDS, "a forward movement was ordered The Forty-Second charges down into the dry bed of a bayou leading directly toward the enemy's batteries. We rush forward fifty paces and halt to examine the ground We dare not go further, for we will be raked from front to rear. The Brigade lies down. A sharp fire continues along the whole line. Balls come, zip-zip, into the trees and ground around us; occasionally, *thud!* a bullet takes some poor fellow, and he is carried to the rear. Two of LANPHERE's guns have crossed and taken position. Col DeCOURCY comes to me and inquires the position of the Rebel batteries. An order is sent back, and one of FOSTER's twenty-pounders is brought up, and takes position to command them. Col DeCOURCY shouts the command, "The Brigade will advance!" Col PARDEE instructs me to form division (that is, a front of two Companies, "A" and "F") as soon as the nature of the ground will permit, and calls out, "Forty-Second Ohio forward!" We turn to the right, out of the bayou, and just as we rise over the bank, four of my men fall together under the fire of two regiments of the enemy. It is a critical moment—the men waver. The Rebels stand firm, their batteries open upon us I call out, 'Forward, boys, they are shooting over us—now is the time—Hurrah!' they are breaking' We raised such a shout that we were heard by the divisions far to our right, infusing courage into the men behind, and adding speed to the now wavering and retreating enemy. Closely we pursued them, unmindful of the storm of canister and shell that rained thickly over and around us. Many Rebels threw down their guns and gave themselves up. I ordered them to the rear, but was astonished, on turning round to point to them the way, to find no one following us The rest of the Brigade had lain down to escape the terrific fire pouring upon it. Fortunately for us, we could separate and shelter ourselves behind trees. The Fifty-Fourth Indiana broke, and the wonder is that more did not, so fearful was the fire which we were required to face. The Rebels, seeing so few of us, endeavored to rally their men. Some turned at bay on our right, but the boys brought them down and pushed on. We now came to the edge of the wood and a piece of fallen timber within three hundred yards of their first line of works. Here we thought best to make a stand till the rest of the Brigade could come up, sheltering ourselves as well as we could, and blazing away at every Rebel that offered a mark."

"Col. DeCourcy now came forward, complimented the men for their gallantry, examined the position, and ordered up Lanphere's Battery. The guns took position just in rear of Company "A's" skirmish line, and for an hour worked as coolly as though shooting at a target, firing fifty rounds from each gun. It would be vain to attempt any description of the noise and confusion of that hour, of bursting shell and shrieking grape, of flying splinters and crashing trees. Three times did shells strike trees behind which I stood, covering me with splinters. One burst not more than a yard in front of Lieut. Chas E. Henry, with nothing in the world to shelter him The fragments passed just over my head, and I turned expecting to see him blown to atoms, but when the smoke cleared away, he stood with a smile on his face as if nothing had happened. He might have been a little blanched, but his complexion was still dark. Gradually the firing on both sides ceased, except an occasional shot along the picket line. We spent the night where we were, without fires, contenting ourselves with gnawing a little hard bread and cold boiled meat. The Rebels made no effort to conceal their numbers, and camp-fires gleamed along their whole line All night we could hear the whistling of locomotives in the direction of Vicksburg, and we knew that heavy reinforcements were continually arriving from Jackson."

Thus ended the second days fighting at Chickasaw In our part of the line the enemy had been driven forward through the woods and across the first bayou, which was deep and impassable except at one or two points, swept at short range by their batteries and defended by entrenched infantry. The work before us was now to provide means for crossing the bayou, go over, flounder through the waste of fallen timber beyond, cross the open field at the foot of the bluff and attack the heights. A serious task it proved, as the record of the next day will show.

Meanwhile, Gen STEELE, commanding the extreme left division of the Federal line, had landed farther up the Yazoo, above the mouth of Chickasaw bayou, and had pressed forward and found it impossible to reach the bluffs from that direction on account of the extent and depth of the swamp. He left a small show of force there and returned by way of the steamboats on the Yazoo, his men being put in on the left of MORGAN's Division, where they occupied a dense thicket and skirmished sharply with the enemy across the bayou on the afternooon of the 28th The bayou could not be crossed in front of Gen. STEELE, and his Division took no further active part in the attack.

During the night the pontoon train came up, a small, shabby affair, and, as we soon discovered, quite inadequate for the needs of that position The boats were heavy, clumsy, and ill-provided. One sank as soon as it was launched. Another was struck by a shell and rendered useless, and when the one bridge that could be made by our pontoon train was laid it was so short and imperfect that it was next to impossible to march the troops across by the flank without breaking the formation of companies and divisions.

With only these imperfect means of crossing, MORGAN, on the

29th, began preparations for the attack. The day before had been bright and warm, but the morning of the assault dawned raw and cloudy, with signs of rain. The ground over which the advance was to be made was that in front of the two left Brigades of MORGAN'S Division, commanded respectively by Gen. FRANK BLAIR and Col. DeCOURCY, and it was to those two Brigades that the assault was entrusted. Along the rest of the line, three or four miles in extent, a show of attack was to be kept up, and at one point in front of A. J. SMITH'S position a real effort was to be made to push across the bayou and sieze a fortified knoll which commanded the direct road from Johnson's plantation along the foot of the bluff to Vicksburgh. During the night of the 28th and the morning of the 29th, skirmishers had crept out and at some cost had examined the ground over which BLAIR and DeCOURCY were to advance. Just in front, immediately at the edge of the wood, was a bayou filled with water too deep to be forded and flanked by steep banks. Along this bayou the artillery was ranged to cover with its fire the advance of the storming columns. Immediately beyond the first bayou lay a tract of rough, swampy ground perhaps fifty rods across, piled and strewn with fallen timber, the heavy swamp woods having been cut down to impede approach and give range to the enemy's guns. Beyond the slashed timber and parallel with the first bayou lay a second and more difficult one. It was in fact a long pool and quagmire of varying width and unknown depth. The road by which DeCOURCY'S Brigade was to advance was a mere path through the woods, entirely obliterated by the fallen trees. Where this path struck the farther bayou it turned abruptly to the left, followed the edge of the water about twelve rods, then turning sharply to the front, crossed the bayou on a rough log bridge or causeway, about ten feet in width, to the solid ground which sloped upward and forward to the base of the bluff. The whole distance from the starting point of the storming columns to the first trenches of the enemy was perhaps three-fifths of a mile. A careful examination of the ground convinced Gen. MORGAN that any assault at that point must end in disastrous failure. The only chance of success had been lost by our three or four days of delay since reaching the mouth of the Yazoo, during which time the enemy had been reinforced until he out-numbered the attacking force. All this Gen MORGAN and his brigade commanders saw, and early in the day he sent Lieut. DENT, a staff officer, with a request that Gen. SHERMAN should come to the field. Together the two Generals rode up and down in front of the line, MORGAN pointing out the difficulties of the advance, the fresh earthworks thrown up by the enemy during the night, and advised against what he and his officers considered a reckless and unavailing sacrifice of life. Gen SHERMAN, disappointed and morose, looked at the ground, and then turning his horse, rode back, without saying a word, to his former position, a mile and a half to the right and rear of MORGAN's line. This was about nine o'clock in the morning. The abrupt departure of Gen SHERMAN from the point of attack left Gen MORGAN in doubt whether the assault would be attempted or abandoned. At all events he determined not to take the responsibility of what he felt sure would be a costly and fruitless experiment without direct and positive orders, and therefore waited in the hope that some other course would be adopted. But at noon an officer from SHERMAN's Staff came to MORGAN and said, "I came from Gen. SHERMAN and will give you his words. He said. 'Tell MORGAN that I wish him to give the signal for the assault, *that we will lose five thousand men in taking Vicksburgh, and may as well lose them now*'" To which MORGAN replied "We will lose the men, but from this position we will not take Vicksburgh."

Nevertheless, there was but one thing to do, obey orders, and

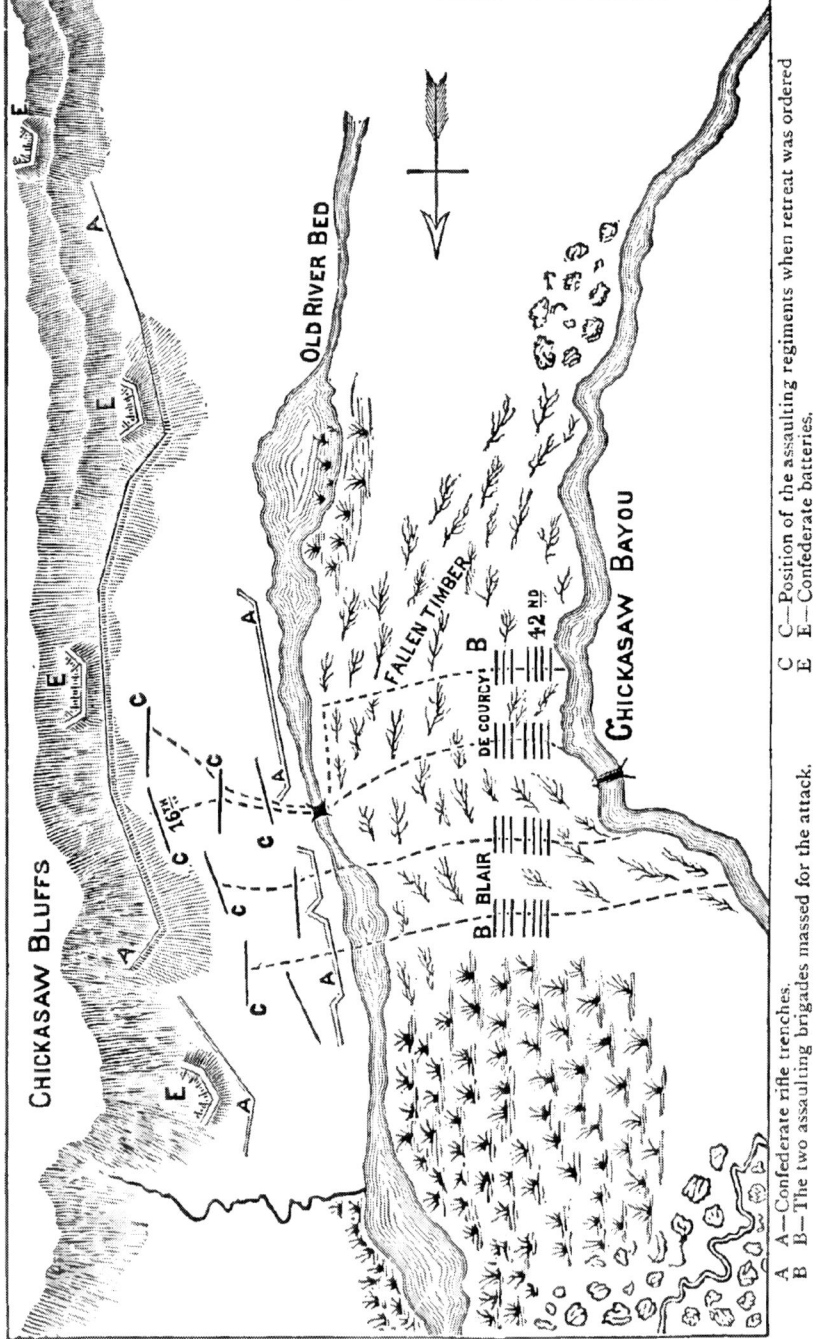

THE ASSAULT AT CHICKASAW BLUFFS.

Gen. MORGAN gave the order to advance. The troops were formed in column of divisions and massed in the formation known as "double column at half distance"—that is a close column in which the right company of each division marched forward by its left flank file right and the left hand company by the right flank file left. By this plan the troops were condensed into a narrow column to cross the slashing and the narrow causeway beyond, but ready to deploy into a column of divisions as soon as the open ground was reached.

DeCourcy's Brigade was arranged as follows First in front, the Sixteenth Ohio, then the Twenty-Second Kentucky, thirdly the Fifty-Fourth Indiana, and last, the Forty-Second Ohio, which having been on duty all night, was by usage entitled to the reserve The Brigade numbered that day not more than fifteen hundred men. BLAIR's Brigade, numbering perhaps two thousand, was about twenty rods to our left, formed in similar order and ready to advance by a route parallel to that of DeCourcy, the two Brigades being prepared to render mutual support.

At a given signal, the batteries of MORGAN and SMITH, posted along the line of the first bayou, opened simultaneously, working as rapidly as possible to keep down the enemy's fire. At the same moment the two assaulting Brigades started forward, each crossing on its narrow and frail bridge under the muzzle of the Union guns and advancing across the slashed timber. The enemy opened fire instantly and swept the whole valley with shells, shrapnel, canister and musketry. Marching in close order, the men climbed logs and tore through tree tops, pushing forward as best they might. The front regiments encountered the most difficulties, and three times during the passage of the fifty rods of fallen timber the Forty-Second and Fifty-Fourth had to lie down and wait for the leading regiments to get forward.

During this part of the advance Col. PARDEE was struck in the leg by a musket ball, but it was partly spent and lodged in his boot. His brother, GEORGE K. PARDEE, received a ball in the breast, but the missile buried itself in a memorandum book carried in his pocket and GEORGE, though knocked down and left for dead, was not seriously hurt. Major WILLIAMS found a straggler from the Twenty-Second Kentucky behind a log, dragged him out and was leading him to the front, when, just as the Forty-Second reached the causeway across the bayou, a bullet killed the Kentuckian, and the Major dropped his prisoner, for whom there was no more fear in this world.

Meanwhile, the three leading regiments had executed the flank march along the bayou and crossed the narrow bridge. Reaching the solid ground beyond, they deployed in column of divisions and marched rapidly up the slope. The Forty-Second followed closely, but before it had advanced fifty yards beyond the bridge, the leading regiments began to melt away under the constantly increasing fire. The proposed point of attack upon the bluff proved to be the interior of an arc or semi-circle, so that as the storming Brigade advanced it found itself in the center of a converging fire, the column raked from batteries and rifle pits directly in front, the divisions enfiladed from either side by cannon posted at each extremity of the crescent. Bravely and determinedly the little column pushed forward, closing up the gaps torn in its divisions by the steady and deadly fire of an enemy now within easy range and perfectly protected. When within a few yards of the trenches at the foot of the hill, the Sixteenth Ohio, which had lost nearly all its officers, including its commander Lieut.-Col. KERSHNER, and had been riddled until its ranks had nearly half melted away, broke and fell back against the Twenty-Second Kentucky. In a moment the utter hopelessness of the assault, which had been apparent from the first, overcame even the discipline of that veteran Brigade, and the leading regiments were thrown into confusion. The order was given to retire. Hardly a shot had been fired by the advancing column. The fire which it faced had been so terrible that it could not stop to fight at such hopeless odds As the broken divisions turned to retreat, the Rebels poured out of their trenches and gathered in such of the Federals as had come too near to escape. The rest, leaving behind the dead and wounded, retired down the slope and re-crossed the causeway, the Forty-Second covering the retreat in good order.

On the left BLAIR's Brigade had gone through a precisely similar experience, with the exception that it had found even a worse crossing than DeCourcy's men and had been longer delayed in getting over the second bayou Gen BLAIR attempted to cross the slough on horse-back, but his horse was mired, and the General, drawing his pistols from his holsters, leaped off and floundered through the mud and water with his men. Like DeCourcy's, BLAIR's advance had nearly reached the enemy's line, but it was one man against three, and both were obliged to retire.

In his "Memoirs" Gen. SHERMAN attributes the repulse to "the failure of MORGAN to support BLAIR's attack with DeCourcy." The fact was that both Brigades were pushing to the same point, DeCourcy slightly in advance, and both retreated at the same time. The statement that DeCourcy's men "could not be moved forward," is answered by the fact that numbers of the Sixteenth Ohio fell within sixty yards of the rifle pits More than this, BLAIR lost in the assault five hundred and five men, while DeCourcy, with inferior numbers engaged, lost five hundred and eighty.

The discomfited Brigades returned to their position in the woods, and for the remainder of the day the fighting was confined to the artillery It was a disastrous and hopeless repulse, as we all knew, and the night, which set in with heavy and continuous rain, was one of gloom, discomfort and discouragement All night long a heavy gun on the heights flashed out at regular intervals, sending a shell over into our drenched and cheerless camp. The night was spent in wondering where the next shell would strike.

Morning finally came, and before mid-day a flag of truce was sent by Capt. LYON of Gen. MORGAN's Staff, to ask a suspension of hostilities until we might gather the wounded and bury the dead who had fallen the day before. The flag was fired upon, the truce failed, and such of the wounded as were still alive were left out in another night of storm and cold. This was the 30th of December. During the day the artillery had kept up its usual steady fire, but with trifling effect. Some of FOSTER's guns, which had got the range with great accuracy, exploded two caissons in the earthworks on the hill and in one of these explosions a son of the Governor of Mississippi, an aide to Gen. PEMBERTON, was killed.

The rain continued through the night of the 30th, and the low, marshy ground upon which SHERMAN's army lay became a miry swamp On the 31st the troops continued to fortify against an attack from the front, and at noon another flag of truce was sent out. By this time Gen. PEMBERTON had arrived from Grenada and taken command, and the flag was respected. A truce of three hours was granted, a road was quickly cut forward to the bayou, the ambulances were sent forward with strong details of men, and came back in long trains laden with dead Many of the poor fellows bore evidence of having been wounded in the assault and subsequently shot and bayoneted by the vandals who came out of the enemy's trenches to strip the dying men of their clothing. After forty-eight hours of thirst, hunger and exposure on that bloody field, two wounded men remained alive, though both subsequently died. The dead were laid in a long line in a cotton field near the scene of our first days fight, and buried without dirge or ceremony.

The enemy was still reinforcing and seemed about to assume the offensive. The front line of Federal pickets was doubled, and all the troops slept on their arms. The rain had ceased and the air had become bitterly cold. It was the last night of 1862. Chilled and cheerless, without fire and still harassed by that all-night gun, the troops lay down in the freezing mud and thought of the New Year's Eve in their Northern homes.

At ten o'clock a staff officer came along the line and whispered a hurried order to the commanders of brigades. Other aids were sent with mysterious messages to colonels and artillery captains. The gunners were roused up and set to work muffling the wheels of the gun carriages with wisps of hay. Then the horses were brought quietly up from the rear, where they had been kept since the evening of the 28th, and in doubled teams, twelve horses to a gun, dragged the cannon out of the miry swamp. The infantry was stirred up, and without a word audibly spoken, the regiments, following the artillery, filed out of the wood and took the road past Johnson's house back to the Yazoo. By day-break the whole army was re-embarked on board the fleet, and the boats began dropping down the river. Such as carried artillery were delayed by the work of embarking the guns from a high, steep bank, and remained to see the Rebel skirmishers come streaming across the cotton fields. They even came close to the landing and fired into the crowded boats, killing several men, but the upper decks were manned with sharp-shooters, and, with the aid of a brisk cannonade from the gun-boats, the enemy's skirmishers were driven back. The fleet steamed down to the mouth of the Yazoo, and the disastrous expedition, the first and worst defeat that the Forty-Second Ohio ever shared, was over.

Concerning the responsibilities of that defeat, there was at the time but one opinion. The case was fairly and impartially stated by Gen. SHERMAN'S official report of the campaign, in which he said. "On the night of the 29th we stood upon our original ground and had suffered a repulse. The effort was necessary to a successful accomplishment of my orders, and the combinations were the best possible under the circumstances I assume all the responsibility and attach fault to no one, and am generally satisfied with the high spirit manifested by all. I attribute our failure to the strength of the enemy's position, both natural and artificial, and to his superior fighting"

As for Gen. SHERMAN'S Army, it retired from this defeat feeling that it had been needlessly punished in an effort to accomplish what had been from the first impossible. It did not know that Gen. SHERMAN'S attack was part of a combination designed to busy the garrison while Gen. GRANT'S column drove PEMBERTON down through Central Mississippi and assailed Vicksburgh in the rear. Gen. GRANT'S column had reached Coffeeville on the 30th of December, when the raid of VAN DORN'S Cavalry upon his line of communications, with the destruction of his depot of supplies at Holly Springs, forced him to turn back, leaving PEMBERTON'S whole force which had been confronting GRANT to return to Vicksburgh and swell the already overwhelming odds against SHERMAN. No news came of the counter-march of GRANT'S column, and SHERMAN went on to carry out his part of the plan by making the attack on the appointed day.

In the absence of any knowledge of the general plan, Gen. SHERMAN'S army, at a loss to account for the curious generalship of the attack, suspected that he might be insane. This was not the opinion of enlisted men merely, but of their officers as well. No army ever better knew when it was ably or recklessly commanded than the legions of the North that fought in the War of the Rebellion, and it is not strange that the excuses and accusations published by the General of the Army thirteen years after the event, reversing his own official report and throwing the responsibility of the failure at Chickasaw upon his troops, have been resented as gratuitous and unjust. Gen. SHERMAN's original report stated the facts fairly, more or less than that is not history

CHAPTER VI.

ARKANSAS POST—THE CAPTURE OF FORT HINDMAN—RETURN TO
YOUNG'S POINT.

When the army returned to the mouth of the Yazoo river on the afternoon of January 2d, it found Major-Gen. JOHN A. MCCLERNAND on board the steamer "Tigress," with orders to supercede Gen. SHERMAN. He brought the news that Gen. GRANT was not coming to Vicksburgh by the interior route through Mississippi, but had turned back from Coffeeville and Oxford to Holly Springs and Memphis. It was this withdrawal of Gen GRANT'S attack from the North, which, as already related, had left Gen. PEMBERTON free to throw his whole army upon us at Chickasaw Bayou.

The fleet, accompanied by the gun-boats under Admiral PORTER, moved ten miles up the Mississippi, and rendezvoused at Milliken's Bend The army, still on board the transports, was re-organized into two Corps—the First commanded by Gen. GEO. W. MORGAN, the Second by Gen SHERMAN, Gen. MCCLERNAND being in chief command. Among the troops there was great anxiety and interest as to what the army would next undertake. Chance threw into the hands of Gen. MCCLERNAND a fortuitous opportunity which he improved in such a way as to inspire his men with new confidence and courage.

While we had been operating on the Yazoo, a small ordnance steamer, the "Blue Wing," coming down with a load of musket cartridges and mails for the army, was captured by a Rebel boat which had come out of the Arkansas river. The captured steamer had been towed up the latter stream to Arkansas Post, or Fort Hindman as it was called, about forty miles from the Mississippi.

The Fort was a heavy, bastioned earthwork, built upon the site of an old Government trading post, the mart for many years of traffic with the Indians. A group of old-fashioned brick buildings with an orchard and a cleared space of perhaps a hundred acres. constituted all that was left of Arkansas Post until the Confederates took possession of it early in 1862 and built Fort Hindman at the head of a long, ox-bow curve in the river. Thus situated, the Fort, which stood on a bluff bank thirty feet above the water, commanded the river both up and down to the extent of the range of its guns. From the rear of the Fort a long parapet, revetted with logs, extended back nearly or quite half a mile facing down the river In front of this parapet, which was guarded by a deep outside ditch, the timber had been cut and arranged as *chevaux de frise*, so that the place, garrisoned by about five thousand Texas troops, was a formidable obstacle to the Federal possession of that country. As long as it remained in Confederate hands, there could be no safety for the communications of an army operating river-ward against Vicksburgh, and Gen. MCCLERNAND, while waiting for the water to rise and the Winter to pass away, resolved to move his whole force against it.

The fleet steamed up, and on the 8th of January reached the mouth of White river, which flows into the Mississippi a few miles above the mouth of the Arkansas. Between the White and Arkansas rivers there is a bayou or cut-off, navigable at ordinary stages of water, and forming a perfect channel of communication. To deceive the enemy as to its destination, the transport flotilla, preceded by three iron-clads, moved up the White river, took the cut-off across to the Arkansas and appeared just below Fort Hindman on the 10th. The landing was difficult, but the troops got promptly ashore on the East bank and moved up towards the Fort, Gen. SHERMAN's Corps in the advance.

About a mile below Fort Hindman was an exterior line of rifle pits strengthened by a levee running from the river to the swamp and enclosing a large village of log huts outside the Fort, in which the majority of the garrison apparently lived. At this point they made their first stand, and Gen. SHERMAN's Corps, coming up to this obstacle, moved by the flank to the right so as to reach round and enclose the entire position.

By the time that MORGAN's Corps was ashore with its artillery and ready to support SHERMAN's advance, the short Winter day was spent. It was followed by a bright and beautiful night with a full moon, and the troops, though moving over strange ground, covered and obscured by dense woods and thickets, rapidly enveloped the Rebel lines. Finding themselves in danger of being surrounded, the Confederates, soon after dark, abandoned their outer line and fell back to a second village standing in a cleared space in rear of the Fort and shielded by dense thickets in front and toward the river. Word was sent to Gen SHERMAN that the enemy had abandoned his front line, and that commander, who was leading STEELE's Division by a long road round the swamp, had to counter-march, and did not get back into position in front of new line until nearly morning.

Just before sunset the Rebels had opened fire from the Fort upon the transports in the river, and by way of keeping them busy and getting the range, the three iron-clads had steamed up and engaged the Fort in gallant style. (It was this fire from the gun-boats in a position from which they could have raked the rear of the cross levee, that forced the enemy to abandon his front line early that night.) The Confederate gunners maintained their fire sharply with two eight-inch smooth bore guns in casemates on the river front, and from a nine-inch columbiad *en barbette* on the Southwest angle of the Fort. The casemates were mailed with railroad iron, closely matched and interlocked, which proved quite an effective armor, but one of the gun-boats got an eight inch shell into a casemate through the embrasure, which destroyed half the detachment working the gun. The duel between the Fort and gun-boats made quite a pretty spectacle, but comparatively small damage was done on either side.

Gen. SHERMAN before daylight had his column well extended round to the right, giving room for Gen. MORGAN to put one division into line. The remainder of MORGAN'S Corps, including DECOURCY'S Brigade with the Forty-Second, bivouacked in some large corn-fields near the landing, known as Lambdin's farm. The night was sharp and frosty, but rails were abundant, and as MCCLERNAND had no special object in concealing his numbers or position, fires were allowed and the bivouac was made comfortable The troops up at the front could hear formidable preparations going on within the enemy's lines Wagons and artillery were moving, and the whole garrison was at work tearing down houses, building rifle trenches, extending the outer parapet and making ready for the morrow.

From some pickets captured soon after landing in the afternoon, it had been learned that two boat loads of reinforcements were expected from Duvall's Bluff and Little Rock, further up the river. A trap was set for them. Two sections of FOSTER'S Battery with two ten-pounders from the Mercantile Battery of Chicago, were sent on board the steamer " Des Arc," to drop five miles down the river, land on the West bank and cross the neck of land to

Smith's plantation, on the river above the Fort. This was accomplished, and before morning the six guns were grinning over the levee near the plantation house, a mile and a half above the Fort, and ready to sink whatever transports might endeavor to pass.

With this disposition, Fort Hindman, before any real attack upon it had commenced, was almost entirely surrounded But one avenue of retreat remained open to the garrison, a road leading up the North side of the river through a dense cottonwood forest, and the chances were that SHERMAN would reach round and occupy that as soon as daylight enabled him to see his way.

Upon this situation the morning sun of Sunday, January 11th, rose cloudless and beautiful. It was such a day as in the latitude of Ohio comes sometimes to break the gloom of November. The Confederate reveille was blown, clear and shrill, at dawn The Federal bugles took up the strain, and the eventful day was opened with as tuneful a morning call as ever woke an army to battle. The Rebels were up promptly and at their posts as soon as the growing light made their position visible. Evidently they had not slept much The long line of out-works running back from the Fort had been strengthened and extended nearly to the dense swamp about a mile back from the river An amazing amount of fresh dirt had been thrown up, and from behind the new parapet the guns of two field batteries peeped out

Through about the center of the isthmus of solid ground between the swamp and river, upon which Fort Hindman and the new earthworks were built, ran a road. SHERMAN'S Corps was ordered to take the right of this, MORGAN'S Corps the left. The plan was that Admiral PORTER with the gun-boats should assail the Fort from the river, while the troops should drive the enemy into their fortifications, work up to within easy distance and capture the works by assault.

DeCourcy's Brigade was astir early in its camp at the landing below. It had lost more than a third of its numbers at Chickasaw Bayou and Gen. MORGAN preferred to hold it in reserve that day unless its services were actually needed. Leaving DECOURCY, therefore, posted so as to watch the road by which STEELE's Division had counter-marched, and to guard the fleet from attack, Gen. MORGAN, with the remainder of his Corps, pushed up to the front.

He had with him A. J. SMITH's Division of two Brigades, commanded respectively by Gen. A. J. SMITH and Col. L. A. SHELDON of the Forty-Second Ohio, and LIGHTBURNE's Brigade of OSTERHAUS' Division, the other Brigade of OSTERHAUS' (DE-COURCY's) being left, as already explained, to watch the White river road and guard the boats. SMITH's Division was put in on MORGAN's right, joining the left of SHERMAN's Corps, and to the left of SMITH, LINDSAY, whose line reached to the bank of the river. McCLERNAND felt sure of his game now and did not force the fighting. He could afford to take the Fort scientifically, and spare as far as possible the lives of his men. They might have charged across the open ground, clambered over the obstructions and through the ditch and captured the works in thirty minutes, or even less, but it would have been at a great sacrifice of life. It was preferable to disable the casemate guns, dismount the lighter ones and give the garrison a good morning's work before making the assault.

Accordingly, all being ready, at 11 o'clock the gun-boats advanced in splendid style and engaged the Fort at short range. They fired rapidly and with such effect that the railroad iron was peeled from the casemates, and before noon the nine-inch barbette gun was struck in the muzzle, split and broken away nearly back to the trunnions. Two twenty-pounder Parrots from FOSTER's Battery were run up behind a large sycamore log on the river bank, three hundred yards from the Fort, and from that advantageous position sent shell after shell into the embrasures of the casemates. These two guns, which were fired with the deliberate accuracy of a sharp-shooter's target rifle, also dismounted and capsized a twelve-pounder iron gun that during the morning had been worked industriously from the Northeastern bastion of the Fort. The other batteries of MORGAN and SHERMAN engaged the field guns behind the parapet and after a sharp duel, in which the Rebel guns used a great quantity of shrapnel and canister, pretty effectually silenced them. An hour of sharp fighting drove the enemy entirely within the works. The assailants had also got so near that no further advance could be made without undertaking a direct assault.

By this time the gun boats had come up directly under the Fort; so near in fact that they actually passed by and opened a reverse fire upon it. But their part was mainly done. The casemates and the water front of the Fort were silenced.

Gen. SHERMAN had extended his attack so far round to the right that his line was weakened on the left, and he called upon MORGAN for reinforcements. MORGAN sent him the three reserve regiments of SMITH'S Division and immediately dispatched a courier to bring up DECOURCY. This gallant Brigade was found ready, and, on receiving the summons, hurried forward at a pace which soon brought it to the front. It was put in between LINDSAY'S Brigade and SMITH'S Division, and formed for the assault in column of regiments, the Forty-Second Ohio in front

While this was taking place a fierce artillery fire opened from the point of land across the river. At first it was thought to be a hostile reinforcement from Little Rock, and LINDSAY'S guns were trained upon it, but just as they were about to fire it was discovered that the guns beyond the river were firing into the Fort and along its West front, enfilading the rear of the Rebel outworks with terrible effect. It was FOSTER, who had been sent up above the night before to intercept any transports that might come with reinforcements from up the river, and who, after watching the battle for some hours, could not keep silent, but had come down on his own responsibility to take a hand in the finish. His fire reached the vitals of the Confederate position, set fire to buildings hitherto sheltered by the Fort, swept the plain in its rear and hastened the surrender.

DeCourcy's assaulting column moved rapidly forward through the brush and across the open space in front of the works. The fire that met this advance was vigorous, but the enemy was excited and aimed wildly They saw the storming column coming and knew that further resistance was useless. Suddenly a white flag was run up at the Northeastern angle of the Fort. The firing suddenly ceased and DeCourcy's men began to cheer. Then the white flag was pulled down and a thin, scattering volley sputtered along the Rebel line. The flag had been unauthorized, and the fight was not yet officially over. Then the whole Federal line, including Foster's guns on the other side, poured in a final broadside, the finishing blow of that day's work. Instantly the signals of surrender appeared all along the enemy's line. White handkerchiefs, tufts of cotton and gray hats were held up on ramrods and bayonets from behind their parapet. The command " cease firing," was given, and in a moment all was hushed excepting a few irregular shots far round to the right. The Rebels stood up behind their works and the victorious army gave three such cheers as are heard but once in a life time. The Forty-Second, already within a few feet of the ditch, swarmed over the parapet and assisted in gathering up the prisoners. Five thousand men, with all that was left of the Fort and its guns, were unconditionally surrendered after a gallant resistance against overwhelming numbers. A horse battery with every animal dead in the traces, lay just to the right of where the Forty-Second crossed the parapet. A large number of Rebel dead had been thrown into a deep gorge, washed out by the rains in rear of the Fort. Others had been burned up in some barns which had been fired by FOSTER's shells. On the whole, the scenes within the works were far worse than on the outside.

The post had been commanded by a Gen CHURCHILL, and the two infantry brigades were led by a Col GARLAND and Gen. DESHLER, the latter a West Point officer. The prisoners stacked their arms and were marched down to the river bank. Their losses, notwithstanding the protection afforded by their works, had been severe, and the wounded and dead lay thick behind the parapet, inside the Fort, and in the large buildings at the rear, which had been used as hospitals By an unfortunate chance these buildings stood in the direct range of the gun-boat shells which over-shot the Fort, they had been riddled and many of the wounded unintentionally killed

Soon after dusk, when every thing had become quiet, two Confederate regiments from Pine Bluff came marching in and found themselves prisoners of war. They piled their guns and were marched to the river bank, venting their feelings, meanwhile, in the hard and picturesque swearing for which Texan civilization is distinguished.

Next morning the prisoners were put on board transports and sent to St. Louis A heavy detail was set to work leveling the Fort and parapet, the casemates and magazines were burned and blown up, and the whole work completely destroyed.

That night there came on a terrible snow storm, and on the morning of the 13th, the battle-field was buried under more than a foot of snow. The troops re-embarked, and through the snow storm dropped down the river and rendezvoused at Napoleon

MCCLERNAND's loss had been about a thousand men killed and wounded, about equally divided between SHERMAN's and MOR-

GAN's Corps. Gen. GRANT did not at first approve the turning aside of the whole army from its attack on Vicksburgh to capture a post on the Arkansas river, but the promptness and completeness of the conquest fully justified the movement, as Gen. GRANT readily admitted. The army came down the Arkansas in splendid spirits and with the demoralization induced by Chickasaw Bluffs thoroughly cured. Gen. GRANT arrived at the rendezvous on the 18th of January, took command of the army and ordered the fleet down the river to Young's Point on the Louisiana side, opposite the mouth of the Yazoo river, where all arrived on the 21st.

CHAPTER VII.

THE CAMPAIGN BEFORE VICKSBURGH—WINTER AT YOUNG'S POINT—THE CANAL—MILLIKEN'S BEND—THE OVERLAND MARCH TO NEW CARTHAGE—GRAND GULF—THE LANDING AT BRUINSBURGH AND THE BATTLE AT PORT GIBSON—ROCKY SPRINGS, RAYMOND, CHAMPION'S HILL AND BLACK RIVER BRIDGE—VICKSBURGH INVESTED—THE ASSAULTS OF THE 19TH AND 22ND OF MAY.

On returning to the vicinity of Vicksburgh, MORGAN'S Corps landed at Young's Point on the Louisiana shore seven miles above the city and encamped wherever favorable ground could be selected in the rear of the levee. SHERMAN'S Corps landed at the same point, but marched three miles farther down and encamped at the base of the long, spear-shaped peninsula opposite Vicksburgh. Across the neck of this peninsula a shallow canal had been cut during the previous year, but the water had subsided before it could be finished, and it had been thus far useless. The river was now rapidly rising, and it was the purpose of Gen GRANT to complete this canal, whether with the expectation that it would open a channel of communication past the city, or simply by way of keeping the troops partially employed during a season of enforced inactivity, was a point on which opinions differed.

The landing of the army was slow and irregular, and the men, who had lived mostly on transports for five weeks with little or no opportunity to cook their rations, were impatient to get ashore. While on board the boats they had been obliged to subsist mainly upon raw pork and hard bread, with no fresh vegetables of any kind During the voyage down from Arkansas Post, the Forty-Second, while foraging on shore one night, had found in a large gin-house several thousand bushels of yams, or sweet potatoes, large quantities had with proper permission been carried on board. These saved the Regiment from scurvy, which by that time had begun to break out in other regiments and to seriously compromise the health of the army With the permanent landing at Young's Point it was hoped that more healthful conditions would prevail, a hope which, as will be seen, was but imperfectly realized

On the 28th of January, Gen MORGAN, our Division and Corps commander since the previous April, was relieved from command at his own request on account of failing health For a month past he had kept the field in defiance of the protests of his surgeon, and upon the re-organization of the army at Young's Point he consented to retire.

The re-organization was by virtue of Military Order, No. 210, of December 18th, 1862, from the War Department, which had been received while the troops were returning from Arkansas Post. It divided the Western armies into five *Corps d'Armee*, as follows· The Thirteenth Corps, commanded by Major-Gen. MCCLERNAND, the Fourteenth, by Major Gen GEO. H. THOMAS, the Fifteenth, by Major-Gen. SHERMAN, the Sixteenth, by Major-Gen. HURLBUT; and the Seventeenth, by Major-Gen. MCPHERSON. Gen. THOMAS' Corps was in Middle Tennessee, HURLBUT'S was at Memphis; MCPHERSON'S in the rear of Memphis, and on its way to join the forces in front of Vicksburgh, and the Corps of MCCLERNAND and SHERMAN, as already stated, were at Young's

Point. The Thirteenth Corps, the largest of the five named, comprised four divisions, commanded respectively by Generals P. J. OSTERHAUS, A J SMITH, E. A CARR and A. P HOVEY. DECOURCY's Brigade, including the Forty-Second Ohio, had been assigned to the Division of Gen. OSTERHAUS, a German officer of admirable qualities, who had distinguished himself at Pea Ridge and in other important engagements in the West.

About the first of February, work was begun on the canal. The river was rising rapidly, and it was necessary that the excavation should be made with all possible dispatch But a small part of the army could work advantageously at one time, and it was arranged that each regiment should excavate a certain number of cubic yards, in proportion to the number of men in the command fit for duty. When the turn of the Forty-Second came, the Regiment, under command of Major WILLIAMS, went down with its rations and blankets, set to work on the 16th of February, and accomplished its task with unparalleled promptness. The work of the Forty-Second became a standard with which that of other regiments was compared from that time forward

By this time, the water had risen to a stage which endangered the camps of the army At several points above, it had broken through the neglected levee, cutting large gaps or crevasses, which poured great streams of water across the country into the bayous which ran Southward, parallel with the Mississippi, into Red River. The Thirteenth Corps was called upon for heavy details of men to work upon the levees, and in this duty the Forty-Second performed its part. The rains were incessant, and the low plantation ground on which the troops were encamped became a vast quagmire. The water broke through the sides of the new canal, which proved a total failure, and backed up, driving Gen. SHERMAN's Corps to the levee. The damp and discomfort began to tell seriously upon the health of the troops, and the hospitals were filled with sick, who died as though stricken by an epidemic. The levee, the only dry ground in the vicinity, was soon honey-combed with graves Finally, about the 10th of March, the Thirteenth Corps was moved upon steamers twelve miles up the river to Milliken's Bend, where fine camps were laid out on the broad, sandy cotton-fields protected by the levee

On the 4th of February, Col. LINDSAY having been relieved from the command of the Second Brigade of the Ninth Division, a reorganization of the Division took place, by which Gen. OSTERHAUS' command was brigaded as follows

FIRST BRIGADE—Gen VANDEVERF, Commanding

Forty-Ninth Indiana Infantry
Sixty-Ninth Indiana Infantry
One Hundred and Eighteenth Illinois Infantry
One Hundred and Twentieth Ohio Infantry.

SECOND BRIGADE—Col J F DECOURCY, Commanding

Forty-Second Ohio Infantry.
Sixteenth Ohio Infantry.
One Hundred and Fourteenth Kentucky Infantry.
Twenty-Second Kentucky Infantry.
Fifty-Fourth Indiana Infantry.

On the 19th of the same month, Col DECOURCY, whose health had failed, went North on leave of absence. He was dissatisfied with his failure to attain his well-earned promotion to a brigadier generalship, and did not return to the army. From that time until the 29th of July following, the Second Brigade was commanded by Col. SHELDON, of the Forty-Second, with conspicuous bravery and ability.

The early Southern Spring had now set in; roses and daffodils were in bloom in the neglected gardens along the river, and the sunshine soon dried and hardened the ground into condition for drilling and reviews. The army was put into fine condition, convalescents were brought up from the rear, equipments perfected, and preparations completed for the Spring campaign. What the plan was we could not guess. That the movement was to be against Vicksburgh was certain, but how or where the attack would be made was as yet a mystery.

On the 16th of March, a part of Gen. SHERMAN's Corps, which had remained at Young's Point, was sent, with several gun-boats under Admiral PORTER, to work a passage through Steele's Bayou, in Mississippi, across to the Yazoo, and endeavor to effect a landing there, from which the army might operate against Vicksburgh. The expedition was conducted with great energy and spirit, but SHERMAN found the Rebels in force at an important point, and the difficulties of the passage so great that the attempt failed altogether in that quarter. The expedition returned to its camps at Young's Point on the 27th of March.

It was demonstrated that the army could not divert the Mississippi from its course, so as to evade Vicksburgh, or gain a practicable base of operations on the east bank of the Yazoo. But two methods remained—to return to Memphis, and move in heavy force down through the interior of Mississippi against the rear of Vicksburgh while the navy threatened the city in front; or, to get past the city, by way of the Louisiana shore, and attack the citadel from below. Gen. GRANT had tried the first of these methods during the previous December, and knew its difficulties. He now chose the latter course, and early in April preparations were made for the Southward movement. Nine miles in the rear of Milliken's Bend flows Willow Bayou, a deep stream, eighty or one hundred feet in width, which runs into the Mississippi at a place called New Carthage, eighteen miles below Vicksburgh. From the river across to this bayou, some miles above Milliken's Bend, was a channel which it was proposed to flood by cutting the levee and dredging out the ditch to a navigable depth, and thus open water communication for the conveyance of supplies to a new base on the river below. Several steam dredges arrived to aid in this work, but the scheme failed, and it was decided to march the troops over-land, and run the gun-boats, with sufficient transports to carry the necessary supplies, past the batteries of Vicksburgh.

This bold and aggressive movement was effected in the night of April 16th. Seven iron-clads, with three large steam transports having ten barges in tow, the latter laden with rations and forage, ran the gauntlet of the batteries under cover of darkness. The scene formed one of the grandest and most picturesque spectacles of the war. The night was dark and still. Admiral PORTER, in the iron-clad "Benton," led the way, followed by the "Mound City," "Carondelet," "Tuscumbia," "Louisville," "Pittsburgh," "Lafayette," and the "General Price," a captured wooden ram, with the transports, "Silver Wave," "Henry Clay," and "Tigress," the three last having the barges in tow. In line and silently the adventurous fleet slipped anchor at eleven o'clock, and steamed down the river. Every port-hole was closed, every light on board concealed, and the "Benton" reached the first water battery without being discovered. But at sixteen minutes past eleven, the black hulks were discovered drifting past, and a terrific fire was opened from the heavy batteries along the face of the bluff. PORTER replied furiously with shell and shrapnel, and the "Carondelet," floating close in by the farther shore unobserved, sent a deadly broadside enfilading the principal street, which was crowded with soldiers and negroes, who had flocked down to see their batteries sink the gun-boats. Steam had been shut off on the transports, and they floated with the current. All were struck many times, and two were drawn into an eddy and floated round and round, up and down before the batteries, not less than three times. The Rebels fired wooden buildings all along the shore, which lit up the river for miles. These lights, with the eddies and cross currents, the blazing guns afloat and ashore, and the great volumes of smoke rolling upward and overhanging the scene, confused the pilots, and some part of the fleet was under fire two hours and forty-six minutes. The gun-boat "Tuscumbia" took the disabled "Silver Wave" in tow, and pulled her safely through. The " Henry Clay " was riddled with shot, set on fire by a shell, and burned to the water's edge. the great flaming hulk floating down the stream as a beacon to the fleet. Finally, the boats got beyond range and came to anchor, or were tied up to the shore to repair damages. The gunboats had not been hurt, and were ready for action in half an hour. The first move in the grand game had been successfully played.

Meanwhile, important progress had been made on land. On the 1st of April, Gen. McCLERNAND had led off with the Thirteenth Corps, marching back from Milliken's Bend, twelve miles to Richmond, on Willow Bayou, which he had bridged and crossed, thence advancing Southward along the bayou to New Carthage, on the bank of the Mississippi, which point his advance guard had occupied on the 6th. The levees had been broken so that the last two miles of the trip had to be made with small boats and yawls. Nevertheless, with heavy labor, one division was pushed over and established on the levee, which was at that time a narrow island. The remaining three divisions of the Corps marched round, following the shore of Bayou Vidal, and struck the Mississippi twelve miles below, at Perkins' plantation. McCLERNAND was with his advance Division, at New Carthage, his headquarters being in a large brick plantation house, the property of a bitter and defiant Rebel. While there, the terrific bombardment at Vicksburgh was heard on the night of the 16th. Next morning every eye was turned up the river to catch the first glimpse of the fleet. About eight o'clock the burning wreck of the "Henry Clay" came floating past. The Rebel proprietor fairly danced with joy. "Where are your gun-boats now?" he tauntingly demanded. "Vicksburgh has sunk them all," and such for the moment, the fact appeared to be. But presently there was a cloud of dark smoke behind the cottonwood forest up the river. The men waited anxiously. It might be the ram which the Rebels had captured in Red River, coming to shell us from the Island. Four field guns on shore were quickly put in position, loaded and pointed up the river. Presently a low, black hulk crept round the curve with a flag flying at its jackstaff. The day was still and the flag hung so close to the staff that its character could not at first be determined. Every glass was levelled upon the banner, and when a puff of wind spread it out so that the Stars and Stripes could be seen, the shouts and cheers were deafening. It was the "Mound City," followed soon after by the "Tuscumbia," with the "Silver Wave" and barges in tow, and, during the afternoon, by all the fleet. It was the Yankees' turn to laugh now, and the desperate Rebel rushed away in a rage, set fire to his own house and fled across the river during the night.

McClernand concentrated his Corps at Perkins' plantation, and immediately began reconnoitering with Admiral Porter, the important position at Grand Gulf, which he had instructions to capture at the earliest moment. The ram "General Bragg" was placed at his disposal and the gun-boats dropped down to draw the fire of the batteries and reveal their strength. The place proved unexpectedly strong. Grand Gulf is a high bluff point at the mouth of the Big Black river. It was armed with thirteen heavy guns in two admirably constructed batteries—one twenty-five feet above the water, the other lower down and near the surface of the river. These guns commanded perfectly the channel of the river up and down, and the mouth of the Big Black.

There was besides an elaborate system of rifle trenches and smaller works armed with field artillery and occupied by a garrison of seven thousand men under Gen. BOWEN.

MCCLERNAND has been censured for not pushing on and capturing Grand Gulf immediately on the arrival of the fleet. The reason why he did not was that Grand Gulf was on one side of the Mississippi while his army was on the other side, and he had not sufficient transports to cross his Corps. He could not cross above and march down upon it because it was protected in that direction by the Big Black, and the impenetrable swamps above its mouth.

GRANT was impatient for the attempt to be made, and on the 24th came down to the front in person He saw the difficulty, and on the 26th six more transports, with twelve barges all laden with rations and forage, ran the batteries at Vicksburgh. One was sunk but five got through and came down.

The Thirteenth Corps had meanwhile marched down to Hard Times, a point on the Louisiana shore three miles above Grand Gulf. Preparations were made to storm the place. Two divisions of MCCLERNAND'S Corps, including OSTERHAUS' with the Forty Second, were crowded upon six transports and moved out into the stream just out of range. Gen. GRANT was on board a tug and MCCLERNAND in command of the troops. The navy was to steam down, engage and silence the heavy batteries, when the six transports would follow, run ashore and land the troops to carry the works by assault.

At eight o'clock in the morning the gun-boats slipped anchor and bore gallantly down They lay close in by the shore and a terrific contest ensued. For five hours and twenty minutes the boats and batteries hammered away at each other at pistol range. The water was so deep that the anchors would not hold, and the gun-boats were kept constantly in motion The parapets were bored through and through, but they were so high above the water that the fleet could not dismount a single gun. At last PORTER, finding that the batteries were getting the best of it, ceased firing and withdrew.

The attack had failed To have landed troops under those still unsilenced guns would have been madness. It remained, therefore, to run past Grand Gulf, march the troops overland and attack the position in the rear from below. The men on the transports were quickly landed and the whole Corps moved rapidly across the point on a high levee, emerging from the cypress woods at DeShroon's plantation, three miles below Grand Gulf on the Louisiana shore.

After dark the gun-boats, followed by the transports and barges, steamed down, ran past the batteries, receiving and returning a terrific fire, and before midnight all were safely below the obstacle. It had been a hot day for the gun-boats One of them had been struck forty-seven times, and a shell had burst in the turret of the "Tuscumbia," killing and wounding a number of men. The loss on the fleet had been eighteen killed and fifty-six wounded

Early next morning the movement was resumed. The nearest landing place on the Eastern shore was at a place called Bruinsburgh, six miles below. The Thirteenth Corps was rapidly embarked on the transports, barges and gun-boats, and dropped down the river to that point By noon two divisions were landed. Barrels of bread, bacon and coffee were rolled on shore and opened, each man having permission to stuff his haversack and pockets with sufficient food to last five days. Very few horses had been brought, Generals being allowed only one, with but two mounted staff officers. Many of the guns had but four horses to each carriage, and even Gen. GRANT, when he arrived that night with no baggage but a tooth-brush, was obliged to borrow a mule for a charger.

The river bottom at that point was a mile in width, flanked by a high bluff to which the road ascended through a deep artificial cut. A brigade of the enemy at that point would have held McClernand in check all the afternoon. But no brigade was there, and McClernand's Staff with a company of infantry, hurried up through the defile, capturing a Confederate Colonel who had been observing the debarkation from the tower of a stately villa which stood embowered in trees at the crest of the hill The Corps moved rapidly up, the regiments cheering when they reached the ridge and stood once more upon solid ground. For five months they had been wading through bayous and the soft alluvial bottom lands of the Mississippi, and the feeling of firm ground beneath their feet gave new life and elasticity to the spirits of officers and men.

Twelve miles inland was the town of Port Gibson on Bayou Pierre, in the midst of a fertile and beautiful country. Toward this point McClernand pushed rapidly, Carr's Division in advance, followed by Osterhaus, Hovey and A. J Smith, in order. The night was intensely dark, and the road, though reasonably smooth, was so narrow that a regiment marching by the flank filled it completely.

At two o'clock a.m., Gen Carr's advance regiment came suddenly upon a heavy infantry force, apparently marching toward Bruinsburgh. Both parties opened fire sharply, and, the enemy proving stubborn, a section of artillery was unlimbered, pushed forward and set to work with canister The enemy retired doggedly a short distance and then, having reached the fork in the road, refused to move farther. Carr, seeing that he had encountered a serious obstacle, ordered his men to cease firing and the whole column sat down in the road to await daylight.

Gen. McClernand with his Staff had the night before gone forward with his leading Division until it had drawn well out on the main road, and had then returned to the large house on the hill, two miles from the river landing, so as to be within easy reach of Gen GRANT, who was expected during the night He had orders to proceed only to Port Gibson, seize the important bridge at that point across Bayou Pierre and await orders No resistance had been expected in that direction, and Gen MCCLERNAND and his Staff, who had not had their boots off since leaving Perkins' plantation, returned to the great house on the hill, anticipating a comfortable night. Hardly had they been an hour in bed when the guns of CARR's advance were heard through the still night, nine miles to the eastward Horses were saddled—enough had been captured during the afternoon to mount the Staff and orderlies— and the General set out at a breakneck pace for the front. Picking his way through the crowded road, MCCLERNAND reached the front just at dawn CARR held the fork of the road with a regiment thrown out a few rods on either branch. Two hundred yards distant, on an oak ridge which crossed diagonally both branches of the road, the hostile line was plainly visible, and a howitzer battery from the right front sent a few shells crashing harmlessly through the trees which surrounded a house at the junction of the roads. Gen. CARR was found on the porch eating a "hard tack" and the dead and wounded of the night skirmish lay on the grass in the yard. It was evident that the enemy had taken a stand and proposed to give battle. The country was broken by parallel ridges, divided by deep ravines filled with a rank growth of timber, cane and vines. The roads followed the ridges, which were alternately timbered and cleared for cultivation, so that the ground abounded in positions which could only be flanked with extreme labor and difficulty and were in every way admirable for defense.

THE BATTLE OF THOMPSON'S HILL.

Dispositions were made for immediate attack. Gen CARR's Division was put into line across the right hand road, OSTERHAUS moved out on the road to the left, HOVEY's Division joined the left of CARR and A. J. SMITH was held for a time in reserve. The sun was just rising, upon such a May day as had been dreamed of but never realized in our Northern clime.

The smoke of the preliminary skirmishing hung in long wreaths over the fields and woods, and warmed and reddened in the morning sunlight like a halo. The trees were in full leaf, and the thickets and canebrakes that filled the ravine were dense masses of fresh, green foliage. "A good day for a fight," observed the gallant CARR, as he rode away on his white mule to put his men into action. OSTERHAUS' Division, the Forty-Second Ohio in front, came gaily up, and took the left hand road The men were munching their hard bread, and taking a few whiffs at their pipes, before the hard work of the day. Capt. OLDS, leading Company "A" at the head of the column, blithely greeted the staff officer sent to guide the Division to its position, with the question: " Where are these Johnnies that have been keeping us here in the road all night?" Poor little Captain! He little dreamed that in the garden which he was then passing he would be buried before another sunrise

The dispositions were quickly made, and the battle opened furiously. HOVEY's men, on the left of the right-hand road, dashed forward to a little wooded ravine and held it a few moments, when the enemy in the thicket beyond attempted to charge across the open space, but was met by a withering fire and driven back in confusion. Seeing the foe retreating in disorder, HOVEY's men leaped from their cover, rushed across the field, cleared the woods beyond, and captured the four howitzer battery, the horses of which had been killed. The first position had been carried, and with it the guns which had already dismounted two pieces of a German battery of CARR's Division, near the forks of the road. The enemy fell back half a mile, chose a new position, and made another stand. HOVEY pressed forward, with CARR on his right now in line and advancing gallantly. Another desperate collision occurred, the Confederates fighting like tigers After half an hour of this, Smith's Division, the rear of the Thirteenth Corps, which had come up and been resting in reserve, was sent to the right of CARR's line to wrap round and take the enemy in flank. It had some distance to traverse, but moved rapidly to its position, attacked vigorously, and before ten o'clock, the whole left of the Rebel line had been broken and driven back to a deep ravine, filled with cane and underbrush, and covered by a steep wooded slope beyond. In these woods and this ravine, the enemy found a new and admirable position, in which from behind a complete shelter he could resist attack from the open ground.

Meanwhile, OSTERHAUS, round on the left-hand road, was hotly engaged. He had found the enemy three-quarters of a mile from the junction of the two roads, strongly posted on a rugged ridge, with his left in a sunken road. OSTERHAUS' Division had here encountered two full brigades, with a six-gun battery, under command of Gen TRACY. As the Federal Division moved to the attack, the battery opened upon it, firing rapidly, but generally too high. FOSTER's Battery went into position near the road, and in less than an hour completely silenced it, dismounting not less than three of its guns. Col SHELDON's Brigade, including the Forty-Second as its right, held the right of OSTERHAUS' line It advanced rapidly across the open ground, charged through a thicket at the foot of the hill, driving out the enemy's skirmishers, and halting in a position which gave some shelter from the enemy's artillery. The Forty-Second, with the Sixty-Ninth Indiana on its left, moved up on the ridge, and found the enemy on a similar ridge, about a hundred yards distant, the two ridges being separated by a deep ravine. The two Regiments were on their mettle, and, as their losses prove, bore the brunt of battle in that part of the field.

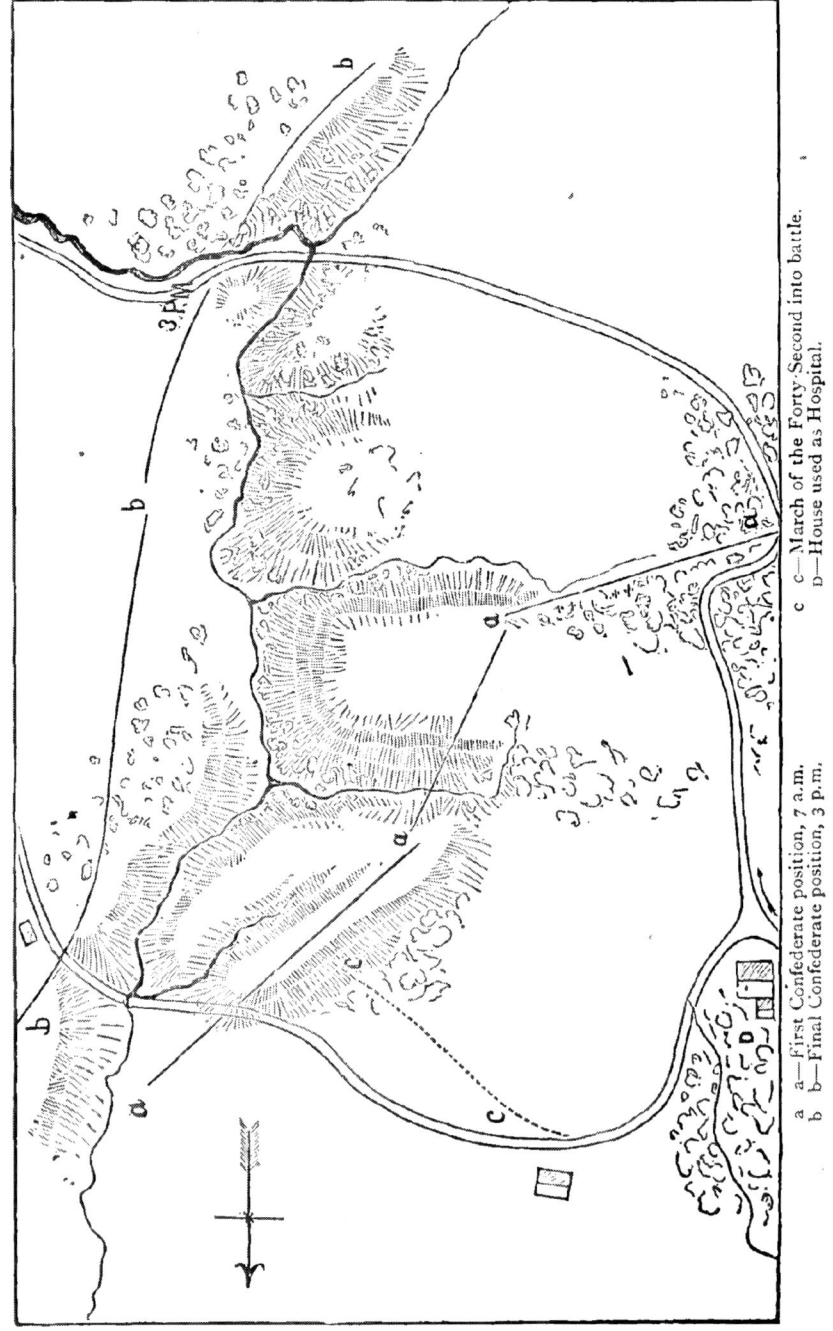

THE BATTLE-FIELD OF THOMPSON'S HILL.

a a—First Confederate position, 7 a.m.
b b—Final Confederate position, 3 p.m.
c c—March of the Forty-Second into battle.
D—House used as Hospital.

Still keeping partly under cover, the men would advance until they got an opportunity for a shot, then lie down or retire and re-load. By this time, the accurate fire of FOSTER'S guns had begun to cut up the Rebel battery The Forty-Second also opened upon it, and the cannoneers were driven into a log hut near by. There they rallied, and making a rush for the guns, tried to get away with the three not yet disabled ones. They first tried to drag the pieces away by hand, but the fire of the Forty-Second and Sixty-Ninth killed the gunners before they could move them an inch. Then, in a desperate effort to save the guns, the horses and limbers came out from behind the log buildings, and made a second dash for the battery, but a volley from the right wing of the Forty-Second brought down every horse, and the guns were lost—it was death to approach them The Forty-Second and the Fifty-Ninth now made two gallant efforts to charge over the hill, down through the ravine, and up the opposite bank. In both instances the dash was successfully made, but failed of its results through the unaccountable stupidity of our own men The two Regiments reached the second ravine and began the ascent, when the Rebels, fearing they were to be attacked at close quarters, advanced to the top of the slope, seeing which the One Hundred and Twentieth Ohio, in the rear and left of the Forty-Second, opened a murderous fire, every shot of which that fell too low, struck among the Forty-Second

Several men, including Lieut CAMPBELL, of Company "G," and IRA OSBORN, of Company "A," were severely wounded, and five or six others killed by this reverse fire in a few moments. Finding itself thus between two fires, the Forty-Second gladly obeyed the order to fall back to its former position on the first ridge. The Sixty-Ninth, which had gone forward at the same time, reached a position sheltered from the fire of our own troops, and held its ground manfully, singing "Rally Round the Flag" as it fought.

After an hour of this, the Sixty-Ninth, whose ammunition began to run low, was ordered back, while the Forty-Second moved forward to occupy its place. The Rebels mistook the movement of the Sixty-Ninth for a retreat of our line, and came down in pursuit, firing furiously, but the Forty-Second charged up gallantly and drove them back. A few moments after, we saw two or three companies detached from the Rebel line, and move round another ravine, separated only by a narrow ridge from the one in which the Forty-Second was then fighting. It was impossible to fire upon them without exposing ourselves to a cross fire. So Col. PARDEE tried strategy. Moving four companies from the Forty-Second round by the right, he gained the flank and rear of the Rebel force, opened a sharp reverse fire upon it, and then charged down, driving the Rebel companies over the ridge into the hands of the main body of the Forty-Second, by whom they were all captured. Eight of the enemy were killed in this little exploit, and more than a hundred prisoners taken.

It was now about noon. For more than five hours the battle had been raging with desperate fury. We could hear the roar of conflict away to the right, and knew by the gradually receding tumult that HOVEY'S CARR'S and SMITH'S Divisions were driving the enemy. Report came that HOVEY'S men had captured a battery—so had we in fact, but we had not yet got our hands upon it. We, in our part of the line, were opposed to a force equal to our own, in a strongly chosen position; and though our whole Division had striven gallantly, the enemy had substantially held his ground.

The roar of our guns that morning had reached the ears of Gen. GRANT, on board of a gunboat at Bruinsburgh, and, borrowing a mule, he had started for the scene. On the way he passed LOGAN'S Division of the Seventeenth Corps, which had crossed the river during the night, and was hurrying forward. GRANT arrived at half-past ten and assumed chief command. LOGAN came an hour later, and one of his Brigades (Gen. JOHN E. SMITH'S) was immediately sent to our aid. It was put in on the left of OSTERHAUS' Division, swung round, and took the enemy in flank. At the same time, our line again charged forward, crossed the second ravine, climbed the hill under a terrible fire, drove the enemy from his position, and rolled his line back in disorder. Gen. TRACY was killed in this final assault, and we found the woods and the open space near the battery and about the log house, strewn with dead. Nearly a mile from his first position the enemy met reinforcements from Vicksburgh, and when we again came up, resisted until night, falling back stubbornly before us until within two miles of Port Gibson, the spires of which we could see shining white and peaceful in the setting sun. Our May-day was over. We had gained a victory, of which every man instinctively felt the importance, but it had been won at serious cost. The loss of the Forty-Second had been twelve killed and sixty-one wounded; that of the Sixty-Ninth Indiana, fifteen killed and forty-one wounded. Ten brigades had been engaged on the Union side that day, and these two Regiments had suffered nearly a quarter of the entire loss. Generals GRANT and McPHERSON, who came with SMITH's Brigade to the left of the field, and watched the charge that broke that part of the enemy's line, personally complimented the Forty-Second and Sixty-Ninth upon their gallantry.

The two roads upon which this spirited battle was fought fork, as already stated, at a point four miles west of Port Gibson. After diverging until nearly two miles apart, they gradually converge and unite again half a mile from Port Gibson.

McCLERNAND, with his three Divisions on the right, continued to press the enemy vigorously all the afternoon. About three o'clock, there arrived two brigades of Confederates from Vicksburgh. They could be seen coming over the hills, swinging their hats and shouting as they hurried into the fight. Their arrival served to cheer the spirits of BOWEN's men, and as still further reinforcements were expected from Jackson, under Gen LORING, the enemy held out stubbornly until dark.

The troops lay down where they stopped fighting, and without fire, awaited the coming of another day. The victory of the Federals had been thus far complete They had captured two batteries and six hundred and fifty prisoners, and held the whole field of the day's battle. The dead and many of the wounded of the enemy were in our hands The Federal loss had been one hundred and thirty killed, and seven hundred and eighteen wounded, of which more than half were in OSTERHAUS' Division. The casualties in the Forty-Second, at the battle of Thompson's Hill, amounted to fifty-nine, this number not including the usual percentage of wounds so slight as not to disable men for immediate service. The official list of killed and wounded was as follows

KILLED

WILLIAM W OLDS, Captain, Company "A."
AARON N ALLEN, Private, Company "A"
JOSIAH ASIRE, Sergeant, Company "B."
PETER MIERS, Private, Company "B"
ABIE D SMALLY, Corporal, Company "C"
ORSON EMMONS, Corporal, Company "E"
GEORGE S HARRIS, Private, Company "E"
JAMES FEAST, Private, Company "E"
HENRY BURDICK, Private, Company "F"
ELI LENOUX, Private, Company "I."
HARRISON CORWIN, Private, Company "I"
GEORGE HARRIS, Private, Company "K"

WOUNDED.

CHARLES HENRY, Lieutenant, Company "A," in hand.
CALVIN RIDER, Sergeant, Company "A," in side
DEWITT GARDNER, Private, Company "A," in shoulder

IRA C. OSBORNE, Private, Company "A," in hip
PETER MILLER, Lieutenant, Company "B," in finger.
GEORGE J. WILLIAMS, Corporal, Company "B," leg amputated.
DARIUS W. SANFORD, Private, Company "B," in leg.
CLAYTON M. VANORMAN, Private, Company "B," in hand
GEORGE MOODY, Private, Company "B," in leg
JOHN WARS, Private Company "B," in arm.
GEORGE MCCRED, Sergeant, Company "C," in arm
DANIEL GROSSCAP, Sergeant, Company "C," in scalp
LEVI H. KIPLINGER, Corporal, Company "C," arm amputated
CHARLES DRAKE, Private, Company "C," in ankle
ROBERT THOMPSON, Private, Company "C," concussion.
SAMUEL KOPP, Private, Company "C," in thigh
EDWARD HISER, Private, Company "C," in thigh
JAMES W. DENSMORE, Private, Company "C," in side.
SAMUEL SWITZERTINAL, Private, Company "C," in side
GAUL TRANGER, Private, Company "C"
WILLIAM L. WILSON, Lieutenant, Company "C," in leg
MELVIN BENHAM, Captain, Company "E," in shoulder.
CHARLES GOODWIN, Lieutenant, Company "E," in thigh
JOHN GRIFFIN, Private, Company "E,' in chest
GEORGE NEWMAN, Private, Company "E," in chest
SAMUEL WELLMAN, Private, Company "E," finger amputated
W. H. STEVENS, Private, Company "E,' in leg
H. C. JENNINGS, Lieutenant, Company "F,' in groin
SAMUEL CORLESS, Private, Company "F," in hand
WALLACE HEFFLEFINGER, Private, Company "F," in arm
GEORGE E. WRIGHT, Private, Company "F," in abdomen
L. B. CAMPBELL, Lieutenant, Company "G," in arm and thigh.
WHEATON GOODWIN, Sergeant, Company "G," in knee
GEORGE STRIKER, Private, Company "G," arm amputated
GEORGE MASTERS, Orderly Sergeant, Company "H," in head
JONATHAN GRIFFITH, Corporal, Company "H," in hip
RICHARD WOODHOUSE, Private, Company "H," in thigh
ROBERT M. SELLERS, Private, Company "H," in abdomen.
ALBERT M. ALLEN, Corporal, Company "I," in chin
WILLIAM GRAY, Private, Company "I," in hip
WILLIAM BYERS, Private, Company "I," in face
ISAAC SHANELY, Private, Company "I," in shoulder
SANFORD TILMAN, Corporal, Company "I," in thigh.
RICHARD NORMAN Corporal, Company "I," in thigh
HENRY SHAUF, Corporal, Company "I," in head
JOSEPH ANDREWS, Private, Company "I," right arm amputated.
JOSEPH THOMPSON, Sergeant, Company "I," in breast

McClernand's orders were to bivouack on the field, and push the attack at daylight. With the first peep of dawn, the men were in line, and the skirmishers advanced through the woods. It was soon discovered that the enemy was gone. The bugles sounded the advance, and the troops, elated with their victory, pushed eagerly forward over the rugged ridges to Port Gibson. Two or three Divisions met on converging roads, at the margin of the town, where the wife of the Mayor was met coming out, in great distress of mind, to surrender the place. Her husband had been out in the volunteer ambulance corps the day before, and had been shot through both legs. He was then lying in the house, with one leg amputated and suffering great pain. His good lady—a Southern dame of thoroughbred ideas—was under pressure of great responsibility in respect to surrendering the town. She wanted to see the Commanding General. A group of ladies who came as her escort, insisted upon the propriety of her demand. A bluff Iowa Colonel referred her to a Captain of McClernand's staff, who happened to be with the advance, who explained that, as the town was already invaded by three columns of troops hurrying through it to wrest the burning bridge from the retreating enemy, the formalities of surrendering it might be safely dispensed with. At this moment, the head of Osterhaus' column had reached the bridge, which was burning, and received the fire of a few sharpshooters on the opposite bank. Foster's Battery went forward at a gallop, unlimbered, and began firing across the stream. The roar of the guns broke up the interview with the lady Mayoress and her suite. They began to shriek and weep, calling upon Heaven to soften the hearts of the invaders and spare the innocent and suffering people of Port Gibson.

The town, though not large, was wealthy and beautiful. The people were mainly at home, and all property except food was rigidly respected. Two bridges spanned Bayou Pierre at or near the town, the lower one on the road to Grand Gulf, the upper one on the road Northeast to Jackson. Both had been important. The lower one was wholly destroyed, but the upper one was of iron, and only the planking, for a distance of a hundred and twenty feet, was burned This was quickly replaced, officers and men working up to their waists in water LOGAN'S Division of MCPHERSON'S Corps came up, and, without waiting for the bridge to be finished, forded the river and started forward. CROCKER'S Division of the same Corps, which had crossed the Mississippi at Bruinsburgh the day before and marched all night, also arrived just as the bridge was finished, and followed rapidly after LOGAN. Prisoners and the wounded in Port Gibson told us that the force which we had defeated the day before had been the garrison of Grand Gulf, seven thousand strong, reinforced by two brigades from Vicksburgh, in all about eleven thousand men—the whole, as we already knew, commanded by Gen. BOWEN. He had expected heavy reinforcements from Vicksburgh and Jackson, but GRANT'S movements had been too quick for him, and he had been struck by MCCLERNAND four miles from Port Gibson, instead of being enabled to pounce upon and destroy the Federal advance at Bruinsburgh Landing. The battle of the day before had exhausted BOWEN'S ammunition, and his troops were greatly demoralized. After this beaten army, MCPHERSON, with his two fresh Divisions, pressed vigorously on, followed by the whole of MCCLERNAND'S Corps. At five o'clock on the morning of the 3d, MCPHERSON overtook the enemy burning the bridge the over North fork of Bayou Pierre, eight miles from Port Gibson. They were driven off, the bridge repaired, and MCPHERSON pushed on, driving BOWEN through Willow Springs, and gaining an important cross-road. Here LOGAN'S Division, accompanied by GRANT in person, was turned back to occupy Grand Gulf, and establish there a new base, while CROCKER'S Division, which had not fired a shot, continued the direct pursuit On the way thither, GRANT learned that Grand Gulf was entirely evacuated and occupied by our navy, so he turned LOGAN's Division Northward toward Hankinson's Ferry, across the Big Black, toward which CROCKER's Division, with McPHERSON in command, was driving the defeated army of BOWEN. PEMBERTON would naturally make a new line of the Big Black river, if GRANT gave him time, and BOWEN was evidently trying to retard McPHERSON's advance to Hankinson's Ferry. At four in the afternoon, BOWEN made a stand, and McPHERSON put CROCKER's Division in line for attack, but at that opportune moment LOGAN came up on the left, and was about to turn BOWEN's flank, when the latter broke and retreated precipitately across the river. This important point being gained, McPHERSON's two Divisions rested for the night, covering the ferry.

McCLERNAND's headquarters, with OSTERHAUS' Division, were moved during the day to Willow Springs His other three Divisions moved by various roads to reconnoiter, and covered as large a tract of country as possible. It was known that reinforcements for BOWEN were on the way from Jackson and Vicksburgh, and, somewhere these bodies or troops might unexpectedly be met. Not finding them, McCLERNAND's Divisions rendezvoused in the neighborhood of Willow Springs, to rest and make further preparations. The movements of the two advance Corps had been so rapid that they had outrun the plans of the commander, and it was now necessary to wait for SHERMAN's Corps to come up SHERMAN was on the way from Milliken's Bend. He reached Hard Times on the 6th, and arrived at Grand Gulf on that night and the following day. McCLERNAND and McPHERSON had, meantime, been living wholly upon the three days' rations which they had brought in haversacks from Bruinsburgh They now foraged vigorously, found plenty of beef and mutton, and with the little corn which the enemy had left in that country, subsisted comfortably Before undertaking a further movement, however, more liberal supplies were needed. The two Corps were wholly without camp equipage, wagons, ambulances, or even cooking utensils Field officers were on foot, and even Division and Corps Commanders were living, like the rest, from hand to mouth. From the 3d to the 8th of May, while McCLERNAND's Corps lay in the vicinity of Willow Springs, the horses, rations, ammunition and other necessaries continued to arrive. The rations included only coffee, salt and bread, but with these and what could be gathered the troops could live.

On the 6th McPHERSON's Corps came from Hankinson's Ferry, passed McCLERNAND and encamped near Rocky Springs On the 8th SHERMAN's Corps arrived, and on the following day the whole army moved Eastward toward Jackson McPHERSON Corps had the left hand road by way of Raymond, McCLERNAND had the right, moving direct from Rocky Springs, while SHERMAN brought up the rear with his Corps divided on both roads, watching carefully toward the left to guard the ferries of the Black River, from which PEMBERTON might emerge and assail GRANT's rear.

Soon after starting, GRANT heard that the enemy in heavy force was fortifying Edwards' Station, on the Vicksburgh and Jackson railroad, six miles East of where the railroad crosses the Big Black He therefore determined to change the relative positions of his three Corps McPHERSON, whose men had done comparatively little fighting, was to continue on via Utica to Raymond and Jackson, at which latter place JOE JOHNSTON was reported to be gathering an army. McCLERNAND was to cross from the right to the left, moving directly Northward, demonstrating against Edwards' Station and striking the railroad East of that point somewhere near Bolton. This would cut PEMBERTON off from reinforcing Jackson, where McPHERSON, aided if need were by

SHERMAN, would capture and destroy the railroads and public buildings, and then return rapidly along the railroad and confront Edwards' Station and Vicksburgh.

From Hankinson's Ferry to Raymond was thirty-five miles, to Jackson was twenty miles further. From Bolton to Jackson was twenty miles, so that by this bold and masterly disposition GRANT avoided fighting PEMBERTON on his own ground, divided PEMBERTON and JOHNSTON, protected McPHERSON from attack from the West, and above all kept his three Corps within supporting distance of each other, no matter from what point they might be assailed.

On the 9th McPHERSON accordingly marched to near Utica on the road to Raymond, and McCLERNAND marched to Five Mile Creek, where he came up with the rear of a Rebel force and skirmished with it without any important result, the enemy falling back without a fight. SHERMAN'S Corps was to the right of McCLERNAND, holding the center of the advance, with headquarters at Cayuga, eight miles beyond Rocky Spring, to which point Gen GRANT removed on the 10th. He had then in hand forty-three thousand of the finest troops in the service. They were all veterans, ably commanded, confident in the ability of their leader and ready for anything. [*Note.*—These figures include BLAIR's Division of SHERMAN's Corps which arrived on the 14th of May, after the capture of Jackson, and McARTHUR's Division of McPHERSON's Corps, two brigades of which only arrived on the 17th, just before the battle of Black River Bridge.]

The important movements of McPHERSON and SHERMAN from the 11th to the 16th must be briefly indicated. At half-past three on the morning of the 12th, LOGAN's Division of the Seventeenth Corps moved towards Raymond, followed, half an hour later, by the Division of CROCKER. At eleven o'clock in the morning LOGAN's leading brigade struck the enemy five thousand strong under Gen. GREGG, two miles West of Raymond. Ordering the trains out of the road, LOGAN's remaining brigade came up on a trot, was deployed, and attacked the enemy with such impetuous fury that before CROCKER's Division could arrive, LOGAN had the enemy routed and flying, with a battery judiciously posted raking the retreating column. The engagement lasted only an hour and a half, but LOGAN's loss was sixty-nine killed and three hundred and forty-one wounded. The enemy lost one hundred killed, three hundred and five wounded and four hundred and fifteen prisoners. A drenching rain came on that afternoon, making the roads almost impassable, and McPHERSON pursued GREGG only to Raymond, where he encamped for the night.

The road to Jackson was now open, and GRANT, hearing that Gen. JOE JOHNSTON was then expecting heavy reinforcements from various points, determined to go there with the Corps of both SHERMAN and McPHERSON. In order to deceive PEMBERTON, who was in position in heavy force at Edwards' Station waiting to be attacked, McCLERNAND was directed to demonstrate strongly in that direction This was done—the skirmish line of OSTERHAUS' Division pushing to within two miles of Edwards' Station, and developing the enemy in force Behind this skirmish line, McCLERNAND, obedient to orders, marched his other divisions Eastward by the flank and pushed on to Raymond, so as to keep within supporting distance of SHERMAN and McPHERSON, who were now hurrying to complete the defeat of JOHNSTON at Jackson

McPHERSON struck the railroad at Clinton on the 13th, cut the road and telegraph, captured some important dispatches going over the wires between JOHNSTON and PEMBERTON, and then hurried on to Jackson, which place was captured by the Fifteenth and Seventeenth Corps on the 14th. JOHNSTON fled with the wreck of his army Northward toward Canton, and SHERMAN's Corps was set to work destroying the railroads, the arsenal, bridges, military stores, and destroying everything of value to the Confederacy.

Resting but one night, McPHERSON's two Divisions, LOGAN in the advance, started back with all speed to the support of McCLERNAND, who was now facing Westward on the line from Raymond North to Bolton Station. HOVEY's Division of the Thirteenth Corps was further East on the Clinton road, but McPHERSON came up with it and both came on together, reaching Bolton Station at night-fall. On the morning of that day OSTERHAUS' advance had captured Bolton Station with a number of prisoners, one of whom a negro, the servant of a brigade commander in PEMBERTON's army, confirmed the report that the whole garrison of Vicksburgh was at Edwards' Station marching Eastward to attack McCLERNAND, GRANT's rear. McCLERNAND accordingly faced his line Westward and the rear of the Federal army became its front.

Three roads lead Westward from between Raymond and Bolton to Edwards' Station. The two most Northerly of these converge and unite at a point six miles East of the Station, known as Champion's Hill. On the right hand one of these three roads was HOVEY's Division of McCLERNAND's Corps, and behind him McPHERSON with his two Divisions commanded by LOGAN and CROCKER. On the center road was McCLERNAND with the Divisions of CARR and OSTERHAUS; on the left hand road, four miles from the center one, were BLAIR's Division, which had just arrived from Grand Gulf with two hundred wagon loads of food, (the only rations received by GRANT's army during those memorable twelve days,) and the Division of A. J. SMITH. SMITH belonged to McCLERNAND's Corps, and BLAIR, from his position, was temporarily under command of that officer.

In this order GRANT's army moved forward. SMITH on the Southern road struck the enemy first at seven in the morning of the 16th, and after a little skirmishing pushed up a battery and opened fire briskly. The enemy, on his way to Clinton by way of Raymond, thinking he had struck the whole of GRANT'S army, withdrew, turned Northward by a lateral road and sought to escape by the Northern route across Champion's Hill and join JOHNSTON at Clinton. Inevitably, PEMBERTON'S advance ran directly into HOVEY. Hearing SMITH'S guns away to his left, OSTERHAUS pushed forward, the Forty-Second Ohio deployed as skirmishers, and encountered a strong Rebel skirmish line in the margin of the woods which cover Champion's Hill. The skirmishers were driven in, uncovering the enemy in heavy force. McCLERNAND'S orders were to feel the enemy sharply, but not bring on a general engagement unless he was sure of success. Meanwhile, he was to establish communication with HOVEY on the right, and BLAIR and SMITH on the left. The responsibility which he felt in this situation was too much for MCCLERNAND. It made him over-cautious, and prevented him from pushing OSTERHAUS and CARR as they should have been pushed on that day. Instead of pushing OSTERHAUS, who had the advance on the center road, MCCLERNAND held him back, and endeavored to establish communications with HOVEY, who, away to the right, was by eleven o'clock furiously engaged. LOGAN came up on HOVEY'S right, went in impetuously, moving far enough round to the right to leave space for CROCKER, who also attacked with splendid spirit.

Nothing in the War surpassed the fighting of those three Divisions from eleven in the morning until three in the afternoon. HOVEY charged up the hill with fearful loss, capturing a battery of five guns. MCCLERNAND'S failure to attack vigorously left the enemy in his front to mass toward the left and wreak his whole fury upon HOVEY and CROCKER. HOVEY'S captured battery was lost, then re-taken, captured and re-captured not less than four times, the Rebel and Union dead being piled around it in heaps.

Champion's Hill is a rough, irregular mound, two hundred feet high, bald at the top, but densely wooded on its slopes, and cut and scarred into rugged ravines, filled with a dense undergrowth, and almost impassable. The hill is two miles in length from North to South, by a mile in width; and the roads upon which McPherson and McClernand respectively were advancing, met at its summit. Upon this hill was Pemberton, with eighty regiments of infantry and ten batteries of artillery—about thirty thousand men. He had, in fact, more men than he could use to advantage, and the density with which his troops were massed only aggravated their slaughter. By two o'clock Logan had pushed his Division clear round the Northern point of the hill, reaching to and occupying the road to Edwards' Station, Pemberton's only avenue of retreat. He soon captured a battery in reserve, standing in the road, when Grant, not knowing the splendid advantage Logan had gained, and fearing he had gone too far, recalled him to form a junction with Crocker's right. Before he had done so, however, Grant threw Smith's and Holmes' Brigades of Crocker's Division into the gap on Hovey's right. The two fresh brigades attacked with superb valor. Hovey's exhausted men were inspired with new courage; Logan charged gallantly up the hill, and after a desperate struggle of forty minutes, the whole left wing of Pemberton was broken and thrown pell-mell over against Osterhaus and Carr, who by that time, two hours too late, had advanced determinedly and become hotly engaged. McClernand, unaware of what had taken place on the right, mistook the horde of fugitives for a massing of the enemy upon him; and instead of charging and completing the wreck of Pemberton, simply held his ground, firing rapidly, but permitting the broken Rebel army to escape down the Southwestern slope of the hill towards Edwards' Station.

The part borne by the Forty-Second in the battle of Champion's Hill has been briefly detailed in the sketch of Major WILLIAMS, in the earlier pages of this narrative. Col. SHELDON was seriously ill, besides suffering from the painful wound in his hand received at Thompson's Hill, and Col. PARDEE was on detached duty at Division Headquarters. Major WILLIAMS was therefore in command of the Regiment. During the advance in the morning, the Forty-Second had been deployed as skirmishers in advance of OSTERHAUS' Division, on the left of the road, and had encountered the enemy sharply at the margin of the wood After halting there for a time, the Regiment was assembled and sent off to the right of the road, to report to Gen GARRETT, commanding one of CARR's Brigades. Major WILLIAMS was ordered to put his Regiment into a line which was then forming to charge through a dense thicket that fringed the wood, and which was filled with the enemy's sharp-shooters, supported, as was conjectured, by heavier masses of infantry in the tall timber beyond. The Forty-Second promptly took position, and at the command moved forward, Major WILLIAMS' only orders being to keep in line with the regiments on either side, and thus avoid exposing his flanks. The line pushed rapidly forward through the thicket, which was so dense that the Companies soon lost sight of each other. The The Forty-Second kept well in line, however, and was charging through the brush in handsome style, when the Regiment suddenly came upon a strong line of the enemy's infantry, which rose and fired through the intervening foliage. The distance between the two lines was only a few paces, but the Forty-Second was so well covered that its losses from this volley were slight. The fire was immediately returned, and a sharp skirmish was contined for several minutes. Major WILLIAMS noticed that the enemy's fire, which at first had been wholly in his front, soon began to wrap round the flanks of his line. He soon saw that the regiments on either side of the Forty Second had stopped some distance back, and that his line was then some twenty rods to the front of everything, and with both its flanks exposed. There was but one way to avoid being surrounded and captured, and this was to retreat and re-establish the line. The Forty Second was therefore ordered back, and not knowing the reason for it, went somewhat precipitately to a ridge some two hundred yards to the rear, where the line was re-established. The enemy followed closely, but at the command the Forty-Second faced about, and sharply checked the pursuers, capturing the battle-flag of a Georgia Regiment in the melee. GARRET's line being established, moved forward rapidly, sweeping through the thicket, and driving everything before it into the woods that covered Thompson's Hill just as PEMBERTON's left, broken and doubled back, came pouring along in retreat. OSTERHAUS, who was up with his front line, saw the situation and finally ordered a brisk advance over the hill, capturing a number of prisoners and cutting off LORING's Division from the line of retreat. LORING abandoned his two batteries in a swamp, made a wide detour to the South and East, and escaped to JOHNSTON's army with the wreck of his Division.

During the fight of the afternoon, the Forty-Second had lost ten killed and wounded, but both of MCCLERNAND's Divisions on the center road felt that they had played a subordinate part in a battle which ought to have captured PEMBERTON's army. Over all the Northern half of Champion's Hill the carnage had been terrible. HOVEY had lost, in killed and wounded, forty-four per cent. of his Division. Thirty pieces of cannon, part of them dismounted and cut to pieces by the Federal artillery, were captured, with many battle-flags, and thousands of small arms. The dead and dying, Union and Rebel intermingled, strewed the ground. GRANT lost four hundred and twenty-six killed, and eighteen hundred and forty-two wounded. The Confederate loss was nearly four thousand killed and wounded, and three thousand prisoners, of whom LOGAN's Division captured thirteen hundred

McCLERNAND's two Divisions came up over the hill, CARR's Division, on the right, being stretched across the road coming up from the Southeast. GRANT met CARR at the fork of the roads, told him that the enemy was in full retreat, and to march by the flank with all speed in pursuit. The order was promptly executed. OSTERHAUS, on CARR's left, also got into the road as quickly as possible, and the two Divisions, maddened by their comparative inactivity during the day, set off at double-quick after PEMBERTON. Five miles away, on the road to Edwards' Station, they struck the rear guard and attacked it sharply. A horse battery was rushed up to the front, and, advancing by sections, shelled the flying column. A body of Rebels, probably a regiment, was seen in a meadow nearly a mile to the left of the road, trying to escape across Baker's Creek McCLERNAND, having no cavalry, sent a gun to shell them A bronze twelve-pounder from an Ohio Battery went down a farm road through the meadow to within half a mile of the fugitives, unlimbered, and sent three shells into a thicket wherein the Rebels had taken refuge. One of those shells, as was afterwards learned, killed Gen. TILGHMAN, one of PEMBERTON's most valuable officers.

It was now six o'clock in the evening. CARR and OSTERHAUS were pushing the retreating army to Edwards' Station. The enemy retired stubbornly, and it was sunset before the Station was reached As the pursuers entered the village, a train of cars standing on the railroad, loaded with bacon, meal and artillery ammunition, burst into flames CARR was sent through the town, and as it was now dark, the pursuit was necessarily suspended OSTERHAUS' Division bivouacked in and about the Station, holding the roads which led North and South, and acting as support to CARR, in case he should be assailed from the front. For three days not a ration had been issued to the Union troops. The men had marched and fought without a murmur, but they were now on the very verge of famine. A party of OSTERHAUS' men, including a number from the Forty-Second, attacked the burning train. In some of the cars shells were bursting and cartridges exploding, but in others were bacon and hams roasting and burning. They had learned to despise danger, and the hungry men broke open the burning cars, speared the roasting meat with their bayonets, and bore it off in triumph. McCLERNAND and his staff found in a house a jar of mouldy crab-apple "preserves," and upon this they fed. HOVEY's Division of heroes—the half of it that was left—remained on the battle-field to collect the wounded and bury the dead. Large field-hospitals were established upon and near Champion's Hill, and in these the surgeons of the whole army worked nearly all night, for they had the wounded of both armies to care for on that field.

BLACK RIVER BRIDGE.

An hour before daylight, the Divisions of CARR and OSTERHAUS were astir. Their men had no toilets to make, for there was no water, no breakfast to get, for they were without food. The drums rattled soon after three o'clock, and the troops had simply to stand up and rub their eyes open, sling their knapsacks, and they were ready for another day's work. OSTERHAUS lay in and about Edwards' Station; CARR's Division was stretched a mile down the road toward Black River Bridge, to which PEMBERTON had fled with his eighteen thousand fugitives the night before. The bridge was but six miles distant, and the road thither broad and sandy. As soon as it was light enough to see, the two Divisions moved, with a regiment thrown forward as an advance guard, and this preceded by a squad commanded by a sergeant. Skirmishers were thrown out on each side to prevent ambuscade

McPherson, the nearest support, had spent the night four miles in the rear of Edwards' Station, near the battle-field of the 16th, and since McClernand was marching with less than ten thousand men to attack nearly twenty thousand, he felt the importance of proceeding cautiously and avoiding pitfalls.

The column moved rapidly until within a mile of Black River Bridge. Here, soon after sunrise, it struck Pemberton's pickets, which were driven in. The road was flanked on each side by woods, and a regiment was thrown out on either flank to cover the advance. In this order the column proceded, pushing the enemy along until the advance line came within sight of a long line of entrenchments, bristling with men. On the right of the road in front of the works was an open beech wood, on the left, a large cotton-field, broken by bogs and marshes. Carr wheeled to the right, and put his Division in line in the beech woods. Osterhaus took the left, and stretched his Division across the cotton-field, his right resting on the road. Thus formed, the line moved up, driving the Rebel skirmishers over behind their parapet, and then lay down, as ordered, to avoid the hot artillery fire, which the enemy had promptly opened.

The Big Black river, at this point, while running toward the West, makes a sharp turn to the South, forming a right angle, whose opening is toward the Southeast. Across this angle, and nearly a mile and a quarter in length, ran a parapet four or five feet in height, and protected in front by a bayou which formed a natural fosse, or wet ditch, which had been further strengthened by being filled with brush. Behind this parapet stood eighteen pieces of cannon, and just as many men as the works would cover—perhaps ten thousand. The remainder of Pemberton's army, with three guns, occupied the high bluff bank beyond the river as a reserve. Through the center of the triangle formed by the river and parapet, ran the Jackson railroad, crossing the Big

Black on a high wooden trestle-bridge, nearly a thousand feet in length. The works, it need hardly be stated, had been built to enable a small force to defend the bridge.

The sun rose bright and cloudless, and before nine o'clock—by which time the two Divisions were in line and wrapped round the Rebel position in the form of a crescent—the heat was becoming oppressive. FOSTER'S Battery took position to the left of the road, in the rear of OSTERHAUS' line, and engaged four or five heavy bronze guns of the enemy, which stood just South of the railroad bridge. In a few minutes, FOSTER got in a center shot and capsized one of them, but a moment later, a shell went through one of his limber-chests, exploding it and frightening the team, which escaped from the drivers, and went scurrying round over the field in which OSTERHAUS' men were lying baking on the dry ground. Both sides stopped firing a moment to watch and cheer the runaway. The boys were not disposed to lose a little fun simply because a battle was going on. The assailants began to grow nervous, and crept up to where they could get a better shot. McCLERNAND, seeing that he was outnumbered by an enemy within permanent entrenchments, had sent back to tell McPHERSON that a battle was imminent, and asked him to come up as support. This McPHERSON did promptly, but he came too late.

The right of CARR'S Division was a Brigade of Iowa troops, commanded by Col. LAWLOR. The heat was intense, and LAWLOR, prancing round without a coat, went down to the river on his right for some water. While there, Col. KINSMAN, of the Twenty-Third Iowa Regiment, pointed out to LAWLOR a small transverse ravine leading to the Rebel works, which they had neglected to fill with brush. Through this a column, four men abreast, might march up, gain the ditch, and climb over the parapet. No sooner said than done. LAWLOR put eleven hundred men in column, and marched them round, Col. KINSMAN at the head, to where, with a short run across an exposed, open place, they could gain the weak point. The column started, but was met by a murderous fire, which killed Col KINSMAN at the head of his Regiment. Not a man faltered a moment. LAWLOR'S movement, though made entirely without orders, was in plain view of both McCLERNAND'S Divisions, the men of which were tired of lying in the hot sun, and were emulous of the renown gained by HOVEY and LOGAN the day before. When they saw LAWLOR'S little column making for the ditch, they thought it a good time for a charge. The whole line sprang to its feet, gave a tremendous cheer, and dashed forward. In less than half a minute LAWLOR'S column, with his supports at its heels, was pouring over the parapet, and the enemy at that end was beginning to break. The two Divisions rushed up to the ditch, meeting a volley but not stopping to fire until within ten yards of the works, when the Rebels gave way and ran like a mob. The Union line poured a broadside into the retreating horde, and, climbing across the obstructed ditch, gave chase. The enemy swarmed to a large bridge made of steamboats, moored across the stream just below the railroad bridge. The battery on the hills beyond the river opened fire to cover the retreat; but it could not check the pursuit. McCLERNAND'S men were now all over the parapet, taking prisoners and driving the frightened enemy into the river. Before the flying host could get across the bridge, some one fired the cotton with which the steamboats were laden, and in a moment the bridge was in flames and impassable. There was no escape now but by swimming, and hundreds of Confederates, including Gen. GREENE, leaped into the river. McCLERNAND'S men shot them in the water, or halted them as they crept up the opposite bank, and made them swim back and surrender. Colonels and captains were captured by private soldiers, and a whole brigade, secreted in a cane-brake, was found and led out as prisoners by a lieutenant and a dozen men.

The victory was decisive and overwhelming. Eighteen pieces of cannon, and nearly two thousand stand of small arms were among the trophies. The entire loss of McClernand's two Divisions was twenty men killed, and two hundred and forty-two wounded.

Had not the bridge been destroyed, McPherson and McClernand, with nearly ten hours of daylight before them, might have chased Pemberton into Vicksburgh, and captured the citadel before the mob could be rallied. As it was, they had to stop and work all day bridging the deep river with timber from the trestles of the railway bridge. The only pontoon train in the army was with Blair's Division, which had crossed that morning through Edwards' Station to Bridgeport, ten miles above, where it was then laying its boats for Sherman's Corps to cross upon. It was not until after dark that McPherson and McClernand could get their bridge finished, but a brigade crossed over in the darkness and occupied the heights. Sherman had reached Bridgeport during the day, found Blair there with the pontoons, and got two of his Divisions across during the afternoon and evening.

Early next morning, the 18th, the three Corps of Grant's army were again marching toward Vicksburgh. Sherman bore to the right, came down in the rear of Haines' Bluff on the Yazoo, found it evacuated, with all its heavy guns left in position, and, turning to the left, closed in upon the defenses of Vicksburgh. McPherson, holding the center, took the direct road to the city, and closed in with his Corps astride the main road to Jackson. McClernand, bearing away several miles to the left, crossed fields and lanes, and finally, later in the afternoon, found the Baldwin's Ferry road, and by marching an hour after dark, struck Pemberton's out-posts two miles outside the defenses. There the Thirteenth Corps rested for the night.

The campaign was now complete. Five times the enemy had

been defeated, a new base of supplies had been established on the Yazoo within easy distance, LORING and JOHNSTON were cut off, with the Black River between them and our rear, and the investment of Vicksburgh was complete. As Gen SHERMAN said that morning when he and Gen. GRANT rode along the abandoned works at Haines' Bluff and saw the Union fleet lying at the mouth of the Yazoo : " This is a campaign, this is a success if we never take the town "

But GRANT had come to take the town. His troops, though weary with constant marching and fighting, their ragged clothing dirty and stained with rain and dust, and their faces thin from long and arduous labor and insufficient food, were in splendid spirits and ready for any task that their commander might assign. It was due to all the circumstances of the case that a vigorous effort be made to capture the city without loss of time. It was now nearly the 20th of May, and the heat and dust were already becoming oppressive Water might fail for the Summer along the rugged hills in rear of the city, and more than all, the victorious army, which had so completely out-fought its enemies in the open field, was in no mood to settle down amid heat and discomfort to trench and sap in a seige that would undoubtedly last until mid-summer. Reliance was placed too on the demoralized condition in which the wreck of PEMBERTON's army had reached Vicksburgh. It was thought probable that if the assault were made at once the works, formidable as they were, might be carried before the *morale* and discipline of the defeated army could be restored These were the thoughts of Gen. GRANT as, on the evening of the 18th, he rode along the Walnut Hills and saw SHERMAN'S Corps close in upon the defenses the city.

Orders were issued next morning to the three Corps Commanders to " Push forward carefully and gain positions as close as possible to the enemy's works until two o'clock p.m.; at that hour to fire three rounds from all the artillery in position. This will be the signal for a general charge along the whole line."

Tuesday, the 19th, the first day of the investment, was one of the most interesting in all that Summer. After six weary months of fighting, marching and digging, the men who had dug the canal and been repulsed at Chickasaw Bayou, were now within sight of the fortifications of which they had heard so much. They came not as a forlorn hope, but as conquerors. and every man from Gen GRANT to the humblest teamster, felt a personal interest in the conquest of the citadel which had thus far locked the Mississippi and held the Confederacy together.

At dawn MCCLERNAND'S Corps, bivouacked in the rugged valley of a creek which flows Southward from the rear of the city, was roused up and started forward. OSTERHAUS' Division was in advance. As the column climbed up out of the ravine it turned a curve in the road near a large white house, which afterwards became the center of a village of field hospitals. Rounding this curve, the great line of defences was suddenly disclosed. For three miles to the right and left, along the whole front, the sharp cut crest of the Rebel fortifications formed the horizon line. Instinctively the men wheeling into view of the scene, began to cheer. A moment after there was a puff of white smoke from the distant parapet, and a shell, singing and shrieking through the air, crashed through a locust tree in front of the house and buried itself in the earth. The gun that had fired it was two miles away, but in the clear morning air it seemed less than a mile. The Corps now moved rapidly up, descended into a series of rugged ravines that lay between the white house and the enemy's line, and deployed for the attack. SMITH'S Division took the extreme right, extending nearly to a junction with QUIMBY'S Division of MCPHERSON'S Corps. Next came CARR, then OSTERHAUS, and HOVEY on the extreme left. The general position of the Corps being established, the troops rested in line, while strong skirmish lines were sent up over the hills toward the fortifications to secure positions from which division, brigade and regimental commanders could carefully reconnoiter the ground. The skirmish line met a sharp, irregular fire, but it pushed bravely up to within three or four hundred yards of the enemy's parapet Gen OSTERHAUS and his officers, following behind on foot, made a careful study of the ground. It proved exceedingly rough and difficult. The enemy's works were built along the crest of a ridge from which deep ravines led down on the Eastern side to the valley in which the reserves were resting The soil, a firm mixture of clay and sand, being cut perpendicularly by the action of the water, maintained a vertical wall or surface for years, so that the sides of the ravines were often so steep that the soldiers could climb them only by using both hands. The hostile line was a series of detached works built upon favorable points and connected with each other by heavy parapets or rifle trenches. The lateral ravines on the Eastern side led up to the slope of this ridge, and in some cases gave a covered approach to within two hundred yards of the line, but in every case it was found that the ravine was swept by the guns of a redoubt or bastion, and the approach finally must be over open space wholly exposed.

By noon the reconnoisance was finished and the troops were moved as far to the front as they could be sheltered to await the signal of attack Batteries meanwhile had been put in position on commanding ridges, and at the appointed hour the signal was fired. The troops moved forward promptly, but the roughness of the ground broke up the line and threw it into confusion. Some regiments had comparatively easy footing and got ahead rapidly, others found declivities up or down which they had to climb almost in single file The enemy's line was crooked and irregular, so that the distances to be traveled by the different regiments and brigades were quite unequal Above all, the Rebel fire was hot and sharp, large guns raking the ravines with great charges of canister, and the musketry fire being severe on all exposed points The ground was moreover strange and had to be crossed cautiously, and the result of all was that night came on before the troops had got up to within charging distance of the works. It was seen that an assault, to be successful, must begin about where the advance of that day had ended, and the situation being alike in all the three Corps, Gen GRANT gave the order to hold the ground then occupied and await further orders BLAIR, in SHERMAN'S Corps had rushed in rashly, been severely cut up, and though fighting like heroes, his men had only the satisfaction of having planted their colors on the counterscarp of a work which they could not enter. So the attack of the 19th failed of its grand object and served only to get the enemy's line closely invested in readiness for a final assault

But the army had done all that it could without food and rest. The enemy had shown unexpected tenacity and spirit. The strength of their defences, the eight thousand fresh troops of the garrison, added, no doubt to a fierce vengeance against the assailants who had so overwhelmingly humbled them in the open field, combined to give PEMBERTON'S army of thirty thousand men fresh courage. It was evident that before attacking such a position, thus defended, GRANT'S army must have sleep and food. Orders were given to this effect. From the new base at Haines' Bluff came trains of wagons bringing rations, clothing, soap, shoes and other luxuries to which the men had long been strangers. Empty barrels were sunk in the ground for wells, springs were sought out, and while some regiments held the advance line, others back in the ravines bathed, changed their soiled clothing, ate and slept. Two days and nights of this set the army fairly on its feet again, and on the 22d the grand final assault was ordered.

The wisdom of this attack has been seriously questioned. In view of its result, it was of course unfortunate, but it is only truth to say that the army desired it and believed that it would succeed. Gen. GRANT under-estimated the strength of PEMBERTON by nearly ten thousand men, and he did not know, as we found to our cost, that the outer line of the enemy was commanded by a second or inner one, and that to hold a captured salient would prove more difficult and dangerous than to take it He knew that JOHNSTON was organizing a formidable army at Canton to attack his rear, the sooner Vicksburgh were captured the sooner he could turn upon that new army and destroy it or drive it from the State.

Ten o'clock a.m., of the 22d was therefore announced as the hour for the grand assault. The artillery was to open vigorously at an early hour, breach the works if possible, and dismount such guns as were exposed through embrasures. The infantry was to advance from the nearest cover in columns of platoons, moving at quick time, with only canteens, ammunition and one days rations, not a gun was to be fired until the outer works had been stormed, and between the columns strong lines of skirmishers were to advance and scale the intervening parapets.

The momentous day came, and at dawn the artillery opened. The cannonade was terrific. Admiral PORTER, with his mortar fleet and three gunboats, was playing upon the doomed city from the river Along GRANT'S line, thirty field batteries blazed and roared from half-past three in the morning until ten. Under this terrific fire the sharp-shooters of the skirmish line crept forward so close that they commanded the enemy's artillery. The gunners could not expose themselves long enough to load their pieces. The watches of the officers had been set with that of Gen. GRANT, and at the stroke of ten the bombardment ceased, and the assaulting columns sprang forward. There was a minute or two of ominous silence, broken only by cheers here and there, as the men climbed up out of the ravines, and rushed across the exposed ground to the ditch. Then, all in a moment, the Rebels' parapet became a fringe of gray and steel, from which streamed a livid sheet of fire. Twenty thousand foes, a double rank along the whole front of the Federal army, rose up behind that parapet, and at from ten to sixty yards poured a withering volley into the the advancing columns. Field guns, double-shotted, were run out over the parapet and fired, and heavy ordnance swept the ridges with canister, raising great clouds of dust that covered the assailants as with a pall of death. Prodigies of valor were performed. In front of CARR's Division, LAWLOR's Iowa men climbed over the parapet into a large lunette, but it was commanded from the interior line, and every man who entered it was shot down. Sergeant JOSEPH GRIFFITH of the Twenty-Third Iowa alone survived, and came out covered with blood and dust, bringing a Rebel lieutenant and thirteen men as prisoners. Nearly every Brigade of OSTERHAUS' Division reached the ditch, but the double line of Rebels within killed them as fast as they could climb the parapet. In several cases they held the ditch until night, defending their lives by watching with uplifted muskets the appearance of a Rebel head, and making it a mortal peril to fire upon them.

The Forty-Second bore an interesting part in the events of that day. On the previous evening, Capt. BARBER was detailed, with his Company ("H") and Company "E," to go at dawn the next morning, and, under cover of the artillery fire that would open at daybreak, explore the ground over which LINDSAY's Brigade was to charge, clear up to the enemy's ditch. He had tried to do this the evening before, but the Rebels were too prompt, and by running out their picket line just at sunset, covered the ground upon which Capt. BARBER wished to operate. Setting out the next morning, therefore, he proceeded with the two Companies— about seventy men—to the head of the ravine up which LIND-

SAY'S Brigade was to advance. When about four hundred yards of the enemy's line, the valley makes a sharp curve, and from that point the men, emerging from behind a clump of willows, were exposed to a concentric fire from the works above. Nevertheless, they got across safely, the bombardment restraining the fire of the enemy Capt BARBER and his men reconnoitered the head of the ravine thoroughly, climbing up the ridges to within fifty yards of the Rebel parapet. Just as he was about to return in person to give his report to Gen. OSTERHAUS, Capt BARBER was shot through the right leg, the ball cutting off both bones below the knee and making immediate amputation necessary. He was taken down the hill and carried to the rear, his men, under a sergeant, holding the advanced position until the assaulting column arrived.

At ten o'clock, the Brigade, headed by the Sixteenth Ohio, moved up the valley to the assault Rounding the clump of willows at the bottom of the ravine, the column was met by a terrific fire, but pressed on to where the shape of the ground afforded partial protection. It was arranged that the Sixteenth Ohio should mount the hill to the left at the head of the ravine, the Forty-Second should take the center, the Twenty-Second Kentucky the right, while the Forty-Fourth Indiana should act as support, and reinforce promptly whichever regiment should first cross the parapet. From the nature of the ground, the Sixteenth, as brave a Regiment as ever marched, having the shortest distance to go, reached the point of attack first Its skirmishers quickly climbed the hill, and made a dash for the ditch. Their appearance was the signal for a terrific volley from the Confederates. The skirmish line was swept away in a moment. The head of the regiment appeared over the crest of the hill, but was literally blown back. The whole surface of the ridge up to the ditch was raked and plowed with a concentric fire of musketry and cannister at pistol range. No man, no company could live to reach the ditch. The few survivors of the skirmish line took refuge in a rugged gorge cut by the water, and held that position. They could neither advance nor retreat.

The experience of the Forty-Second was similar, except that its advance was checked by the experience of the Sixteenth. Lieut. Col. PARDEE was in command, Col SHELDON being off duty by reason of illness and his wound received at Thompson's Hill. Marching quickly across the exposed place in the valley, the Forty-Second climbed the hill, meeting just such a fire as had checked the Sixteenth The skirmishers rushed out upon the exposed ground, but were instantly covered and hidden by the dust raised round them by the terrible rain from the enemy's artillery. It was seen in a moment that the point of attack assigned to LINDSAY's Brigade was a re-entrant angle of the enemy's line, and that the head of the ravine was the focus of a converging fire from three points, armed by heavy batteries. As a result, there was no part of the enemy's ditch in that quarter which, if captured, could be held for a moment. Every part of it was enfiladed from the hostile parapet, which was too high to be climbed without bridges or scaling ladders. Col LINDSAY, up at the extreme front, saw that no column could live to reach the ditch, nor if it did reach that point, could escape. At some places in the enemy's line there were exterior angles at which the ditch offered some protection, but there was no such point in his front. He could see to the right the heroes of CARR's Division retiring from their superb assault, leaving the ground blue with the dying and dead. The parapet in LINDSAY's front was manned by WALL's legion of Texas troops, one of the finest divisions in the Confederate service, and they were so massed that by exchanging places they were able to pour down a continuous fire To push his remaining regiments into such a death-trap, to continue an assault that was already failing along the whole line, would be a needless and unsoldierly sacrifice, and the Forty-Second, after the repulse of its skirmishers, was not again ordered to attack.

The skirmishers, though losing several men, had been momentarily fortunate. The distance was so short that the canister, not having range to scatter, struck in masses, and the enemy's musketry fire was too high. In the midst of a perfect hail-storm of shot they were, for the moment, miraculously preserved. The Regiment lay down behind the crest of the ridge and awaited new orders It held the point all day under the hot sun, keeping up a sharp fire whenever a Rebel head appeared, and meeting considerable loss.

The assault, which at several points was renewed in the afternoon, failed along the whole line The enemy's works were of immense strength, the difficulties of approach were too great for any courage or discipline to surmount, and the garrison, if we had but known it, was almost equal in numbers to the assailants. It only remained, therefore, to hold what ground had been gained and conquer Vicksburgh by siege

CHAPTER VIII.

THE SIEGE OF VICKSBURGH—CAMPAIGNING WITH THE AXE AND SHOVEL—BLACK RIVER BRIDGE AGAIN—THE CAPITULATION—PURSUIT OF JOE JOHNSTON—THE JACKSON CAMPAIGN—RETURN TO VICKSBURGH.

Although the losses of the National Army in the assault of the 22d of May had been fully three thousand men, though the ground between the hostile lines was left strewn with Union dead festering in the sun, the troops were neither dismayed nor discouraged. They had come to take the citadel that obstructed the freedom of the Mississippi; and if men enough could live to do it, they, like their commander, were ready to work and fight until the grand purpose was accomplished. Bringing away their wounded on the night of the 22d, the three corps settled down in that torrid climate, without adequate water, or any comfort beyond the barest necessities of existence, to a siege which lasted forty-seven days. Ground was cleared for camps as near to the front as tenable locations could be found, dwellings were dug in the hillsides and roofed with cane, and every precaution taken to promote, as far as possible, the health and comfort of the men.

The siege began on the 23d. Batteries were pushed forward to favorable points, within close range of the enemy's line, and protected by heavy earthworks thrown up by night, trenches and covered ways were cut connecting the batteries with the ravines. The extraordinary ruggedness of the ground, which had been such an obstruction to the assault, now proved of great advantage to the besiegers. In front of nearly every division was a natural covered approach, through some defile, to within three or four hundred yards of the enemy's line—in some cases these distances were less than one hundred yards

At these advanced points the sap began, and the first and second parallels incident to ordinary sieges being thus rendered unnecesary, were omitted. There was a serious lack of experienced engineer officers to conduct the siege Generals SHERMAN and McPHERSON were themselves educated engineers, and kept an intelligent supervision of their own operations; but McCLERNAND knew nothing of such work, and the trenches of his right wing were in charge of a Lieutenant of Engineers, a graduate of the class of 1861 at West Point, and those of his left wing were managed by an enlisted man of the Forty-Second Ohio,* who studied "Mahan" and the work of McPHERSON's Engineers as the siege progressed. Col HARRY WILSON, of Gen. GRANT's staff, maintained an informal oversight over the operations in front of the Thirteenth Corps, and saved the novices there from making any serious mistakes; but from want of experienced direction at the start, many a useless shovelful of earth was thrown, and the excellent ground in front of HOVEY's Division was not utilized until the latter part of the siege. But with all the difficulties, progress was rapid and substantial. The wonderful ingenuity and adaptability of that army of mechanics, farmers and tradesmen shone out conspicuously from first to last. Men who

---

* For these and other services during the campaign of 1863, Private F H MASON was promoted during the year by the Secretary of War to Captain and A D C

had never heard of a gabion or fascine, were taught in an hour to make them acceptably of cane and grapevines.

Admiral PORTER lent Gen. GRANT a heavy battery from the fleet, and volunteers who had never trod a deck in their lives, hauled them up, put the mysterious navy carriages together, mounted the guns, and worked them with consummate skill. Sap-rollers were made by fastening two barrels head to head and wrapping them with the cane that grew plentifully in the ravines. The trenches were revetted with cotton bales, with empty bread and flour barrels, or when better work was required, with gabions and fascines, made in the manner already described. A heavy parallel trench, or rifle-pit was cut along the front, in many cases within fifty yards of the hostile salients. These trenches were wide and spacious, with banquettes for riflemen, who ingeniously protected their heads with sand-bags, or by laying heavy green logs, notched on the under side, along the parapets. These advanced trenches were occupied during the day by sharpshooters, who stood with their rifles pushed out through the loop-holes, ready to shatter any head that appeared above the enemy's parapet. Batteries were advanced and shifted from point to point, as closer observation suggested, the field-guns were brought up so close that they could fire through the embrasures of the hostile line, and actually forced the enemy to withdraw his heavy guns to save them from destruction. In all, eighty-nine different earthworks were built during the siege for the protection of GRANT's artillery, which, on the 5th of June, numbered two hundred and twenty guns. The ingenuity displayed in protecting these guns in advanced positions from the enemy's sharpshooters, was one of the curious incidents of the siege. The trenches advanced rapidly, the work being done, as usual, mainly at night. It soon became a matter of extreme difficulty and risk to secure ground upon which the zigzag approaches could advance.

In some places this was done behind sap-rollers, but work by that method was necessarily slow, from the limited number of men who could be employed. The plan that suited the ardent volunteers best was to push forward the picket-line at sunset, secure ground enough to work upon during the night, and then boldly dig the trench from the top downward. This method was extensively practiced in front of the Thirteenth Corps.

The Rebels had from the first thrown out a strong picket-line at night, to hold the besiegers as far back as possible and prevent night assaults. Soon the two picket-lines came together, talked over the situation amicably, and agreed not to fire upon each other at night without first giving warning. This suited the besiegers; but, as they were advancing all the time, and needed to push the Confederates back about thirty feet further on each succeeding night, the harmonious relations were not preserved without great tact and diplomacy on the part of the Union sentinels and their officers. On several occasions, when crowded too far, the Confederate officers swore they would no longer submit to such aggression, gave notice of hostilities, and withdrew within their works. At such times the Union soldiers retired within their advanced trenches, let the enemy blaze away for a time, gave them as good as they sent, taking good care that the enemy gained nothing by such peevishness. The policy was adopted of concentrating all the Union batteries within range upon such portions of the Rebel line as showed any such perverseness, and several highly-spirited and picturesque bombardments ensued from these causes, in which the Rebels invariably got the worst of it. They lost many in killed and wounded, their men were prevented from sleeping or cooking by night, and more than all, nothing was gained—the persistent Yankees kept on digging and advancing as before. As each evening came on, the Federal pickets would emerge from the front trenches and advance until they met the Rebel line Lying down within a few yards of each other they discussed various questions—the origin of the war, the emancipation proclamation, the battles of the May campaign, probabilities of the siege, etc., etc. Hot disputes sometimes arose, but no actual collision occurred. On the narrow belt of neutral ground between the two lines the officers of both armies met, West Point classmates in blue and gray chatted over school-boy reminiscences, and agreed that it was a monstrous pity for two such armies of the same race to be cutting each other's throats.

In all this hard, but varied and interesting work, the Forty-Second bore its full share until Monday, the 22d of June, thirty-three days after the investment. The front held by LINDSAY's Brigade being, as already stated, within a re-entrant angle of the enemy's line, was unfavorable for siegeing operations, which were directed mainly against the salients. The work of the Forty-Second had been largely guard duty and sharp-shooting at the front, and special fatigue duty at other points of the line On the 18th, several Companies of the Regiment were engaged in planting some heavy guns on the right near the Jackson railroad, and on returning to camp found orders issued to pack knapsacks, cook two days' rations, and be prepared to march at a moment's warning Ever since the siege began, every intelligent soldier in Grant's army saw that the greatest danger threatening them was not in front, but at the rear. Gen. JOE JOHNSTON, one of the ablest of Confederate Generals, was at Carthage, a few miles North of Jackson, in the midst of a rich country, collecting and organizing an army with which to fall upon GRANT's rear and raise the siege.

On the 16th of June, prisoners captured by the small force of Cavalry which Gen. GRANT kept reconnoitering beyond the Big Black river, had reported that JOHNSTON's army already amounted to thirty thousand infantry, six field batteries, and two thousand cavalry. Of this force, ten thousand were veteran troops from BRAGG's army in Tennessee, and the garrisons of Mobile, Port Hudson and various other places had been reduced to the smallest safe proportions to fit out this army to save Vicksburgh, or at least to extricate its garrison. Gen. GRANT's watchful eye had not failed to note carefully the progress of JOHNSTON's preparations. Our reinforcements that had come down the river during the siege, including two Divisions of the Ninth Corps under Gen. PARKE, had been sent to confront this army in the rear.

On the 22d positive information was received that JOHNSTON with a heavy force was approaching the Big Black. OSTERHAUS was immediately detached from the Thirteenth Corps, and with his fine Division marched on the afternoon of that day to Black River Bridge, the point at which McCLERNAND and McPHERSON had crossed on the 18th of May. The Division reached the railroad bridge at ten o'clock in the evening, and having a high, bluff bank from which to guard the crossing of a deep river with low ground beyond, OSTERHAUS' position was one of great strength.

The country was moreover pleasant and healthy, and the Forty-Second, like the rest of the Division, was not sorry to be out of the broiling trenches and where duty did not occupy two-thirds of the entire time. All felt sure that Vicksburgh was surely ours, and there was a pang of regret in the thought that after all the hard fighting of the past six months we should not be in at the death, but the consciousness of guarding at Black River one of the most important approaches by which the rear of the besiegers could be attacked, fully consoled the Division for giving up its share in the siege.

Gen. SHERMAN had meanwhile been detached from his Corps and sent back to take command of this army in the rear. His command included Gen. PARKE'S two Divisions of the Ninth Corps, reaching from Haines' Bluff to the Benton, or ridge road, then TUTTLE'S Division of the Fifteenth Corps, then MCARTHUR'S Division of the Seventeenth, and finally, OSTERHAUS' at Black River Bridge—five Divisions of the finest troops in the service. A line of rifle pits, armed with several field batteries was now quickly cut across the neck of land between the Big Black and the Yazoo, eight miles wide, and occupied by SHERMAN'S command.

BLAIR'S Division went on the 26th and destroyed all the food and forage through the country between the two rivers for a distance of sixty or seventy miles to the Northeast. JOHNSTON could not march an army in by that route without hauling his subsistence, and that GRANT was certain he could not do. After that MONROE'S Brigade was sent up the Yazoo river to Mechanicsburgh to watch the crossing there and at Bridgeport on the Big Black, and to obstruct the roads.

OSTERHAUS, finding that JOHNSTON had not come, crossed the Big Black with a strong force, gathered cattle and forage, destroyed what he could not bring away, and likewise obstructed the roads. This done he remained on the defensive, and the Forty-Second in its pleasant camp took occasion to wash its clothing free from the red earth which had been ground into it during its days and nights in the trenches at Vicksburgh.

On the 30th the Regiment was mustered for pay, always an event of interest, and on the following day the monotony of camp life was varied by the report of a hot skirmish between OSTERHAUS' Cavalry Regiment across the river and a force of Confederate cavalry, in which the latter were routed and driven. Thus the days wore on until the night of July 3d, when a courier came with the news that negotiations looking to the surrender of Vicksburgh were in progress, and that it was expected that the evacuation would take place on the morrow. This was great news, all the greater in that the capitulation was to be consummated on Independence Day. The telegraph along the railroad had been repaired back to the city, and we had regular reports. Capt Ross and several other members of the Regiment were back at the lines on the Fourth, and returned that night, bringing full news of the surrender which they witnessed. It was a happy, glorious day!

Not a moment was lost in idle rejoicings. Gen GRANT was not even present when the Confederate army marched out and stacked its arms. He was in his tent dictating instructions to Gen SHERMAN to immediately cross the Big Black, defeat JOHNSTON, and drive him from the State. For this purpose there was to be sent to his support the remaining three Divisions of the Thirteenth Corps, to which was also attached LAUMAN'S Division, and the remaining two Divisions of SHERMAN'S own Corps, (the Fifteenth.)

On the 19th of June, Gen. McCLERNAND had been relieved from the command of the Thirteenth Corps, and sent home to Springfield, Illinois. His place was filled by Gen E. O. C. ORD, one of the most accomplished officers in the service. On the afternoon of the Fourth of July, within six hours of the surrender of Vicksburgh, ORD's Corps was on the march. The weather was intensely hot and dry, and the march was begun at night to save the strength of the men. OSTERHAUS' Division at Black River prepared the floating bridge, and, when the Corps came along early next morning, took the advance of the column. The Thirteenth Corps was now reunited, and, with LAUMAN's Division, was nearly twenty thousand strong. Gen. ORD got his Corps across by noon of the 6th, and marched that afternoon to Edwards' Station. The Fifteenth Corps crossed at Messenger's Ford on the 5th and 6th. PARKE'S two Divisions of the Ninth Corps crossed at Birdsong's Ferry, and the three columns converged on Bolton Station. The march was one of terrible suffering. The atmosphere was like an oven. JOHNSTON, on hearing of the surrender at Vicksburgh, on the 4th, had retreated with his army to Jackson, and, with the hope of making the country impassable for an army, had driven animals into the few ponds and springs, where they were shot down and left to fester and poison the water. The weather was excessively dry, and this, with JOHNSTON's efforts, had made water fit for drinking practically unattainable. The men almost perished from heat and thirst. Scores were prostrated by sunstroke in a single day. The men filled their canteens from muddy, stagnant pools, green and poisonous with slime and filth, and this water, drank by the heated and perspiring men, induced nausea and serious digestive difficulties. It was not known precisely where JOHNSTON had gone, and each of the three columns, marching toward a powerful enemy, was not only obliged to march by daylight, but to proceed with the greatest caution. The troops were therefore kept tramping over the dusty roads through the long, broiling days, and angry complaints were heard against what was mistaken for the careless cruelty of the commander. ORD's column moved on the road past the bloody battle field of Champion's Hill, where the atmosphere was still heavy and fetid with the miasma of death. Horses and men had been buried, but the soil on the rocky hill was thin and the graves were shallow. On the night of the 7th, ORD's Corps reached Bolton, and on the afternoon following SHERMAN's three columns were concentrated in the neighborhood of Clinton. During the day JOHNSTON's cavalry had been hovering round our front, and in one or two skirmishes with the advance had lost a number of prisoners. SHERMAN with his three Divisions now pressed forward and drove JOHNSTON into the entrenchments of Jackson, which had been greatly enlarged and strengthened since the capture of the city in May. The Union army closely invested the place, with the exception of the Eastern side, which it could not reach on account of the Pearl river. ORD'S Corps held the right of the line of investment, SHERMAN'S the center, and PARKE'S the left, the wings reaching to the river above and below the town. It was not SHERMAN'S purpose to assault the works—they were too strong and well defended for that; but he closed in his lines and shelled the town from every direction. One of ORD'S Brigades (LAUMAN'S, which had arrived before Vicksburgh from the North on the 24th of May, and had taken only a small part in the siege) was anxious to distinguish itself, and got in too close to the enemy's works, where it met a large Division of troops from BRAGG'S army and was very roughly handled. LAUMAN had exceeded his orders and was relieved from command. The enemy, on the 11th, also sallied against SHERMAN'S lines, but was promptly repulsed with considerable loss. On the 13th, the heat being still stifling, a truce of four hours was arranged, and the dead that lay between the lines of the two armies were buried. Sherman bombarded the town heavily on the 15th, and had arrangements in progress to throw his wings across the river, but on the following morning the works were found deserted JOHNSTON had evacuated the place during the night, escaping with everything but four field-guns, leaving a swarm of stragglers who were captured and paroled.

STEELE'S Division pursued the fugitive army Eastward to Brandon, but JOHNSTON was gone, the weather was too hot to pursue, and Gen SHERMAN gave himself up to the work of destroying past all repair the railways of Central Mississippi. The Forty-Second aided in this work on the 18th, 19th and 20th. On the morning of the 21st it marched at 5 a m., its faces again turned Westward, and after another scorching day's walk through the dust, encamped for the night at Mississippi Springs, on the road to Raymond. Next day it rained, and the Forty-Second, being in advance and homeward bound, struck out and marched twenty-five miles, reaching its camp on the Black River soon after dark. There being no enemy in the country, Gen. SHERMAN allowed the troops to march back somewhat at will.

On the 13th, the Forty-Second, with the remainder of OSTERHAUS' Division, having sent its sick to Vicksburgh by rail, struck tents early and marched to the captured city, encamping at night in a clean, comfortable place in rear of the works. Next day camp was broken again, and the Division, with colors flying and its bands playing national airs, marched through the city in splendid style and encamped on the large plain between the bluff and the river below the town. The goal of nearly a year's work was reached—we were encamped inside the walls of Vicksburgh. Boats lay at the landing, but they all wore the national colors; sentries paced along the formidable water batteries, but they were men of LOGAN'S Division, our own comrades and friends. The plain upon which we were encamped was an old race-ground, where the beauty and chivalry of Vicksburgh had assembled in former days to witness the scrub-races that answered for sport among that liesure community. Directly across the river lay the abortive canal on which the Regiment had worked last February; and on the shores near our tents was the battery which the Rebels had built to command its mouth.

The Regiment cleared up and occupied a neat, regular camp, drew new clothing, and on the 30th received two month's pay. The weather, from extreme drouth had changed to regular and heavy rains, the heat still remaining constant and intense. The air was laden with miasmatic vapors, and sickness spread through the camp, attacking nearly a third of some companies, and deaths were frequent. Company "G" lost three men in a single day. The Regiment had a fine parade ground, and there being only guard-duty to perform, it resumed the regular camp routine, including three hours of brigade drill, with formal daily guard-mounting and dress-parade. The convalescents and a few recruits were brought down to the several companies, and the Forty-Second, while spending its leisure in walking over the vast and formidable fortress, was rapidly prepared for new duties in another department.

CHAPTER IX.

TRANSFERRED TO THE DEPARTMENT OF THE GULF—DOWN THE RIVER TO NEW ORLEANS—BRASHEAR CITY AND THE TECHE COUNTRY—THE WINTER AT PLAQUEMINE—BATON ROUGE AND RED RIVER—MORGANZIA AND THE WHITE RIVER—A BUSY BUT AIMLESS SUMMER—THE RETURN HOME—MUSTERED OUT OF SERVICE.

It is on record that when Gen. GRANT's army passed below Vicksburgh in the Spring of 1863, it was with a more or less definite design of landing in Mississippi, marching down to Port Hudson, assisting Gen BANKS to capture that place, and then returning with the armies of GRANT and BANKS united to operate against Vicksburgh, having a new basis of supply at New Orleans. But when GRANT failed to take Grand Gulf by attack in front, he was obliged to capture that important stronghold by a flank movement, and the important victory at Thompson's Hill on the 1st of May effected that result. With BOWEN's force defeated, and his army thoroughly established on the Mississippi shore, Gen. GRANT, contrary to the judgment of President LINCOLN and Gen HALLECK, turned Northward and fought the superb campaign which terminated with the capitulation of Vicksburgh.

All this time Gen Banks had been begging Grant to send him reinforcements. Not less than three times, during the May campaign and the siege which followed, did the commander of the Gulf Department send the most urgent appeals to Gen. Grant to send him sufficient troops to capture Port Hudson and drive the Rebel forces from the Red River country. Finally, during the siege, Grant had written to Banks explaining the importance of his operations and his inability to spare a single man, closing his letter with the promise that "when I get through with this job I will send you a Corps of as good troops as ever marched on American soil."

Accordingly on the 13th of August, the Forty-Second, with the remainder of Osterhaus' Division, went on board transports at Vicksburgh and started down the river. The great work of opening the Mississippi was now complete, and the future service of the Forty-Second was to aid in defending what had been gained. The weather during the trip down was bright and beautiful, though warm, and the troops, now quite accustomed to the heat, enjoyed the voyage thoroughly. The fleet had in tow several barges loaded with wagons and mules, one of which was snagged and sunk, two of the guards on board being drowned. The boats passed Port Hudson, Natchez and Baton Rouge, and on the night of the 15th reached New Orleans. The Division immediately debarked and marched to the pretty suburban village of Carrollton, four miles above and in the rear of New Orleans, on the road to Lake Pontchartrain. Here, on a beautiful lawn, a clean, dry and healthful spot, Osterhaus' war-worn Division encamped in luxurious style. Tents and camp equipage were in perfect order, and the troops, with no enemy to oppose, divided their time between drilling and exploring New Orleans. Provisions of all kinds, fruits, fish, etc., were abundant and cheap, and the Forty-Second, having been recently paid, fared sumptuously.

While at New Orleans, Liet.-Col PARDEE was detailed as Provost Marshal General of the Gulf Department, with headquarters at Baton Rouge, with Lieut. CHARLES E. HENRY of Company "A" as Provost Judge. Col. SHELDON returned from sick-leave and assumed command of the old Brigade, Major WILLIAMS being left in command of the Forty-Second.

The pleasant episode at Carrollton lasted from the 15th of August until the 6th of September, when Col. SHELDON'S Brigade was ordered to Brashear City, near the coast, about a hundred miles Southwest of New Orleans. Up to this time it had been expected that the next point of attack would be Mobile, and this was indeed Gen. GRANT'S intention, but the inefficiency of ROSECRANS in Tennessee induced the Government to recall the captor of Vicksburgh to that important department, and the movement against Mobile was postponed. In its stead, the troops at New Orleans were headed toward Texas.

Gen. BANKS' Department, West of the Mississippi, had by this time lost all importance as a part of the Rebellion to be crushed. The fighting that should close the war was to be done East of the great river. But Louisiana and Texas were wealthy with cotton; a heavy crop of sugar was ripening, and it was of the greatest importance that those States should be kept sufficiently under Federal control to permit the cotton and sugar to be gathered and marketed. For some purpose of this kind, or as a start toward Texas—we could never ascertain precisely which—the Brigade, on the 6th of September, marched to the landing, and leaving tents and knapsacks behind, took steamers and dropped down the river to Algiers, opposite the lower part of New Orleans, where the troops went on board trains and at 4 p.m. started Westward. At ten in the evening the train stopped at Bayou Boeuff, seventy-five miles from New Orleans, but in the absence of orders the men remained on board the cars during the night. Next morning the Brigade having all arrived, the troops were unloaded and put into camp. The weather was extremely hot, and the water in the bayou was found to be salt. The tide in the stream rose and fell about two feet, and when it was out the Forty-Second skirmished up and down the sand in a brisk and interesting hunt for crabs. They were plentiful, and the haversacks of the Regiment were soon filled. The Brigade, being wholly destitute of tents or camp equipage, bivouacked on a plantation near the railroad. Here it remained until the morning of the 11th, when it broke camp and marched ten miles Westward to Brashear City, the terminus of the railroad. The march was rendered especially trying by the excessive heat and want of water. The only reliance of the people for water was upon rain cisterns, and these of course could not be relied upon to supply a regiment, much less a brigade. Before reaching Brashear City, many of the men, unable to endure their thirst, rushed to the brackish streams that crossed the road and drank of the warm, salt water. By this mistake many were rendered sick, and the road was strewn with stragglers unable to walk. They came up after sunset, however, and found the camp at Brashear City, on the large bayou, twenty-five miles in length, which connects Grand Lake with the Gulf. Here the difficulty about water was again encountered, but the men immediately dug holes in the sand in which small quantities were collected, and this, with what could be obtained from cisterns and the oranges which grew abundantly everywhere, served to assuage their thirst. It was also found that a strong North wind filled the bayou with fresh water from the lake above, and the rare opportunity thus offered was improved by filling what tubs and barrels could be found. After ten days in camp at Brashear, heavy and continuous rains set in, and the troops, still without tents, were badly exposed. On the 27th, however, the tents arrived, but the rains continued until the camp was flooded. A few of the prudent ones, who always spend their leisure in providing against emergencies, had built bunks or shelves to sleep on, supported by stakes several inches above the ground. As they lay in these, they could hear their less fortunate comrades calling out, in imitation of the steamboat leadsmen, "Two feet!" "Two and a half!" "Quarter less twain!" "No bottom!" The veteran volunteer had by that time become a creature whose logical hilarity no misfortune could suppress.

After something more than two weeks at Brashear, during which time the Forty-Second received two months' pay, the Brigade set out, on the 3d of October, for Opelousas, a hundred miles to the Northwest. The country was overrun with Confederate guerrillas, but having no mounted troops, Col. SHELDON could neither pursue nor fight them advantageously. On the fourth day the column reached New Iberia, where the troops went into camp and remained until the 8th, when Gen. ORD arrived, the remaining three Divisions of the Thirteenth Army Corps having been, as we learned, transferred to the Gulf Department. On the following day SHELDON's Brigade again moved, marching twenty miles during the day and encamping beyond Smithville. The Nineteenth Army Corps was in our front, skirmishing with the Rebel forces under Gen. DICK TAYLOR, and on the night of the 10th the Forty-Second passed some of these troops on picket. Apparently, therefore, we had come to reinforce the army with which Gen. BANKS was operating in the Teche country. The 13th was election day in Ohio, and after brigade and division inspection, the Ohio regiments cast a unanimous vote for Hon. JOHN BROUGH, adding their mite to the overwhelming majority under which their loyal State buried Mr. VALLANDIGHAM. After remaining in camp till the 16th, the Division again moved forward, and after two days' marching reached Opelousas. From here five Companies of the Forty-Second were sent back to

Iberia to convoy a provision train, and did not return until the 22d.

OSTERHAUS' Division encamped, on the night of the 17th, near Vermillionville, where it remained until the 23d, during which time the remainder of the Thirteenth Corps came up. The Forty-Second had been reduced by sickness and other causes to about three hundred enlisted men present for duty, and while in camp at Vermillionville, Companies "F" and "G" were broken up and distributed among the others, the Regiment thereafter having but eight Companies.

After two days at Opelousas, the Thirteenth Corps was faced about and started back to Brashear City. There was no enemy of any serious strength in that country, and the Nineteenth Corps was abundantly strong for all defensive purposes. After a rapid but pleasant march, SHELDON's Brigade reached its old camp at Berwick Plantation, opposite Brashear City, on the night of the 10th of November. The march to Opelousas and back, though involving some hardships, was in the main a pleasant one. The weather had become cool, with intervals of rain and sunshine, and the foraging was unrivalled. The country along the Teche is a high rolling prairie, fertile and swarming with cattle, ponies and hogs. The ponies were caught in great numbers, and the cattle and swine made fresh meat a daily luxury to both officers and men. Enormous sweet potatoes could be had for the digging, oranges grew along the road plentifully as apples in Ohio, and poultry was so cheap and abundant that the army rations, except coffee and sugar, were almost untouched.

On the 25th of October, while on the return march, a party from the Forty-Second had been out foraging, and while twelve of the men were at dinner at a sugar plantation they were approached and captured by a squadron of Rebel cavalry in Federal uniform. The infantry observed them coming, but supposing them to be Union cavalry belonging to the Nineteenth Corps, permitted them to surround the house and get possession of the muskets, stacked in the yard. This misfortune produced an order which from that time forward greatly restricted foraging.

After remaining at camp at Berwick until the 18th, SHELDON's Bridade, now including the Forty-Second Ohio and the Seventh and Twenty-Second Kentucky, crossed to Brashear City. The next day Col SHELDON was ordered to reinforce Gen. BIRGE at Thibodeaux. The Brigade went by rail to that point, where it reported to Gen BIRGE, debarked and marched up Bayou Lafourche to Donaldsonville on the Mississippi, where it took steamers for Plaquemine, a town of three or four thousand inhabitants, on the Western shore of the river, one hundred and ten miles above New Orleans. While returning from Opelousas to Brashear City, it had been confidently expected that OSTERHAUS' Division would be ordered to Texas; in fact, orders were issued to be ready to embark for Galveston as soon as transportation by sea could be procured. The transfer to Plaquemine was so abrupt and hurried that it was evident that the entire plan had been changed. A force of four or five thousand of the enemy had appeared in the rich country West of Plaquemine, and it was found, upon our arrival there, that the Brigade, with Col SHELDON in command, had been ordered to fortify Plaquemine, and hold it as a base of operations during the Winter. This announcement was hailed with delight. For more than two years the Forty-Second had been in the field, without a week of what was known in the army as "soft" duty. Not a man in the Regiment had seen the inside of a barrack, or—with the exception of the few weeks of hard work—had it at any time formed part of the garrison of a permanent post. Always in the field, often without tents, the men had learned to take life as it came and ask no questions.

Plaquemine was a clean, healthy, beautiful town, the people

were intelligent and cordial, and the Regiment settled down to its Winter in the South with bright anticipations. The Brigade included, besides the Infantry Regiments already named, the Second Ohio and First Indiana Batteries, and a Company of the Fourth Wisconsin Cavalry.

Immediately upon his arrival, on the 21st of November, Col SHELDON gained information that the enemy, four or five thousand strong, under Gen WALKER, was raiding through the interior and threatening Plaquemine. One or two expeditions were made to meet this enemy, but the Autumn rains had set in, the plantations were flooded, artillery could not be moved, and even infantry was often obliged to leave the roads and travel along the levees that lined the bayous and inland creeks. Forty or fifty prisoners had been captured in these expeditions, however, but finding that WALKER was not disposed to bring on a real engagement, Col SHELDON settled his command down to the work of repairing the levees and fortifying the town. A bastioned earthwork with an area of two acres was built, with magazine, drawbridge, etc., and armed with fourteen guns. The exterior slope and glacis were neatly turfed, and the work when completed made a very creditable appearance. All this was completed by the 1st of January.

Meanwhile, considerable work of a miscellaneous kind had been done. Our tents, left in Brashear City on our departure for Opelousas three months before, had been issued to other troops, and were permanently lost to us. To supply their place, barracks were built at Plaquemine, old buildings in and about the town being torn down to furnish lumber for the purpose. A strict provost guard was organized, the most rigid garrison discipline established, and with better acquaintance the relations between the inhabitants and the garrison soon became intimate and cordial. Christmas and New Years day passed off with great eclat, the third year's holidays we had seen in the field, and the last, thank God! What a twelve-month of peril, adventure and victory since the last New Year's night, when the Army of the Mississippi, repulsed and disheartened, was slinking away from the miry swamp and bristling heights of Chickasaw! Could it be possible that only a year had passed since then?

Among the inhabitants of Plaquemine was a French soldier of fortune, an adroit fencing master and musician. He had been band-leader in a Confederate regiment, but when his band had been converted into soldiers, he had retired from service and returned to civil life. His accomplishments and his Confederate service paved the way for his prompt admission to Plaquemine society, and, in the general dearth of young men, the young cavalier had almost monopolized the maiden sentiment of the place. Upon the arrival of the Union troops, the more ambitious members of the Forty-Second organized a fencing class, of which the French gentleman gladly took charge. He introduced his new friends to the families which he visited, and before midwinter the rare opportunity thus offered had been so well improved that Plaquemine society was ready to declare that it had no idea such refined and intelligent gentlemen could be found in the Yankee army. The soldiers were dined and entertained, and young ladies who had sung the "Bonnie Blue Flag" and "My Maryland" since Sumter fell, hid their blushes behind the argument that "These Ohio soldiers are not Yankees, but Western people like ourselves."

The establishment of the post at Plaquemine had created a mart where the people of a rich district, long shut out from every market by the blockade and military regulations, could sell their valuable products for the luxuries and necessaries of life. The coming of the troops, so far from an affliction therefore, had been an emancipation; and while the maidens and the soldiers wooed and sighed, the town rose to new prosperity and importance

On the 27th of January, the Kentucky regiments were transferred to Baton Rouge, and the garrison was thereby reduced to the Ohio troops and the artillery During the Winter an opportunity was given for such as wished to re-enlist in the regular army as cavalry, and a number of the members of the Forty-Second, who had determined to remain in service at least till the end of the war, took advantage of the chance thus offered

Spring set in soon after the middle of February, and by the first of March peach trees and roses were in bloom, and the roads dry and fine as in June As the season advanced the spirit of unrest began to develop, and when, on the 24th of March, orders were received to prepare for immediate removal, the announcement was received with cheers and rejoicing. A steamer with FOSTER'S Battery came up from New Orleans on the 26th, bound for Red river. On the same day the Forty-Second received the first outfit of dress-coats that had been issued to it since enlistment. After two years and a half of service, and just as it as was about to take the field for the last campaign, it received the uniforms that could be of no possible advantage, and only an incumbrance on the march. There was a theory in the army that soldier's luxuries always came in that awkward way

On the 26th of March, the Forty-Second, bright and neat in its new uniforms, marched down through the town and took the steamer for Baton Rouge The farewell was an ovation to the Regiment Citizens of all colors, ages and of both sexes, crowded along the line of march to wish the departing braves God-speed The young ladies were unconsolable, and wept and waved their handkerchiefs as their cavaliers marched away An irreverent scoffer, who drove a mule team, said that the scene was entitled to a place in poetry beside that of "The Last Sigh of the Moor "

The Gulf steamer upon which the Regiment had embarked, sped rapidly up the river and about sunset reached Baton Rouge. The Forty Second promptly went ashore, marched half a mile from the landing, and encamped in some wedge tents, which had been left by some troops which had gone up Red river with the expedition under Gen. Banks. It being apparent, the next day, that the Regiment might remain there some days, the men gathered some lumber, raised up the tents, and put them in a condition more in keeping with the luxury that they left behind at Plaquemine. Company "A" was detailed as provost guard, and was quartered in the city. The remainder of the Regiment performed various duties. The city and State were under martial law, and the administration of justice, the control and protection of the immense trade that then centered at the State capital, and the management of the gangs of idle and dissolute negroes that thronged the city, gave the little garrison abundant scope for its energies. The department had been stripped of troops for the Red River Expedition, and very soon the news from Alexandria began to assume a serious character. It was evident that Gen. Banks had found a stronger enemy than he had expected. The whole Confederate army West of the Mississippi, reinforced by thousands of paroled prisoners who had surrendered at Vicksburgh and had not yet been exchanged, had concentrated in Louisiana, and, with the desperation of a final effort, had set out to reclaim the State.

About the 1st of May, Col. Sheldon was ordered with his Brigade to Alexandria, on the Red river, the center and base of Gen. Banks' operations. He sent the One Hundred and Twentieth Ohio by the only steamer that could be secured; but when the boat with that Regiment on board came within twenty miles of Alexandria, it was fired upon by a battery behind the levee, the boat disabled, and the men slaughtered like sheep. Of the

the entire Regiment, only ninety men escaped. On the following day a transport, having on board the Fifth Sixth Ohio Veterans, bound for home, was attacked at the same place, the boat sunk, and the Regiment nearly all killed or captured. The seventy men who swam to the opposite shore marched down the river several miles, hailed a boat bound up the river, boarded and turned her back to Baton Rouge in time to meet a steamer bearing the Forty-Second and save us from a similar fate. By this time news came that Gen. BANKS had given up the contest in that quarter, and begun his memorable retreat to the Mississippi. Col SHELDON, with the Forty-Second, was ordered to Simmsport, twelve miles up the Red river, to assist in covering the retreat of the army. At the mouth of Red river Col SHELDON reported to Gen. CANBY, and was sent on to Simmsport, where the road, coming down the South shore of the river, crosses Atchafalaya Bayou. There three Regiments—the Thirty-Fourth Illinois, and the Twenty-Second and Twenty Third Iowa—were added to the Brigade, which was set to work to construct bridges across the Atchafalaya for the passage of BANKS army, which was at that time crossing Yellow Bayou, six miles distant, under heavy pressure. A. J. SMITH'S Division—our old comrades of the Thirteenth Corps—was rear guard that day, and fought like tigers for seven hours. At Yellow Bayou was a bridge, defended by an earthwork and rifle pits. These works were obstinately defended, but the Rebels, in the hope of destroying the bridge and capturing the remainder of BANKS' army, charged the fort repeatedly, but were as often repulsed with heavy loss. Col SHELDON made two applications to Gen WARREN, in command at Atchafalaya, for permission to march with his Brigade to the support of SMITH, but consent was refused, and the Brigade set briskly about the work of bridging the bayou. Two bridges were constructed, one of timbers and planks resting on wooden cribs, the other by mooring transports alongside of each other and laying a roadway across their forecastles. Hardly were these completed when the retreating army appeared and began marching across The transit occupied several hours, SMITH's Division, the rear guard, coming in weary and powder-stained, and crossing after dark The Forty Second was in charge of the bridges, and as the three Divisions of the Thirteenth Corps came along, many rueful greetings were exchanged Before the last Regiment had reached the Eastern shore, both bridges were loosened at the Western end and swung out into the stream. The steamers were loaded with wounded and exhausted men, the other bridge was broken up, and the army, with SHELDON's Brigade as rear guard, moved down the river, marching rapidly and reaching the mouth at daylight. After a brief halt for breakfast, the column moved on down the Mississippi to Morganzia Bend, fifteen miles below, where it arrived on the 22d and went into camp, the Nineteenth Corps on the right, facing the river, and the Thirteenth on the left The knapsacks and blankets had been left on the steamers in Red river, and as they did not come down until the 23d, the troops spent two uncomfortable nights on the ground The baggage and tents finally arrived, however, and the army was snugly encamped. Hardly had the pickets been established at Morganzia, when they were attacked from the rear, and a constant skirmish kept up during the day The Forty-Second lay on its arms all day and night, ready to march at a moment's notice to whatever point was seriously threatened, but the Rebels were not in force, and no serious collision occurred The troops were leaving by steamers for New Orleans as fast as boats could be procured

While at Morganzia the Forty-Second was assigned to the First Brigade, Third Division of the Nineteenth Army Corps, and expected to return with the remainder of that Corps to the Army of the Potomac, a result which was only prevented by the fact that the Regiment had only a few weeks more to serve. Soon after this assignment, a competitive drill between all the Companies of the Nineteenth and Thirteenth Corps was ordered, and after a spirited trial, Company "E," of the Forty-Second, carried off the first prize. From the day of its departure from Camp Chase, until the close of its service, the Regiment never met its superior in the manual of arms or battalion drill.

By the 29th, four Divisions had gone, and the Forty-Second received orders to be ready to start at four the next morning, with two days' rations. At daylight the column, including the First and Third Divisions of the Thirteenth Corps and one Division of the Nineteenth, started out in a Westerly direction, leaving knapsacks and all dispensable equipments behind, and halting during the heat of the day until five o'clock, when the march was resumed and continued until two at night. At this hour the advance Division reach Bayou Grossette, and the whole force encamped on a fine old plantation. In the morning our Cavalry attacked a Rebel force of five hundred men encamped four or five miles distant, capturing forty or fifty men and their stores. During the forenoon, SHELDON's Brigade was marched a mile or two from the main road and encamped in a heavy wood, where the Forty-Second men found a bee-tree and captured a princely ration of honey. After a day or two of mysterious marchings and counter-marchings, the whole force returned to its camps at Morganzia Bend.

It was now the 3d of June, and the mid-summer heats had fairly set in. It seeming probable that we might remain some time at Morganzia, the camps were neatly laid out and trellises covered with boughs built in front of the tents. The other troops were gradually leaving, and by the 7th of July there remained but one Division of the Thirteenth Corps and a brigade of negroes

On the 12th SHELDON's Brigade embarked for the White river in Arkansas, at the mouth of which stream it arrived on the 18th, landed and went into camp. On the evening of the following day a detachment of one hundred and fifty men from the Regiment under command of Col. SHELDON crossed the river and went on a night expedition against a force of cavalry under a Major MONTGOMERY, who with a section of horse artillery, was hanging round the rivers firing into boats and doing various mischief. The force was surrounded and captured, not one of MONTGOMERY's fifty men escaped. While the party was gone Private FRANK HENDERSON of Company "A," who had been left in charge of the small boats by which the expedition had crossed, was captured by four or five straggling Confederates. He was taken some distance, but escaped, swam the Mississippi river with his clothes on and rejoined the Regiment. The expedition returned on the 20th and next morning started up the White river.

After considerable trouble, all the boats running aground several times, the fleet reached St. Charles on the 23d, landed and learned that eight thousand Rebels under Gen. MARMADUKE were stationed within twenty-five miles. The whole Brigade immediately commenced fortifying, the men working day and night in reliefs of two hours. After forty-eight hours of this labor the defences were so far completed that no further danger was apprehended, and, the anticipated attack not being received, a scouting party of two regiments, one of which was the Forty-Second, made a raid to DeWitt, the seat of Arkansas County, fifteen miles distant. The expedition was a fruitless one, only a few fugitive Rebels being picked up, and after two days hard marching the regiments returned to camp. The Brigade remained at St. Charles until the 5th of August, when it was replaced by another brigade, and immediately took steamers for Morganzia Bend, where it arrived on the 12th, and again went into camp.

In this aimless and trifling business the Summer was frittered away. The men marched hard, suffered fevers, heat and thirst, lived on green corn, dug entrenchments, and all availed nothing. The practical veterans of the Forty-Second were rapidly growing disgusted with such service.

On the 2d of September they were again ordered to prepare for an expedition, without tents or baggage. Twenty days rations were to be taken. The point of destination was once more the mouth of the White river, where the Brigade arrived on the 8th, and once more established itself in camp.

There was evidently no work of importance remaining to be done in that quarter, and the Regiment, weary of fruitless voyagings up and down the river, began to think longingly of home. The three years for which the Forty-Second had enlisted were drawing to a close. On the 25th of September Companies "A," "B," "C" and "D" would be entitled to release. Barely a week remained after the final arrival at White river before the survivors of those four Companies would begin the homeward journey which for so many weary months had loomed up in the future as the bright, joyous mile-stone at the end of their soldier lives. But the members of the four first Companies, envied though they were, did not wholly enjoy the prospect. After three years of service together it seemed awkward and unfortunate that all the Companies of the Forty-Second could not be simultaneously discharged. Eager as they were to return, the men sincerely regretted that instead of returning to Ohio as a Regiment, with their war-worn equipments and tattered battle-flags, they were to come in detachments, a few Companies at a time, and with none of the formality of a victorious return. But there was no help for it, and preparations were made for the final breaking up. The four Companies to be first discharged were ordered to be in readiness to embark for Cairo on the 17th. Those who were to go began distributing their various warlike property among those who were to remain. Cooking utensils, the rude apparatus of the soldier's mess table, tobacco, pipes, stationery and supplies of various kinds, were turned over by the four happy Companies to the other less fortunate ones, with many good wishes and much solemn advice. For three days the men who were to stay busied themselves with writing letters to fill the knapsacks of those who were going home.

The night of the 16th was devoted to cooking rations for the homeward bound veterans, bidding elaborate farewells and telling over for the last time the camp stories which had served so long. The fires blazed brightly, though the night was mild, and before morning biscuits enough had been baked to load the haversacks of the returning braves. It was thought a felicitous thing that our last Government rations should be so conspicuous a luxury as the amateur biscuit, which, though unctuous with bacon fat and tawny with saleratus, had made for us so many oases in the arid, hard-bread desert of the past three years. With the end of the biscuit baking the preparations were complete, and after a night only a fragment of which was wasted in sleep, the four Companies, early on the morning of the 17th, went on board the steamer "Julia." Amid the cheers of those on board and ashore, the boat swung out into the stream and headed toward Memphis. The voyage up the river was a succession of joyous hours, illumined by bright anticipations of home. The "Julia" touched at Memphis, and, with only a brief delay, continued her voyage to Cario, where she arrived on the 20th. Here the veterans of the Forty-Second landed, and with a last look across the river at Confederate soil, they boarded a train of freight cars which was found in readiness to convey them to Columbus.

The route was by way of Indianapolis and occupied nearly three days. It was not until the 23d that the detachment, weary and disgusted with its slow journey, arrived at Camp Chase, the dreary village of white-washed barracks which the Forty-Second had left thirty months ago. The return, though joyous in itself, was not without many sombre suggestions. Compared with the full Companies which had gone out from those barracks in 1861, how small seemed these returning squads of brown faced men! Of the thousand who had gone forth, how many would return no more!

Without delay preparations were made for the final muster and discharge from service. Rolls were made out and signed, arms and equipments turned over, pay received, and on the 30th of September the veterans of Companies "A," "B," "C" and "D," free once more, shook hands and dispersed to their homes.

The other Companies which had been left at the mouth of White river were soon ordered to Duvall's Bluffs, on the Arkansas, where they remained several weeks. Companies "E" and "F" returned to Camp Chase on the 10th of November, and were mustered out on the 25th. The two Companies remaining, arrived a few days later and received their final discharge on the 2d of December.

There were detailed while at Duvall's Bluff one hundred and one men, members of different Companies, who had enlisted in 1862, and whose term of service had therefore not expired. They were organized as a Company under command of Capt. CAMPBELL of Company "G," and assigned to the Ninty Sixth Ohio. As part of that Regiment they were transferred to the command of Gen. CANBY and participated in the siege and capture of Mobile, which practically closed the war in the Department of the Gulf.

The battle flag of the Forty-Second Regiment hangs with the other tattered banners which Ohio cherishes so proudly, in the Capitol at Columbus. It was borne through eleven battles and many more skirmishes. Though often in danger it was never in the hands of an enemy.

The losses of the Regiment by battle and disease are shown in detail by the aggregated muster roll of the Regiment which forms the succeeding chapter. The killed and wounded number in all nineteen officers and three hundred and forty-five enlisted men

CHAPTER X.

PERSONNEL OF THE FORTY-SECOND—SURGEON POMERENE—THE COMPANIES AS INDEPENDENT ORGANIZATIONS—A FULL ROSTER OF THE REGIMENT.

Concerning the Field Officers of the Forty Second Regiment, some detailed personal account has been elsewhere given. No history of the Regiment would be complete, however, which should fail to pay some tribute to the services of Major JOEL F. POMERENE, the accomplished and devoted Surgeon who, from the earliest organization of the Regiment until after the close of its important work in 1863, was the constant and unwearied guardian of the health of all its members. Enviable and envied as the Forty-Second was in many respects, it was in nothing more fortunate than in its Surgeon. At home a physician of high attainments and extensive practice, he left his patients and his studies and went out to the laborious and trying duties of a Field Surgeon, in obedience to that high sense of duty which in those days constrained so many of the best men of every loyal community to sacrifice personal ease, profits and prospects for the future, to the supreme duty of the hour. Surgeon POMERENE went into the service with his whole heart enlisted in the cause. He soon knew every man in the Regiment by name. He watched over their food, their camps and their health as though each soldier had been his own son or brother. He stood between the men and all the annoyances of red tape, the rapacity or indifference of quarter-masters and commissaries, and no medicine or comfort that foresight and solicitude could secure was ever wanting from the hospital tents of the Forty-Second. If the Regiment was in a malarial atmosphere, the Doctor and his rations of whisky and quinine were unfailing. If a tired soldier or a sick one gave out on the march, it was Surgeon POMERENE who never failed to have a place in an ambulance or wagon for the sufferer if that were possible, at least he would find some way of relieving the sick one of his burthen. It was no uncommon sight to see the horse of that Samaritan in uniform laden with the knapsacks of men too weak to carry them, and the Doctor leading his laden steed while he chatted with the men on foot. There was a theory among the men that the good Doctor never slept. It was never too late or too early for him to look after a sick or wounded man who needed attention. During a battle he was generally up at the front when the first gun was fired, and the earliest wounded were carried off the field under his orders, or, if that were impossible, were treated where they fell. Broad and active as were his sympathies, he was not a man who could be imposed upon, and after the first few weeks in the field it was understood that there could be no "soldiering" on the Doctor. Naturally, he was a warm favorite with the officers and men, and though in constant demand as Medical Director and Brigade Surgeon, he never failed to avail himself of the first opportunity to return to his own charge. If in the subjoined roster of the Regiment there were affixed a star to the name of each man who at one time or another were owed the saving of his life to Surgeon POMERENE, the list would be a long one.

THE FIELD AND STAFF

of the Regiment, as shown by the final muster roll, was as follows

NAME	RANK	REMARKS
James A Garfield	Colonel	Promoted to Major General
Lionel A Sheldon	Col and Bv't Brig Gen	Discharged, expiration term service
Don A Pardee	Lt-Col Bv't Brig Gen	" " "
Frederick A Williams	Major	Died, July 25th, 1862.
Wm H Williams	Major	Discharged, expiration term service
Joel F Pomerene	Surgeon	Resigned, July 20th, 1863
Joseph C Kalb	"	" August 30th, 1864
Harrison McFadden	Assist Surg	Discharged, expiration term service
Joseph W Harmon	"	Resigned, November 9th, 1863
John W Driscoll	"	" July 1st, 1863
Isaac N Minor	"	Died, December 13th, 1862
Jefferson H Jones	Chaplain	Resigned, April 18th, 1863
Joseph D Stubbs	R Q M	Promoted to Capt and A Q M
Alvin J Dyer	"	Discharged, expiration term service
Wm W Olds	Adjutant	Killed in battle at Thompson's Hill
Wm H Clapp	"	Promoted to Regular Army
Chas E Henry	"	Discharged, expiration term service
Chas P Goodwin	"	" for wounds rec in battle
George K Pardee	"	Promoted to Capt Company "D"

NON COMMISSIONED STAFF

Horace S Clark	Serg't Major	Promoted to Lieutenant
Albert L Bowman	"	" "
Edmund P Smith	Q M Serg't	Discharged, expiration term service
Owen J Hopkins	"	" " " "
Lester A Lewis	Com Serg't	" " "
Cyrus A Richards	"	" " "
David B Elson	Hospt Stw'd	" " "
Wm F Hathaway	"	" " "
Henry B Roff	Prin Mus'n	Discharged, expiration term service.
Wm Fisher	"	" General Order 126, A G O.

NAME	RANK	REMARKS
Wm B Osborn	Prin Mus	Discharged, expiration term service
Reuben Falconer	"	" " "
John Pany	"	" " "
Samuel Fisher	"	" for disability
P. B. Johnson	Wagon Mast'r	

BAND

NAME	RANK	REMARKS
John W Ford	Leader	Discharged by Order War Departm't
Wm H Park	1st class Mus'n	" " "
Chas E Mason	"	" " "
Aaron G Hollister	"	" " "
Wilson O Hart	"	" " "
Daniel Chase	2d Class	" " "
Enoch Elber	"	" " "
George Gemchis	"	" " "
Philip Harper	"	" " "
Henry Morrison	"	" " "
Edward F Smith	"	" " "
Henry H Bryant	3d Class	" " "
Sylvester Couch	"	" " "
Thomas H. Gibson	"	" " "
Frank B Hale	"	" " "
Johnson Hutchins	"	" " "
Wm B Hollister	"	" " "
Enos Kelly	"	" " "
Jacob F Lewis	"	" " "
Lewis F. Nitts	"	" " "
Milo B Parsons	"	" " "
Marion Wood	"	" " "

THE COMPANIES

Company "A" was the prompt and spontaneous outgrowth of two war meetings held in Portage County during the month of September, 1861. The Union armies had been defeated at Bull Run and Big Bethel, and the Confederates were everywhere victorious and confident. It seemed too obvious for denial that the Southern men, more accustomed than those of the North to the use of arms, were, in the outset at least, the better soldiers, and this, though something of a damper to the ardor of those who had been disposed to regard the conquest of the South a holiday campaign, roused in the hearts of others a determination that Northern valor should be vindicated.

On the evening of the 10th of August, a meeting was held in the Disciples Church at Hiram. Mr. GARFIELD, then State Senator, was present and spoke with an earnest eloquence that stirred every heart. It was during the long Summer vacation. The students were scattered to their homes, and the recitation rooms were silent and deserted. A few of the students and alumni, living within eight or ten miles of the College, had heard of the meeting and came up to attend it. To these were added the people of the village generally, and so earnest was the feeling that when the meeting dispersed, fifty young men, mostly students, had signed the enlistment roll.

On Friday of the same week, a Military Convention was held at Ravenna, under the auspices of the County Committee. The news of Monday's enlistments had been widely circulated, and at the Ravenna Convention the Company was not only filled to the maximum, but a good beginning was made toward the enlistment of what afterwards became Company "F." With the exception of a squad of recruits brought from Mantua by Mr. H. S. BATES, the material of Company "A" was almost exclusively students and graduates of Hiram Eclectic Institute, then in the zenith of its popularity and usefulness.

As soon as the roll was full, the Company held an election for the choice of officers. The election was entirely harmonious, and resulted in the choice of FREDERICK A. WILLIAMS, of Ravenna, as Captain; H. S. BATES, of Mantua, as First Lieutenant; and WM S. CLAPP, of Hiram, Second Lieutenant. Next morning, the 21st of September, the Company started via Cleveland, for Camp Chase. It reached Columbus in the evening, slept in the chamber of the Supreme Court in the Capitol, and on Sunday marched out to its quarters in Camp Chase. The rank and file of the Company included an unusually large proportion of highly educated and intelligent men. Many of them were promoted during the three years' service of the Regiment to commissioned officers in other Regiments and staff positions. Others were in constant requisition for detached service, in situations where intelligence and education were required for the performance of special duties. This was true in a remarkable degree of several other Companies in the Regiment; and it was one of the difficulties of commanding officer of the Forty-Second, that his command was constantly drawn upon by special details for duty at brigade, division and corps headquarters. The roster of Company "A" was as follows:

NAME	RANK	REMARKS
FREDERICK A. WILLIAMS	Captain	Promoted to Major
WM W. OLDS	Captain	Killed in battle May 1st, 1863
JASPER S. ROSS	"	Discharged, expiration term service.
HOWARD S. BATES	1st Lieut	Resigned March, 1862.
CHAS E. HENRY	1st Lieut and Brevet Capt.	Discharged, expiration term service
WM H. CLAPP	1st Lieut	Promoted to Captain and A. A. G.
MATHIAS RODOCKER	1st Lieut.	Discharged, expiration term service.
THOMAS C. PARSONS	2d Lieut	" " "

NAME	RANK	REMARKS
Pembroke M. Cowles	Color Seig't	Discharged, expiration term service.
Calvin Rider	Sergeant	Killed in battle May 1st, 1863
Ambrose C. Mason	Sergeant	Com Capt in 105th O. V. I
David A. Gates	"	Discharged, expiration term service
Joel M. Seymour	"	" " " "
Newel N. McIntosh	"	" " " "
Bazel G. Hank	"	" " " "
Wm. M. Hattery	Corporal	" " " "
Osmer C. Hill	"	" " " "
Edward L. Lemert	"	" " " "
Ransom V. Young	"	" " " "
Manning H. Case	"	" " " "
Peleg C. Mason	"	" " " "
Frank M. Clover	"	" " " "
Henry Barholtz	Musician	" " " "
Ebenezer Bissell	Private	" " " "
George Briggs	"	" " " "
Henry Briggs	"	" " " "
Daniel W. Bidlake	"	" " " "
David D. Carlton	"	" " " "
Wm. H. Reynolds	"	" " " "
Calvin N. Campbell	"	" " " "
Alfred Churchill	"	" " " "
Charles H. Chapman	"	" " " "
Ephriam Cook	"	" " " "
Judson Cramer	"	" " " "
Geo. W. Carson	"	" " " "
Harvey Durkel	"	" " " "
Orlando L. Earl	"	" " " "
Hiram Finch	"	" " " "
Stephens R. Freeman	"	" " " "
DeWitt C. Gardiner	"	" " " "
David Hall	"	" " " "
Cornelius Finch	"	" " " "
Sherman M. Leach	"	" " " "
Wm. H. Monroe	"	" " " "

NAME	RANK	REMARKS
Frank H McClintock	Private	Discharged, expiration term service.
Nathaniel Parker	"	" " " "
Vincent Reynolds	"	" " " "
Sherman Rowley	"	" " " "
John W. Risk	"	" " " "
Frank W Robbins	"	" " " "
Amos T. Roys	"	" " " "
Samuel Shattuck	"	" " " "
Perry C Stafford	"	" " " "
Joseph H Stafford	"	" " " "
Coe J. Stanford	"	" " " "
Ezekiel D Taylor	"	" " " "
Aaron Teeple	"	" " " "
Isaac Teeple	"	Killed in battle May 16th, 1863
Fred E Underwood	"	Discharged, expiration term service
Wilson B. Osborn	"	" " " "
Edward H Rogers	"	" " " "
Elijah L Mason	"	" for disability June 3d, '63
Sutton P Newcomb	Corporal	" to rec. com in Col. Reg't
George Hayden	Corporal	" for disability June 23d, '63
Henry Hayden	Private	Killed in battle December 29th '62
Frank Udell	Musician	Discharged for disability 1862
John Hewitt	Private	" for disability Jan 31st, 1864
Frederick Bard	"	" for disability Oct 24th, 1862
Selley Chapman	"	" for disability July 17th, 1862.
Charles W Clark	"	" to rec. com. Corps D'Afrique
Washington Ellinwood	"	" on ac't of wounds rec. battle.
John I Hastings	"	" for disability, 1863
Hyal B Hart	"	" to Reg Army as Hos St'd
Jefferson H. Jones	"	" for disability February, 1862
Origin C. Loomis	"	" for disability, 1862.
Frank H. Mason	"	Promoted to Capt and A D C
Richard C Norton	"	Disch'd, for disability March 18th, '63
Henry B Nornon	"	" for disability Sept 17th, '63
Timothy G Parsons	"	" for disability April 8th, '64
Horace Winchell	"	" for disability Aug 18th, '62,

THE FORTY-SECOND OHIO INFANTRY.

NAME	RANK	REMARKS
Elam H Chapman	"	Died March 28th, 1862, disease
Ira C Osborn	Corporal	Died May 13, '63, wounds rec battle
Aaron N Allen	Private	Killed in battle, Thompson's Hill
Comfort Bennett	"	Died March 14th, 1863, of disease
Moris M Brewster	"	Died January 4th, 1862, of disease
Baldwin Bently	"	Died February 10th, 1862, of disease
Frank B Cowles	"	Died March 28th, 1862, of disease
Albert Curtis	"	Died December 12th, 1862, of disease
Amasa B Cook	"	Died Jan 5, '63, wounds rec'd battle
Zina Jennings	"	Died May 25, '63, wounds rec battle
Cyrus A Mead	"	Died March 27th, 1862, of disease
Martin W Ray	"	Died Sept 29th, 1863, of disease
Samuel Wooley	"	Died July 24th, 1863, of disease
Abel P Winchll	"	Died Dec 12th, 1861, of disease
David M Andrews	"	Discharged, expiration term service
George Dean	"	" " "
George Finney	"	" " "
Thomas Drennen	"	Died at Camp Chase, 1862
Henry Flemming	"	Discharged, expiration term service
Richard B Hobbs	"	" " "
Frank L Henderson	"	" " "
Samuel D Ray	"	" " "
Wm H. Rothrock	"	" " "
David R Rothrock	"	" " "
Wm A Sypher	"	" " "
George P Young	"	" " "
Charles G Rolph	"	" " "
Joseph Rudolph	"	Disch'd to rec com in Subsis't Dep't
Peter White	"	Discharged, expiration term service.

COMPANY "B"

The organization of Company "B" has already been described at some length in the biographical sketch of Major WM. H. WILLIAMS. It was recruited almost entirely in Medina County, more than two-thirds of the men being enlisted by Major WILLIAMS. The first detachment of eighty men reached Columbus on the 24th of September, and spent the first night in the rotunda of the Capitol, enjoying everything but sleep. From the day of its arrival at Columbus, Company "B" developed an especial talent for that curious, many-sided drollery which was so characteristic of the volunteer soldiers of the Union army. There was nothing too difficult or extraordinary for a soldier to do in those days, provided it were not absolutely criminal and was reasonably original and "odd." Company "B" began its hilarity even before it was mustered into service. Within twenty minutes of its arrival in the State House, some one in the Company had found an old violin, and not being under camp discipline, the frisky recruits organized a dance which was kept up until long after midnight. Meanwhile, a verdant volunteer had been captured and brought before a mock court-martial for trial upon a charge of having attempted to break guard. He was solemnly convicted and sentenced to be shot at sunrise. He was terribly frightened, but soon after his sentence was pronounced, Sergeant BEACH appeared on the scene, dissolved the court, stampeded the guards and released the trembling culprit.

In Camp Chase, private ANDREW HUNTINGTON attained great repute by his exhibitions of an elephant, constructed of two men and an army blanket. LYMAN THOMAS developed great talent as a serio-comic orator, and his stump speeches on politics, love and war entertained the camp on many a pleasant evening.

Company "B" was made up of clever, intelligent men, who soon acquired thorough proficiency in all their military duties

Being a flank Company, it was almost constantly on duty either as skirmishers or rear guard. It was commanded by Capt. WILLIAMS until his promotion to Major in April, 1862, and from that time until the expiration of its term of service by Capt. HORACE POTTER. The names of its members were as follows:

NAME	RANK	REMARKS
WM. H. WILLIAMS	Captain	Promoted to Major
HORACE POTTER	"	Discharged, expiration term service.
HENRY A. HOWARD	1st Lieut.	Transferred to Company "C"
JOSEPH LACKEY	2d Lieut.	Resigned, for disability
JOHN McDONALD	1st Sergeant	Discharged, expiration term service.
JONATHAN M. BEACH	Sergeant	" " "
PETER MILLER	"	" " "
LYMAN C. NICHOLS	"	" " "
AMOS T. BOYCE	"	" " "
ALVIN J. DYER	Corporal	" " "
ALLEN POMEROY	"	" October 4th, 1862, disability.
ALBERT W. GREEN	"	" Sept. 8th, 1862, disability
AARON M. ROSS	"	" expiration term of service
JAMES C. KELLOGG	"	" March 24th, 1863, disability
GEORGE W. WALTZ	"	" expiration term of service
EDWIN R. RICE	"	" October 6th, 1862, disability
JOHN W. BOWMAN	"	" expiration term of service
CHARLES H. CRANDALL	"	" " "
ALONZO P. MAINE	Private	" " "
REUBEN H. FALCONER	"	" " "
JOHN P. WALTZ	"	" " "
SETH AULT	"	" Dec. 10th, 1863, disability.
NATHAN H. ALVORD	"	" expiration term of service
JAMES C. BOYCE	"	" September 20th, 1862
GEORGE BRUST	"	" February 28th, 1862
LEVI BOWMAN	"	" expiration term of service.
ISAAC L. BURTON	"	" March 10th, 1863.
HENRY BURNETT	"	" expiration term of service
LEVI A. CHASE	"	Died, June 2d, 1863, of disease.

NAME	RANK	REMARKS
Calvin Chapin	Private	Discharged, expiration term service.
Henry Chapin	"	" " "
David Caswell	"	" January 22d, 1863
Orville D. Colton	"	" expiration term of service
Austin W. Cotton	"	Killed, Dec 30, '62, Chickasaw Bluff
Aaron Clark	"	Discharged, expiration term service.
Wm. E Carlton	"	" " "
Wm Eddey	"	" " "
Geo W Foote	"	" " "
George Frazier	"	" " "
Ezra Futz	"	" " "
Josiah Foust	"	Killed in battle, May 19th, 1863
Wm. Griswold	"	Discharged, Dec 9, 1861, disability.
David Grandy	"	" expiration term of service
Eli B Harris	"	" " "
John H Horton	"	" " "
Henry W. Horton	"	" " "
Frederick Howard	"	" " "
Wm H Hickox	"	" " "
James Huffman	"	" " "
John Halliwell	"	" " "
Andrew J Harrington	"	" March 24th, 1863, disability
George W. Jordian	"	" expiration term of service
John J Jordian	"	" " "
David E Johnson	"	Died of disease
Chester Loomis	"	Discharged, expiration term service
Curtis F Lutz	"	" " "
Lister A Lewis	"	" " "
Abram J Lance	"	" Jan 26, 1864, to re-enlist
Charles N Lyon	"	" expiration term of service
George C Moody	"	Died, July 31, '63, wounds rec battle
Miles Mark	"	Discharged, expiration term service
John B McConnell	"	" " "
Peter Milks	"	Killed in battle, May 1st, 1863
George Messmer	"	Discharged, Jan 26, 1864, to re-enlist
Alonzo H Miller	"	Discharged, expiration term service

THE FORTY-SECOND OHIO INFANTRY.

NAME.	RANK	REMARKS
Elliott McDougall	Private	Discharged, expiration term service
Chales H Millington	"	Died, March 25th, 1862, disease
Harnson B Orin	"	Died, March 11th, 1862, disease
Ebin Phinney	"	Discharged, expiration term service
Horace F Prouty	"	" " "
Jasper Powers	"	Died of wounds in battle, May 4, '64
Ben Pittinger	"	Discharged, expiration term service
George F Porter	"	Died, February 20th, 1863
Wm H Richards	"	Died February 21st, 1862
Hinsdale Richards	"	Discharged, July 25, 1862, disability
Merritt A Rice	"	" " "
Ruben Ream	"	" expiration term of service
Frank Richardson	"	" Dec 1st, 1861, for disability
George Randall	"	" expiration term of service.
Himan Ross	"	" Oct 1st, 1862, for disability
Jonah Stiles	"	" " "
Daniel T Smith	"	" expiration term of service
Andrew J Smith	"	" for disability
Edwin F Smith	"	" for disability.
Porter H Smith	"	Died, January 1st, 1862
Timothy H Smith	"	Discharged, expiration term service
John V K Sulley	"	" for disability
Edwin A Streeter	"	Died April 20th, 1862
Darius W Sanford	"	Discharged, expiration term service
John Staddler	"	" April 8th, for disability
James H Snyder	"	" expiration term service
James W Slocum	"	" August 13th, 1862
Lyman Thomas	"	Died, March 4th, 1862
Oliver O Van Orman	"	Discharged, expiration term service
Clayton M Van Orman	"	" " "
Wm Varney	"	" " "
Ephriam Watkins	"	" February 28, 1862, disability.
John L Waltz	"	" Sept 19th, 1862, disability
Wm Wheeler	"	" expiration term of service
George J Williams	"	" Oct 29, '63, wounds rec in bat
Ludwick Wagoner	"	" expiration term of service

NAME	RANK	REMARKS
WM H LIE	Private	Discharged, expiration term service.
WESLEY A. SEELEY	"	" " "
JOHN MAIN	"	" " "
JOSIAH OSIRF	"	Killed in battle, May 1st, 1862
JACOB WORTING	"	Discharged, expiration term service
DANIEL W EVANS	"	" " "
HENRY FINCKA	"	" " "
NELSON A BARRETT	"	Died, May 23d, 1863, in Hospital.
ABSALOM BROWN	"	Died, 1864.
WM. J. BENNER	"	Died, December 25th, 1862
HOWER CHASE	"	Died, March 18th, 1863
WM DOBSON	"	Discharged, Sept 22, '63, disability.
EDWIN GIER	"	" expiration term of service.
HENRY C. HOTCHKISS	"	" " "
DANIEL P HECKERT	"	" " "
WM. O LANCE	"	Died, May 30th, 1863
EDWARD HOWARD	"	Discharged, expiration term service
SOLON D MOODY	"	Died, February 23d, 1863.
FRANCIS MACK	"	Discharged, expiration term service
SALMON A POWERS	"	" Oct, 31st, 1863, for disabilty
LUTHER C. PROUTY	"	" expiration term of service
HENRY RUDD	"	Died, March 21st, 1863
JASPER N RICHARDS	"	Died, February 16th, 1863
WM A. SNYDER	"	Died, May 31st, 1863
FREDERICK SPORN	"	Discharged, August 13th, 1863
HARRISON S SOMERS	"	" expiration term of service.
JOHN H. WASS	"	" " "
ROBERT F. BROWN	"	" Sept. 22d, 1863, for disabilty
EDGAR O. HAWLEY	"	" expiration term of service

COMPANY "C,"

The Color Guard of the Forty-Second, was organized on the 10th of September, 1861, at Ashland. It was recruited mainly by T. C. BUSHNELL and WILLIAM H. STARR, the former of whom was made Captain and the latter First Lieutenant.

JOHN R. HELMAN also secured a number of enlistments in the Company and was chosen Second Lieutenant. The men were mainly from Sullivan, Montgomery, Perry, Orange, Clear Creek, Troy and Milton townships, and were a fine, intelligent and patriotic Company.

Unlike the men of some other Companies in the Regiment, the members of Company "C" were in the main neighbors and acquaintances, and went into the service with the advantage of knowing who and what their immediate comrades were. When Capt. BUSHNELL and his recruits arrived in Camp Chase, they had some intention of joining the Sixty-Fourth Regiment, but the high character of the field officers of the Forty-Second offered strong attractions, and the Ashland Company very promptly transferred its allegiance to Col. GARFIELD's Regiment. It was the third Company to report, and was assigned to the Colors at the center of the line. The battle-flag of the Regiment was carried by Color Sergeant P. M. COWLES, of Company "A," and Company "C" was its faithful and devoted guardian. Capt. BUSHNELL was an officer of high character, and his command reflected many of his best qualities. After his resignation in October, 1862, Company "C" was commanded until the end of its service by Capt. WM. H. STARR, an officer of sterling merit. The muster roll of the Company was as follows:

NAME	RANK	REMARKS
T. C. BUSHNELL	Captain	Resigned, October 22d, 1862
W. H. STARR	Captain	Discharged, expiration term service.
H. A. HOWARD	1st Lieut	" " "
J. R. HELMAN	2d Lieut	Transferred to Capt. of Co. "H"

NAME	RANK	REMARKS
J S Bowlby	2d Lieut	Discharged, expiration term service
R. D Kiplinger	Sergeant	" " "
G. McCrea	"	" " "
W H Martien	"	" " "
Frank Otto	"	" " "
John Fisher	"	" " "
John Shriver	Corporal.	" " "
A J Snowberger	"	" " "
W S Chamberlain	"	" " "
Daniel Drach	"	Joined Regulars
Charles Bundy	"	Discharged, June 20th, 1862.
Frank Beer	"	" expiration term of service
Chester Drake.	"	Reduced to Ranks
George Lee	"	Discharged, expiration term service
William Rudd	Musician.	Died, September, 1863
J B Dorrow	"	Discharged, expiration term service
Adam Emmens.	Private	Died at Vicksburg, August, 1863
John Albright	"	Died at Memphis, January, 1863
Ernest Aler	"	Killed, Champion's Hill, May 16, '63
James Anderson	"	Discharged, August 19th, 1862.
John D Ankeny	"	" expiration term of service
Wm S. Atew	"	" " "
W. S Brown	"	" " "
S G Brown	"	Transferred to 96th Reg't, O V I
D. W Brandt	"	Discharged, expiration term service
George Burd	"	" " "
James Beer	"	Died, Cumberland Gap, Aug 30, '62
Israel Border	"	Died, Ashland, Feb 17th, 1862.
George Cassell	"	Discharged, expiration term service
Albert H. Chambers	"	" " "
Edward O Clark	"	" January 1st, 1863
Rice S Crial	"	Transferred to 96th Regiment
J R. W Dinsmore	"	Discharged, expiration term service.
Horace Deibler	"	" " "
J H. Doll	"	" " "
Marcuss Dimoss.	"	" November, 1862,

THE FORTY-SECOND OHIO INFANTRY.

NAME	RANK	REMARKS
David Ecker	Private	Died at Carrolton, La., Sept, 1863.
A. C. Ecker	"	Discharged, expiration term service
J. P. Ely	"	" June 20th, 1862
Zachariah Emery	"	" expiration term of service.
Henry Forney	"	" " "
Jacob Freedlein	"	Died, from wounds received in battle
George Foll	"	Died at Carrolton, La., Aug, 1863
Lewis Fullington	"	Died at Ashland, Feb 14th, 1862.
Josiah Fike	"	Discharged, expiration term service.
Daniel Fike	"	" " "
Daniel Grosscup	"	" " "
J. A. Helman	"	" " "
J. D. Helman	"	" " "
Jessie Hines	"	" " "
James Hull	"	Joined Regulars, November, 1862.
A. A. Hamilton	"	Discharged, expiration term service
A. F. Hettinger	"	" " "
O. I. Howard	"	Transferred, to the 96th Regiment
E. I. Heiser	"	" " "
Jeremiah Johnson	"	Promoted to Corporal
L. H. Kiplinger	"	Discharged, wounds received in battle
Samuel Kopp	"	" expiration term of service
Jacob Kart	"	Died at Rows, Ohio.
J. P. R. Kramer	"	Died, at Carrolton, Miss., Aug., '63
W. J. Lowfrie	"	Discharged, expiration term service.
C. G. Martin	"	" " "
J. C. Musser	"	" " "
William Mish	"	" " "
Jeremiah Mish	"	" " "
Adam Maurer	"	" December 15th, 1861
J. C. Connell	"	" expiration term of service
Wm. McBride	"	" " "
Wm. Maxhammer	"	" October, 1862.
David Mundorff	"	Killed, December 29th, 1862
Benj. F. Martin	"	Discharged, December 22d, 1863
B. F. Nelson	"	" January, 1863.

NAME	RANK	REMARKS
Otto Frank	Private	Discharged, expiration term service
J. W. Over	"	" " "
E. L. Over	"	Transferred to 16th Reg't. O. V. I.
Robert Patterson	"	Discharged, expiration term service
Robert Pollock	"	Wounded at Champion Hill, May '63
John Pollock	"	Discharged, 1862.
T. D. Park	"	" expiration term of service
Joseph Palmer	"	" " "
Aaron Plank	"	Died at Ashland, March 28th, 1862
Herbert Persons	"	Discharged, expiration term service
George Pomeroy	"	" 1863.
T. B. Patterson	"	Died at Rows, Ohio, Sept. 1863
Lewis Rote	"	Died at Carrolton, Sept. 1863
Peter Rote	"	Wounded at Chickasaw, Jan. 1st '63
John Rote	"	Discharged, for wounds rec. in battle
A. D. Smalley	Corporal	Killed in battle, May 1st, 1863
Rudolph Suter	Private	Died at Vicksburg, Miss., 1863
John Sower	"	Discharged, expiration term service
Joseph Swartz	"	" " "
John Shafer	"	" " "
Jacob Snowberger	"	Died at Ashland, August, 1863
Isaac Shockey	"	Died at Carrolton, Sept., 1863
Shriver Milton	"	Died at Ashland, Feb. 14th, 1862
Harvey Simmons	"	Discharged, expiration term service.
John Saddler	"	" " "
Russell Smith	"	Died at Sullivan, Ohio, May 13, '62
Robert Smiley	"	Discharged, expiration term service
Samuel Switzer	Corporal	Died at Carrolton, La., Sept., 1863
J. B. Switzer	Private	Transferred to 96th Regiment
J. M. Lavalley	"	Discharged, expiration term service
R. M. Thompson	"	" " "
Paul Franger	"	" " "
Andrew Utz	"	" April, 1862,
Dennis Vanderhoff	"	Discharged, expiration term service.
A. D. White	"	" " "

NAME	RANK	REMARKS
JOHN WISE	Private.	Discharged, expiration term service.
JACK WILES	"	" November, 1862
D B ELSON	"	Discharged, expiration term service
F P SMITH	"	" " " "

COMPANY "D"

This Company was made up mainly of volunteers from Noble County. The first organization of its members was at Summerfield, in that County, whence they were transferred to camp at Mount Ephraim early in September, 1861. The Company was soon filled to the maximum number, and chose as its officers Capt. JAMES H. RIGGS, First Lieut. HERMAN SUIBADISSER, and Second Lieut WM L WILSON. Thus organized, the Company reported at Camp Chase on the 25th of September, and was assigned to the fourth place in the line Capt RIGGS served until December, 1863, during which time the Company performed its full share of all the duties devolving on the Regiment At Cumberland Gap the Company was on detached service several weeks, felling timber and building fortifications on the Southern front of the mountain Lieut WILSON, who was wounded in the battle of Thompson's Hill, remained with the Company until the close of its service in September, 1864 M D RODOCKER, whose service began as Corporal, was promoted to First Sergeant, and afterwards to Lieutenant During the last few months of the Regiment's service, he was assigned to Company "A." Company "D" was peculiar in the fact that its members were at first, almost without exception, unknown to all other members of the Regiment Among the other Companies there was from the beginning a more or less general acquaintance in civil life Companies "C" and "H" came from Ashland County, Companies "B" and "E," and part of "K," from Medina County, Companies "A" and "F" were almost wholly from Portage County, and so on, a thread of personal acquaintance running through all these organizations, which made them from the day of their arrival at Camp Chase ready and quick to coalesce into a genial and harmonious Regiment Company "D" was in every respect an admirable body of men, and although it came among strangers, it soon established its claim to the most cordial fraternity and respect. Its muster roll was as follows:

NAME	RANK	REMARKS
James H Riggs	Captain	Discharged, Dec., 31, 1863, disability
Porter H. Foskett	Captain	" expiration term of service
Herman Suabedison	1st Lieut	" April 1st, 1862, for disability
Wm L. Wilson	1st Lieut	" expiration term of service.
M D. Rodocker	2d Lieu	" " "
Robert Stephenson	1st Sergeant	" " "
Wm J Nicholson	"	" " "
Robert P Willson	"	" " "
Gideon O Pringle	"	" " "
George W Wilfy	"	" " "
Hugh M Shipman	Corporal	" " "
Asa D. Hallett	"	" " "
John McCarty	"	" " "
Wm Brandi	"	" " "
Thomas R Henthorn	"	" " "
James Lindsey	"	" " "
Charles W Farley	"	" " "
Patrick Batts	Private	" " "
Gustav A L. Brothers	"	" " "
Nelson Brooks	"	" " "
Aaron B Browning	"	" " "
Lewis Bates	"	" " "
James W. Buckingham	"	" " "

NAME	RANK	REMARKS
Cyrus Balis	Private	Discharged, expiration term service
Thomas G. Buckingham	"	" " "
Wm F Carter	"	" " "
James Currey	"	" " "
Robert W Calland	"	" " "
Azaniah C Cooper	"	" " "
Samuel B Clemens	"	" " "
Richard B David	"	" " "
John B. Davis	"	" " "
Samuel A Davis	"	" " "
Joseph T Eagler	"	" " "
George Fogle	"	" " "
John L Glasner	"	" " "
John Horton	"	" " "
Henry Hickman	"	" " "
Wm H. Harrison	"	" " "
Wm M Kayes	"	" " "
Abraham Kent	"	" " "
Isaac Larrick	"	" " "
John Moore	"	" " "
Wm Marsh	"	" " "
Elisha F. Morrison	"	" " "
Edward Maginnis	"	" " "
Shamger Morris	"	" " "
Harrison Nichols	"	" " "
James T Nowell	"	" " "
Edward T Petty	"	" " "
Marion Polson	"	" " "
Peter T Patterson	"	" " "
Otho Pennington	"	" " "
Rufus Pryer	"	" " "
Bethel B D Rucker	"	" " "
Wm. Rosenbush	"	" " "
John W Ruby	"	" " "
Benjamin F Rose	"	" " "
John M. Ryan	"	" " "

NAME	RANK	REMARKS
Michael Shepherd	Private	Discharged, expiration term service
Benjamin F. Scott	"	" " "
David Turner	"	" " "
John W. Miles	"	" " "
James Wise	"	" " "
Hiram Glasner	"	" " "
Josiah P. Kernan	"	" " "
Isaac Marlon	"	" " "
John Milligan	"	" " "
Nathan Stephens	"	" " "
James Yohr	"	" " "
H. B. Newton	"	" " "
Hershel V. Webster	"	" Oct 1, '61, writ Hab. Corp.
Joseph H. Stivers	"	" " "
Hugh McDonald	"	" " "
Benjamin Oakey	"	Discharged, May 23, 1862 disability
Ezekel Farley	"	" Sept 19th, 1862, disability.
Enoch Archer	"	" Oct 26th, 1862, disability
Isaac N. Hickle	"	" Oct 2d, 1862, disability.
Samuel Porter	"	" March 13th, 1863, disability.
James W. Robinson	"	" November 4th, 1862
Wm C. Frost	"	" April 4th, 1863, disability.
Timothy B. Rucker	"	" May 1st, 1863, disability
Wm H. Sommers	"	" Acc't wounds rec'd in battle
Stephen D. McIntire	"	" March 1862, disability
John H. Hiddlebach	"	" February 2d, 1864, disability
Burna Batts	"	" April 20th, 1864, disability
Samuel Grigg	Sergeant	Died, Nov 1st, 1861, of disease.
Joseph C. Clark	Private	Died February 8th, 1862, of disease.
John C. Hanson	"	Died Feb 27th, 1862, of disease
David H. Shepman	Corporal	Died March 3d, 1862, of disease
Isaac Dickinson	Private	Died March 6th, 1863, of disease.
Samuel Johnson	"	Died March 6th, 1862, of disease
Wesley Hickman	"	Died April 21th, 1862, of disease
John M. Piper	"	Died May 28th, 1863, of disease
Nicholas Gebhart	"	Died Sept 10th, 1862, of disease

NAME	RANK	REMARKS
Edward Forbes	Private	Died, Feb 11, '63, wounds rec battle
Wm Pringle	"	Killed in battle, May 15th, 1863
James F Matheny	"	Killed, May 16, '63, Champion Hill
George C Brown	"	Died May 3d, 1863, of disease
Abraham McConnell	"	Died June 5, '63, wounds rec battle
Benjamin Willson	"	Died July 6th, 1863, of disease.
John H Grant	"	Died July 23, '63, wounds rec battle
Michael Dougherty	"	Died January 9th, 1863, of disease
Josiah M Davis	"	Died May 15th 1862, of disease
Smith Groves	"	Died August 14th, 1863, of disease

COMPANY "E."

Company "E," of the Forty-Second, was recruited mainly in Medina County. The men were enrolled by Chas H Howe and Melvin L. Benham, though the enlistments were largely due to the labor and influence of Col. Sheldon, who had already accepted a place among the field officers of the Regiment. Mr Howe became Captain and Mr. Geo F. Brady First Lieutenant of the Company, Mr Benham receiving his first commission as Second Lieutenant. The high character of all these officers had secured for the Company some of the best material in the County. The men of Company "E" were, as a whole, younger than those of any other Company, but they were bright, intelligent and ambitious, and became a model Company. Their perfection in drill and all the duties of the infantry service was exceptional, and when in September 1864, the crack Companies of the Thirteenth and Nineteenth Army Corps held a competitive drill at Morganzia, La., Company "E" brought conspicuous honor upon Ohio and the Forty-Second by winning the first prize. The Nineteenth Corps was made up of Eastern Regiments, trained in the Army of the Potomac, and the victory of an Ohio Company from the Thirteenth Corps was a surprising result. No one, not even the defeated contestants, questioned the justice of the award. Capt. Howe resigned in May, 1863, when Lieut. Benham succeeded to the command. Lieut. Brady having resigned in March, 1862, Chas. P. Goodwin, originally an enlisted man of Company "E," who had been Sergeant Major, was promoted to Second and afterwards First Lieutenant. He was appointed Adjutant in June, 1863, and was mustered out of service in August following for disability from severe wounds received in service. Company "E" performed conspicuous duty in the battle of Thompson's Hill, where all its officers were wounded, Capt. Benham very dangerously. He recovered, however, and remained at the head of his Company until its final discharge from service in November, 1864. The following were members of the Company:

NAME	RANK	REMARKS
Charles H. Howe	Captain	Resigned, March 2d, 1863
Melvin L. Benham	"	Discharged, expiration term service
George F. Brady	1st Lieut	Resigned, March 27th, 1864
John T. Flynn	1st Lieut	Discharged, expiration term service
Chas. P. Goodwin	1st Lieut	Disability, August, 1863
A. L. Bowman	2d Lieut	Discharged, expiration term service.
Wm H. H. Bryant	1st Sergeant	" " "
Wm. R. Moses	"	" " "
John Lonesbrough	"	" " "
Leonard G. Loomis	"	" " "
Orrin L. Campbell	"	" " "
Wm H. Jaques	Corporal	" " "
Chas. R. Turner	"	" " "
Wm Zemen	"	" " "
Henry R. White	"	" " "
Charles O. Boynton	"	" " "
Benjamin Phinney	"	" " "

THE FORTY-SECOND OHIO INFANTRY.

NAME	RANK	REMARKS
Thomas Howers.	Corporal	Discharged, expiration term service
Rolland G Abby	Private.	" " "
Franklin F Allen.	"	" " " "
James Blorige.	"	" " " "
Harrison H Bates.	"	" " " "
Edmond E Buell	"	" " " "
Henry Burnett	"	" " " "
Freeman L. Cooley	"	" " " "
George Fenney	"	" " " "
Edwin Gould	"	" " " "
John Griffin	"	" " " "
Nathan Holmes	"	" " " "
Lewis L Hanchet	"	" " " "
John Hudson	"	" " " "
Henry D Johnson	"	" " " "
Charles B Jordan.	"	" " " "
Stephen L Ketchum	"	" " " "
Henry McNeily.	"	" " " "
Frank W. Mackert	"	" " " "
George Moe	"	" " " "
George H Raymond	"	" " " "
Wm Stephens	"	" " " "
Ebenezer P. Sexton	"	" " " "
Ambrose Sawyer	"	" " " "
Mason Terry	"	" " " "
Stephen Taylor	"	" " " "
John B Underhill	"	" " " "
Wm H Websdale	"	" " " "
Joseph Wilford	"	" " " "
James Yohr	"	" " " "
Benjamin Morehouse.	Corporal	Died, February 6th, 1862
Charles O'Brien	"	Died, May 18th, 1862, disease.
Owen Emmons	"	Killed in battle, May 1st, 1863.
George H Harris	Private	" " "
Martin Lilley	"	Killed in battle, December 31, 1862
Milo W Morse.	"	Killed in battle, May 20th, 1863

NAME	RANK	REMARKS
Frederick Watson	Private	Killed in battle, July 12th, 1863
Frederick R Brooks	"	Died in Hospital
Reuben Blunt	"	Drowned, January 20th, 1862
Malon B Cozzens	"	Died, February 28th 1862
John Carl	"	Died, January 30th, 1863
David B Dyer	"	Died, February 27, 1862
Christopher Drummack	"	Died March '63, wounds rec'd battle
Milton Flint	"	Died, February 1st, 1862
Luke Flint	"	Died, February 8th, 1862
George Goldsmith	"	Died, February 12th, 1863
Wm C Hubbard	"	Died, February 1st, 1863
Nelson Herrick	"	Died, February 1st, 1863
Henry Hebner	"	Died, August 19th, 1863
Lyman Hawley	"	Drowned, March 12th, 1864
George W Lee	"	Died, January 12th, 1862
Alfred Lucas	"	Died, May 6th, 1863
Freund M Neal	"	Died, March 20th, 1863
Sanford Phinney	"	Died, May 18th, 1862
Luther A Sweet	Corporal	Died, March 29th, 1863

COMPANY "F"

This Company was made up almost entirely of volunteers from Portage County. It was recruited by H H Willard of Ravenna, O. C Risdon of Shalersville, and S H Cole of Franklin Mills, who became respectively its Captain and First and Second Lieutenants. Its first squad of forty men arrived in Camp Chase on the 10th of October, and by the close of the month the Company was filled to the maximum. Lieut. Cole resigned during the April following, and was succeeded by H C. Jennings, who had been Third Sergeant on the original organization of the Company Company "F," like Company "A" from the same County, was made up of young men from the leading families of that region, and served faithfully and well throughout the whole career of the Regiment. At Thompson's Hill it suffered severely, having two of its officers (Lieutenants CAMPBELL and JENNINGS) wounded—the latter so severely that his life was for a time despaired of He was shot through the groin, and when brought off the field his hands were cold and his lips blue He lived however, and, although partially disabled, subsequently became Sheriff of Portage County.

Company "F" performed considerable detached service, always with credit to itself and the Regiment Shortly after its discharge from service, a history of the Company and its adventures was published at Columbus, which forms a valuable contribution to the records of the Forty-Second The roster of the Company was as follows

NAME	RANK	REMARKS
H. H. WILLARD	Captain	Resigned, July 4th, 1864
O C RISDON	1st Lieut	Discharged, expiration term service.
S H COLT	"	Resigned, April, 1862
H C JENNINGS	2d Lieut	Discharged, expiration term service
W B BINGHAM	1st Sergeant	" " "
E ANDERSON	Sergeant	" " "
W L WHARFIELD	"	Discharged for disability.
H S CLARKE	"	" expiration term of service
W PARMELEE	Corporal	" " "
A DICKINSON	"	Died, July 18th, 1864, of fever
G HILTON	"	Died, December 18th, 1863
A F PRICE	"	Discharged, expiration term service
J R BARTON	"	Promoted to 2d Lieut 53d U S C I
J L BEARDSLEY	"	Died, April 9th, 1862
R B CUTTS	"	Discharged, expiration term service
M H JUDD	"	Promoted to 2d Lieut 53d U S C I
H WHITLOCK	Musician	Discharged, expiration term service
J H. WHITE	Wagoner	Died in Hospital

NAME	RANK	REMARKS
E Ailey	Private	Discharged, expiration term service
J H Albright	"	Died, February 17th, 1862.
J W Bury	"	Died, Oct 12, '63, in hos , N Iberia
J Bradey	"	Discharged, expiration term service
A Beach	"	Died, February 18th, 1863.
J Bowker	"	Discharged, expiration term service
H Burdick	"	Killed, battle, May 1,'63, Pt Gibson
F H Coffin	"	Died, of wounds, Jan. 18, '62.
S Carlisle	"	Discharged, expiration term service.
T C Conway	"	Died, May 9, 1862, at Ashland, Ky
C Carlton	"	Discharged, wounds rec'd Jan 10,'62
T H Clark	"	Discharged, expiration term service.
J H Carle	"	" " "
G A Case	"	" transferred
H G Carmer	"	" for disability
H Case	"	" "
E E Converse	"	Died, of fever, at Camp Chase
D Dull	"	Discharged, expiration term service
J B Edson	"	" for disability.
C Foote	"	Died, Oct 15, 1863 Carrollton, La
T C Foote	"	Killed, in battle, May 17th, 1863
J Fuse	"	" in battle, May 1, '63, Pt. Gib.
C S Fenton	"	Discharged, expiration term service
E Gilbert	"	" " "
A Gillett	"	" " "
W P. Gray	"	" " "
H Hentz	"	" " "
H Hartelroad	"	" " "
G W Hartelroad	"	" " "
A Hartelroad	"	" " "
C Hartelroad	"	" for disability
D Hurger	"	Died at Kent, O
H Hurger	"	Discharged, for disability
J C Hillabidle	"	" "
Charles R. Hart	"	Died, April 9th, 1862
G Huffman	"	Died, January 30th, 1862.

NAME	RANK	REMARKS
George Hallman	Private	Discharged, for disability
Thomas Heath	"	Died, Aug 22, '63, Memphis, Tenn
G Ilsler, Jr	"	Discharged, expiration term service
S Johnson	"	" " "
Silas Johnson	"	Died, February 7th, 1863
L Johnson	"	Discharged, expiration term service
Aug Johnson	"	" " "
W R Kelso	"	" " "
Harrison Kelso	"	Died, March 29, 63, at Ashland, Ky,
H P King	"	Died, Feb 4, 1863. "
A King	"	Died, Feb 20, 1872, "
L. D Levings	"	Died, March 19, 1862, "
H Lord	"	Discharged, expiration term service
H G Mills	"	" for disability
W C. Micle	"	Discharged, expiration term service
E G Myers	"	" for disability
N M Combs	"	Discharged, expiration term service
J G McBride	"	Died, Feb 7, '63, at Young's Pt, La.
E Morrison	"	Discharged, expiration term service
F Niles	"	" " "
A Palmer	"	" " "
D. M Pereira	"	" " "
J Primey	"	" " "
W Remalia	"	" " "
I Remalia	"	" " "
John Remalia	"	" for disability
W. C Ray	"	" "
W J Root	"	Died, Jan 19th, 1865, at Kent, O
George Retting	"	Discharged, for disability
S Risk	"	" expiration term of service.
L J Rhodes	"	" for disability.
E D Sawyer	"	Discharged, expiration term service
S K Stom	"	" " "
G Stewart	"	" " "
J Smith	"	" " "
C Stephenson	"	" for disability

NAME	RANK	REMARKS
H. H. Steward	Private	Died May 22, '64, at Baton Rouge.
H. Southmayd	"	Died, of lung fever and wounds
C A Tyler	Corporal	Discharged, special order Sec War
J L Woodard	Private	" expiration term of service
H S Walcutt	"	" for disability
G E Wright	"	" expiration term of service
S S Yale.	"	Died, of fever, at Camp Chase.
John Dull	"	Discharged, for disability
P Black	"	Discharged, expiration term service
E W Grindle	"	" " "
G Rapelje	"	" " "
James Boyd.	"	Died, February 8th, 1863
C Davis	"	Discharged, expiration term service.
G. Derenberger	"	" " "
P Faber	"	" " "
J S Glenn.	"	" " "
W. Heffenger	"	" " "
D Horn	"	" " "
J E Hostman	"	Died, wounds rec'd at Chick Bayou.
M A Honsholder	"	Discharged, expiration term service
J C Hull	"	" " "
S Laman	"	" " "
W McLain	"	" " "
A Morris.	"	" " "
J Otto	"	" " "
A Reynolds	"	" " "
S Remik	"	Killed, battle, May 17, '63, Bl'k Riv.
J M Smith	"	Discharged, expiration term service
E Shriver	"	" " "
M R Smitiser	"	" ' "
A Smith	"	" " "
E J Vanniman	"	" " "

COMPANY "G"

Company "G," of the Forty Second, was the outgrowth of an independent militia squad, organized in Newburgh during the Summer of 1861, under the name of Ellsworth Cadets. The Company included forty or fifty of the most popular young men of Newburgh, and had hosts of friends On the 19th of September a ball was given at the Cataract House, under the management of these amateur Cadets. The ball-room was filled with a merry company In the midst of the festivity, Col. GARFIELD, who was then making speeches throughout Northern Ohio, and gathering recruits for the Forty-Second, appeared on the scene. He was welcomed by Capt JEWETT, the commander of the Company, and, being well known to the people of Newburgh, was urged to address the assembly. Mounting the stage on which the musicians were seated, Col GARFIELD began with the thrilling passage from Childe Harold·

> "There was a sound of revelry by night,
> And Belgium's Capital had gathered then
> Her beauty and her chivalry"

The effect was electrical After speaking twenty minutes, Col. GARFIELD produced a blank enlistment roll Capt. CHAS. P. P JEWETT came up and signed it, and when the ball ended that night there were sixty names upon the roll. By the 3d of October the Company had been increased to eighty men, and on the following day it reached Camp Chase. Here a combination was made with a squad of twenty men from Medina County, by which the organization was raised to a hundred men The detachment from Medina County received by agreement the choice of First Lieutenant and Second Sergeant, and the election of Company officers resulted as follows Captain, C P JEWETT, First Lieutenant, T. G LOOMIS, Second Lieutenant, A J. STONE.

The Company was assigned to the letter "G," and faithfully shared the service of the Forty-Second until the day of its final discharge.

In some respects the Company was peculiar. There was among its men a greater variety of age, nationality and character than among those of any other Company. They included natives of seven different countries, and their ages ranged from sixteen to fifty years. Nearly all trades and professions were represented in Company "G." Its men were the life of the Regiment. They were as ready for an escapade as they were for a fight, and whenever a detachment of the Forty Second was caught on a lark, and brought to camp under guard, Company "G" was apt to be more or less fully represented. Among its special characters were MIKE O'BRIEN, a perfect type of the volatile, convivial Irishman, and a soldier who was known by the name of "The White Officer." It may fairly be doubted whether the war developed any more advanced example of the original and talented "forager" than the "White Officer." He reduced the methods of predatory subsistence to an absolute art. On one occasion he sold one pair of shoes five times to a Kentucky mountaineer, who was peddling bread and pies through the camp—stealing them back and bartering them again as fast as the bread merchant could bind them to his saddle.

Company "G" was ably officered during its entire term of service. Capt. JEWETT, one of the most efficient officers of his rank in the Regiment, served until July, 1863. Capt E. B. CAMPBELL, a veteran of the British army, entered Company "G" as a private, and after earning two promotions for meritorious service was mustered out as Captain in 1865. Most of the survivors of Company "G" still live in Cleveland, of which city Newburgh now forms a part. The Company muster roll bears the following names:

THE FORTY-SECOND OHIO INFANTRY.

NAME	RANK	REMARKS
Charles P. Jewitt	Captain.	Resigned, July 11th, 1863
E B Campbell	"	Transf'd to 96th O. V. I. Nov. 18, '64
Timothy G. Loomis	1st Lieut	Resigned, July 4th, 1862
James T. Henry	"	Resigned, July 1st, 1864.
Calvin Pierce	"	Discharged, expiration term service
Andrew J. Stone	"	Died, March 9th, 1862
Calvin A. Marble	Sergeant	Discharged, disability, March 25, '63
Noble P. Wiggins	"	Discharged, expiration term service
John Hull	"	" " "
DeWilson J. Wilder	"	" " "
J W Hofste	"	" " "
Daniel Underhill	"	" " "
John R Bailey	Corporal	" " "
Alfred D Stryker	"	" " "
Edward Caim	"	" " "
Norman F Deane	"	" " "
Edward H. Williams	"	" " "
Henry Collins	"	" " "
John Brown	"	Discharged, disability, May 3d, 1863
Thomas Mapes	Wagoner	" " Dec 4th, 1863
Charles G Anderson	Private	Discharged, expiration term service
John Brayton	"	" prom to 1st Lieut U S C I
Peter Carlin	"	Discharged, expiration term service.
Lorenzo D Cox	"	" " "
Robert Corlett	"	" " "
Eben S. Chapin	"	" " "
Wm. Clarey	"	" disability
Jesse Fetterman	"	Discharged, expiration term service
George D. Farr	"	" disability
Willard M Farr	"	" prom to 1st Lt 118 U S C I
Amasa S Garfield	"	Discharged, expiration term service
Philip S Goodwin	"	" " "
Noah Griswold	"	" " "
James Gazelly	"	" disability.
George Haycox	"	" "
Joseph D. Howes	"	" "

21

NAME.	RANK	REMARKS.
Julius A. Harris	Private	Discharged, for disability.
R. C. Huntoon	"	" prom. to 2d Lieut U. S. C. I.
Calvin M. Homer	"	" disability
Emanuel Heffinger	"	" "
Wm Johnson	"	" Writ hab corpus, Jan 10, '63.
Jacob James	"	" disab., wounds rec'd in battle.
George M. Kelly	"	Discharged, expiration term service.
James McGregor	"	" " "
John McGregor	"	" " "
James McGuirl	"	" " "
Patrick Murphy	"	" " "
John McMahon	"	" Louisville, Ky., Aug 19, 1862
Nicholas Moore	"	Transferred to Invalid Corps
Michael O'Brien	"	Discharged, for disability
Leroy B. Owen	"	Discharged, expiration term service.
George M. Phelps	"	" " "
Wm Parmeier	"	" for disability
Seymour Ruggles	"	Discharged, expiration term service
Warren Rathburn	"	" for disability
Frederick J. Switze	"	Discharged, expiration term service
Michael Shelvin	"	" " "
Harrold Shattuck	"	" " "
Wilson Shepard	"	" " "
Herbert L. Styles	"	" " "
Chas Stanbury	"	" " "
Levi D. Smith	"	" " "
Giles G. Sheldon	"	" for disability
George G. Stryker	"	" Oct 24, '63, wounds in battle
Wm Lemon	"	" for disability, April 22, 1863
Cornelius Smith	"	" wounds received in battle
Wm P. Williams	"	" for disability
James Williamson	"	Discharged, expiration term service
Avery A. Clark	"	" " "
Lorenzo D. Crosier	"	" " "
Robert W. Codding	"	" " "
Wm Durham	"	" " "

THE FORTY-SECOND OHIO INFANTRY.

NAME	RANK	REMARKS
George Emerling	Private	Discharged, expiration term service
Newel J Fuller	"	" " " "
Orsemus Graves	"	" " " "
Stephen T Harrington	"	" " " "
Edward Mabury	"	" " " "
James Monroe	"	" Apr 2, '63, wounds in battle
Philander F. Vaughn	"	" at Vicksburgh, July 6, 1863
Wm H Wheeler	"	" " " "
Patrick Hayes	"	Killed Dec, 29,'72, Chickasaw Bayou
Alfred Faulkner	"	Killed May 30, '63, Vicksburgh
Wheaton Goodwin	Sergeant	Died, May 20, '63, wounds, Pt Gib
Henry C. Morgan	Corporal	Died, July 27, 1863, at Vicksburgh
Egbert C Harris	"	Died, at Plaquemine, Feb 24, 1864
Wm. Gardiner	"	Died, Jan 12, '62, wounds in battle
Adelbert A Dix	"	Died, Jan 4, '64, at Memphis, Tenn
John Quiggin	"	Died, Aug 3, '63, New Orleans, La
John Archer	Private	Died, Apr 27, '63, at St Louis, Mo
Thomas Corlett	"	Died, Feb, '62, at Warrensville, O
Junior R Cox	"	Died, Sept 18, '62, at Cumb'd Gap
Wm. Case	"	Died, April 18, '63, at St Louis, Mo
Daniel B Clark	"	Died, July 27, '63, at Vicksburgh
Aaron Farr	"	Died, March 27,'63, Young's Pt, La
Bela W Porter	"	Died, Jan 1, '63, at St Louis, Mo
Arthur T. Strong	"	Died, Feb, 1862, at Ashland, Ky
George Swift	"	Died, Jan 8, '63, wounds rec. battle
John W Thomas	"	Died, July 8, '63, at Milliken's Bend
John G Warren	"	Died, Feb, '62, at Ashland, Ky
Frank Williams	"	Died, July 27, '63, at Vicksburg
Leander Loomis	"	Died, at Clarksfield Hollow, O

COMPANY "H."

Company "H" was organized in Ashland, and, like Company "A," had for its basis the students of a school. About the 1st of November, 1861, Col. GARFIELD, Capt. BUSHNELL of Company "C," and Quartermaster STUBBS came to Ashland on a recruiting expedition. Several Companies of the Forty-Second were already in camp and it was well understood that it was to be one of the crack regiments of Ohio. The fact that Ashland County had already one company in its ranks served to greatly stimulate local interest in the success of the Regiment. On the evening of the 2d a meeting was held in the Court House, at which Col. GARFIELD and Capt. BUSHNELL made stirring speeches in favor of enlistments and the vigorous prosecution of the War. EDWIN C. LEACH and J. F. ROBINSON enlisted that night and great interest was awakened. Among the most interested of those present was Mr. S. M. BARBER, the Superintendent of the Public Schools. He held a position of delicate responsibility to the parents of his pupils, and although all his inclinations and his sense of duty constrained him to enter the service, his duties at home made him hesitate. But his indecision was brief. On the day after the meeting he came to the Court House with his mind fully made up. He signed the enlistment roll, and his example was followed by every boy in the school capable of carrying a gun. Mr. BARBER did not even return to the school house. His whole energy was, from the moment of his enlistment, given to the organization of his Company. Thirty Alumni of the Ashland school formed the basis of the organization, and to these were added many more of the students then in attendance. Other young men from the country came in and enlisted, and by the 15th of the month a large detachment of recruits was forwarded to Camp Chase. Col. GARFIELD went to Troy and other townships in Ashland County, made speeches and enlisted recruits, so that before the close of the month, Company "H" was in camp, filled to the maximum.

Mr. BARBER was of course made Captain, and from that time until he was carried from the field in front of the entrenchments at Vicksburgh with a wound which cost him his right leg, he was the guardian and the inspiration of the Company. He was an unusually conscientious and earnest man, and the strong influence which he had acquired over a majority of his men while in the relation of teacher and pupil at home, gave him complete control over his Company. They were quiet, well-behaved soldiers, ready for any duty. The loss of his leg of course put an end to Capt. BARBER's active service in the field. He was transferred to the Veteran Reserve Corps and remained on duty until July, 1866. He was brevetted Major "for gallant and meritorious services at Vicksburgh," and was subsequently again brevetted Lieutenant-Colonel "for gallant and meritorious services during the War." He was succeeded in the command of Company "H" by Lieut.-CHAS. B. HOWK, who had been First Lieutenant since the organization of the Company. Company "H" contained some of the best soldiers in the Regiment, and left a spotless record.

NAME	RANK	REMARKS
SETH M. BARBER	Capt. & Bv't Lieut. Col.	Transferred to V. R. C., Feb. 1864
JNO. R. HELMAN	Captain	Discharged, expiration term service
PETER MILLER	1st Lieut.	" " "
W. J. SPENCER	1st Lieut	Resigned
EDWIN C. LEACH	2d Lieut	Resigned
CHAS. B. HOWK	2d Lieut.	Resigned
JNO. F. ROBINSON	Sergeant	Promoted to Major, 53d U. S. C. I.
GEO. B. MASTERS	"	Discharged, expiration term service
GEO. MITCHELSON	"	" " " "
JNO. H. BOWMAN	"	" " " "
ELISHA BRIGGS	"	" " " "

NAME	RANK	REMARKS			
Geo Taylor	Corporal	Discharged, expiration term service			
Jos B F Sampsell	"	"	"	"	"
Eli Wertenberger	"	"	"	"	"
Elmore Evans	"	"	"	"	"
Wm Sloan	"	"	"	"	"
Wm H Nickerson	"	"	"	"	"
Sol. Barrack	Private	"	"	"	"
David Buffenmire	"	"	"	"	"
Henry Burge	"	"	"	"	"
Jno J Buzzard	"	"	"	"	"
Wm Chambers	"	"	"	"	"
Chas Crosier	"	"	"	"	"
B D Clugston	"	"	"	"	"
Jno Davidson	"	"	"	"	"
W Davidson	"	"	"	"	"
Jas A. Darrow	"	"	"	"	"
LeGrand Drown	"	"	"	"	"
Oel Durkee	"	"	"	"	"
L M Fast	"	"	"	"	"
W B Fasig	"	"	"	"	"
F. A. Ford	"	"	"	"	"
Josiah Hardy	"	"	"	"	"
N S Hendryx	"	"	"	"	"
Jacob Hart	"	"	"	"	"
Chas W Kelley	"	"	"	"	"
Jno E King	"	"	"	"	"
Fred. K Long	"	"	"	"	"
A A Leach	"	"	"	"	"
Horace Morehouse	"	"	"	"	"
John Peters	"	"	"	"	"
Wm Robinson	"	"	"	"	"
Hiram Raker	"	"	"	"	"
Peter Royer	"	"	"	"	"
Alvin J. Stanley	"	"	"	"	"
David Schrobl	"	"	"	"	"
Jas B Smith	"	"	"	"	"

NAME	RANK	REMARKS
Jos. Spencer	Private	Discharged, expiration term service
Wm. Swineford	"	" " " "
Jno Wells	"	" " " "
Rich P Woodhouse	"	" " " "
Fred Byers	"	" for disability.
Jacob Barrack	"	" "
Jos. Brown	"	" "
Henry O. Briggs	"	" "
Henry Burton	"	Re-enlisted 1st Wisconsin Battery.
W H Buchan	"	Promoted, 2d Lieut, 53d, U.S C I.
Andrew J Burns	"	" " " "
W H Mason	Corporal	" for disability.
Nelson Scott	"	" expiration term of service
Gibbon A Case	"	Discharged for disability
David Doty	"	" "
Chris Eppier	"	" "
Daniel Fike	"	" expiration term of service
David Garver	"	" for disability.
Austin Hayls	"	" "
Samuel Hart	"	" expiration term of service
Rufus King	"	" for disability
Adrian K Hoffman	"	" to enlist in Miss. Marine Brig.
Samuel Kopp	"	" expiration term of service
Jacob Newcomer	Private	" for disability
Henry Onstott	"	" "
Henry Perky	"	" "
Jas Pollock	"	" expiration term of service
Daniel F. Pocock	"	" " " "
Geo M Reed	"	" for disability
Geo. Riggs	"	" "
Thos. G Ryall	"	" expiration term of service.
Jno Sours	"	" " " "
Wm A Smith	"	" for disability.
Andrew Shoemaker	"	" "
Jno Shoemaker	"	" "
Harmon Stanley	"	" expiration term of service.

NAME	RANK	REMARKS
Jno Strayer	Private	Discharged, expiration term service
Lewis Taylor	"	Discharged for disability
Jno Warren	"	"
Chas B Wickman	"	"
Kluben Wall	"	"
Phil Youngblood	"	"
A D Atkinson	Sergeant	Transferred to 96th O V I
Wm. L Aton	Private	"
Jno C. Baum	"	"
Samuel G Brown	"	"
Robert M Cellers	"	" to V R C, March 28th, '62
Royce S. Crial	"	" to 96th O V. I.
George Full	"	" to Co C, 42d O. V I
Jno W Fry	"	" to 96th O V. I
Jos Finley	"	"
Edmond J Heiser	"	"
Orin J. Howard	"	"
Isaac Buchanan	"	"
Jos Ingman	"	"
Jacob Kosht	"	" to V. R. C
Jos Moodey	Sergeant	Promoted to 2d Lieut. in Co "I"
Wm Maxheimer	Private	Transferred to Co "C."
Edmond Naylor	"	" to 96th O. V. I
Elijah J Pocock	"	"
Jno W. Smalley	"	"
Jno B. Switzer	"	"
Curtis Swineford	"	"
Paul Trauger	"	"
Isaac Wertenbergler	"	"
Thos. B White	Sergeant	Transferred to V. R C
Geo. N. Ryall	Corporal	Died, May 18, wounds rec in battle
Jno Beachley	Private	Died, January 21st, 1862
Henry Beer	Sergeant	Died, November 30th, 1863
J. L. Chapman	Private	Died, December 19th, 1862
Jas Crawford	"	Died, December 19th, 1862
Christian Deel	"	Died, July 19th, 1863

NAME	RANK	REMARKS
JNO. ERNST	Private	Died, May 1st, 1863
JONATHAN GRIFFITH	Corporal	Died, July 19th, 1863
JACOB GRIFFITH	Private	Died, August 19th, 1863
JACOB HINES	"	Died, March 26th, 1862
LAMUS O. HUMPHREY	"	Died, December 30th, 1861
ADAM INNES	"	Died, March 28th, 1863
DANIEL KESSLINGER	"	Died, February 23d, 1862
DAVID E. LONG	"	Died, April 10th, 1862
ALEX MASTERS	"	Died, May 1st, 1863
ANDREW McCOMBS	"	Died, May 30th, 1862.
CHAS C MARTIEN	"	Died, February 25th, 1863
ELISHA STARKWEATHER	"	Died, February 26th, 1863
TOBIAS SPIKER	"	Died, September 22d, 1863.
CHAS D TOWSLEY	"	Died, July 14th, 1862
GEO VANOSTRAND	"	Died, March 19th, 1862
WM SHEETS	"	Muster'd out honorably, Columbus '65

COMPANY "I"

Company "I" was recruited in Miami, Shelby, Clarke and Logan counties, and therefore represented a part of Ohio somewhat remote from the homes of the other Companies, which, as has been seen, were mainly in the Northeastern part of the State. The Company was recruited without any definite preference for any particular Regiment, but on its arrival at Camp Chase the fine appearance and general popularity of the Forty-Second soon attracted the notice of the new-comers, and they willingly accepted a place in its line

In the first organization of the Company, DAVID SCOTT was made Captain, MARION KNIGHT, First Lieutenant; and R. B. LYNCH, Second Lieutenant. Capt. SCOTT resigned on the 28th of February, 1862, and Lieut LYNCH, who had shown especial capacity as an officer, was promoted to his place. Upon this, Lieut KNIGHT resigned and was succeeded by Lieut. PORTER H. FOSKETT, with DAVID N. PRINCE as Second Lieutenant. Capt LYNCH remained at the head of the Company until the 3rd of March, 1863, when he resigned and was succeeded by Capt FOSKETT, who was subsequently transferred to the Captaincy of Company "D." This led to the promotion of Lieut. PRINCE to the Captaincy of Company "I," and he remained in service until the final discharge of the Company.

Company "I" lost seven men killed in battle, and twenty-three discharged for disabilities, mainly resulting from wounds received in action It also received a number of recruits, seven of whom were transferred to the Ninety Sixth O V I, in 1864, when the remainder of the Forty-Second Regiment was mustered out of service The personnel of Company "I" was as follows

NAME	RANK	REMARKS			
DAVID SCOTT	Captain	Resigned February 28, 1862.			
R B LYNCH	"	Resigned March 3d, 1863			
PORTER H FOSKETT	"	Transferred to Co D, June 23, 1864			
DAVID A PRINCE	"	Discharged, expiration term service.			
MARION KNIGHT	1st Lieut	Resigned June 28, 1862			
JOS D MOODLY	1st Lieut	Discharged, expiration term service			
WM I STEWARD	2d Lieut	Resigned November 15, 1862			
JNO T KNOOP	Sergeant	Discharged, expiration term service			
NORMAN W CADY	"	"	"	"	
DAVID WALLACE	"	"	"	"	
JOS W LEEDOM	"	"	"	"	
SYLVESTER COUNTS	"	"	"	"	
A W ALLEN	Corporal	"	"	"	
JNO W ANDERSON	"	"	"	"	
ORRIN APPLE	"	"	"	"	
W H BYERS	"	"	"	"	

NAME	RANK	REMARKS		
R R Earson	Corporal	Discharged, expiration term service		
Jos H Loudenbach	"	"	"	"
Jno Shanley	"	"	"	"
W H Dodson	Musician	"	"	"
W H Moore	"	"	"	"
Jas Apple	Private	"	"	"
Jas Blair	"	"	"	"
Daniel Baker	"	"	"	"
R M Coffenberger	"	"	"	"
Albert J Corry	"	"	"	"
Jno. B Deweese	"	"	"	"
Jos W French	"	"	"	"
Chas L Fenton	"	"	"	"
Wm M Good	"	"	"	"
Wm G Gay	"	"	"	"
Christ Guess	"	"	"	"
Benjamin Haines	"	"	"	"
Wm P Haines	"	"	"	"
Ephraim Heath	"	"	"	"
Arteman O Knodl			"	
Gurdon H Killinger	"	"	"	"
Lorenzo Krause	"	"	"	"
Jason P Keie	"	"	"	"
Oliver P Longfellow	"	"	"	"
Chauncey M McIntosh	"	"	"	"
Samuel March	"	"	"	"
Jno Morris	"	"	"	"
Amos J McElroy	"	"	"	"
Granville B Overhulls	"	"	"	"
Wm Palmore	"	"	"	"
Archibald J Powells	"	"	"	"
Isaac Shanley	"	"	"	"
Cameron L Stewart	"	"	"	"
Benjamin P Taylor	"	"	"	"
Jno L Troy	"	"	"	"
Wm J. Verdle	"	"	"	"

NAME.	RANK	REMARKS
Samuel Williams	Private	Discharged, expiration term service
Benjamin Watson	"	" " "
Jos H Wilson	"	" " "
Jas H Corwin	"	Killed in battle May 1, 1863
Eli Lemon	"	Killed in battle May 1, 1863
Denton O Miller	"	Killed in battle December 28, 1862
Jas McConnaughey	"	Killed in battle December 29, 1862
Jos Bishop	"	Died May 11th, 1863
Daniel J Conner	"	Died October 8th, 1863
Darius Comer	"	Died January 31st, 1864
Isaac Di boy	"	Died February 15th, 1862
Wm Gray	Corporal	Died of wounds rec'd in battle
Andrew Hulman	Private	Died February 28th, 1863
Jos Kitchen	"	Died January 10th, 1863
Wm R Kune	"	Died January 18th, 1863
Ackley Knowlton	"	Died of wounds received in battle
Jas W Lyon	"	Died of wounds received in battle
Jno Miller	"	Died March 25th, 1863
David Newell	"	Died January 29th, 1863
Zachariah Fritz	"	Died April 19th, 1862
Geo Anderson	"	Discharged for disability
Thos Brevard	Corporal	Discharged for disability.
Jno A Breedlove	Private	Discharged for disability
Jno F Brown	Private	Discharged, expiration term service
Wm Campbell	"	Discharged for disability
Nathaniel Briner	"	Discharged, expiration term service.
Jacob Couchman	"	Discharged for disability
Michael J. Cruger	"	Discharged for disability
John A. Dodson	"	Discharged for disability
Jno F Faust	"	Discharged for disability
Geo Foster	"	Discharged, expiration term service.
Ira B Granby	Sergeant	Discharged for disability
Cyrus Gurley	Private	Discharged for disability
Henry Heiner	"	" " "
Evans Jenkins	"	" " "
Wm Jones	"	" " "

NAME	RANK	REMARKS
Wm Knoop	Private	Discharged, for disability
Geo H Lippincott	"	" " "
Robert McIntosh	Corporal	" " "
Jasper Noe	Private	" " "
Samuel Peter	"	Discharged, expiration term service
Jno H Rutherford	"	Discharged for disability
Jno W Smith	"	" " "
Chas Smith	"	" " "
Augustus F Smock	"	" " "
David Snively	"	Discharged, expiration term service
Henry Stauffer	"	" " "
Jno L. Taylor	"	Discharged for disability
Abraham Van Sickles	"	" Wounds rec in act'n, Dec 29, '63
David Weikle	"	Discharged for disability
Benjamin Wenrich	"	Discharged, expiration term service
Geo R Crawford	"	Transferred to V R C Feb 15, '64
Hiram B Glazier	"	" to Co F, Nov 2nd, 1864
Jon Milligan	"	" to 96 O V I Nov 19, 1864
Isaac Marlow	"	" to 96 O. V. I Nov 19, 1864
Nathaniel Stevens	"	" to 96 O. V. I Nov 19, 1864
James Yoho	"	" to Co E, Oct 29th, 1864
Howard B Newton	"	" to 96 O V I Nov 19, 1864.

COMPANY "K"

This Company was recruited principally in Logan County by ANDREW GARDNER, Jr, although it contained volunteers from various other parts of the State Thirteen of these, enlisted by PORTER H FOSKETT, came from Medina County THOMAS L HUTCHINS of Bellefontaine, also assisted in recruiting the Company, and at its first organization the following officers were chosen Captain, ANDREW GARDNER, Jr ; First Lieutenant, THOS L. HUTCHINS, Second Lieutenant, PORTER H. FOSKETT.

Captain GARDNER resigned on the 28th of January, 1863, and Lieut HUTCHINS was promoted to the vacancy thus created Capt. HUTCHINS continued in command until the final discharge of the Regiment from service. Lieut FOSKETT was promoted to First Lieutenant, and afterwards to Captain, and transferred to Company "I" Thence he was transferred to Company "D," and finally resigned in 1864 ALBERT L BOWMAN, who was originally an enlisted man of Company "K," was made Sergeant-Major of the Regiment, then promoted from that grade to Lieutenant, and was mustered out at the close of three years' service as First Lieutenant of Company "K." GEORGE K. PARDEE, an another enlisted man of the same Company, joined the Regiment in the Autumn of 1862 on its arrival at Oak Hill, after the Cumberland Gap campaign. After the three days' fighting at Chickasaw Bluffs, during which he had behaved with conspicuous credit, he was promoted, upon the recommendation of Col SHELDON, to a Lieutenancy. He was consequently made Adjutant, and in the latter part of 1863 received promotion to a Captaincy He commanded various companies during the temporary absence of their officers, and was finally transferred to the Captaincy of Company "D," which command he retained until the regiment was mustered out of service Company "K" lost six men killed in battle, and at the breaking up of the Regiment in Arkansas in November, 1864, sent twenty-nine of its men, who had enlisted in 1862, to join the Ninety-Sixth O V. I. The history of the Company is the history of the Forty-Second Regiment ; all of whose services and perils it shared bravely and faithfully from first to last. The following is the record of its organization

NAME	RANK	REMARKS
Andrew Gardner, Jr	Captain	Resigned, Jan. 28th, 1863
Thomas L Hutchins	"	Discharged, expiration term service
George K Pardle	"	Mustered out at expiration of service as Captain of Co "D"
Porter H Foskett	"	Transferred to Company "I"
Albert L Bowman	1st Lieut	Discharged, expiration term service
Geo D Douglas	1st Sergeant	" " "
Owen J Hopkins	Sergeant	" " "
Wm H Leister	"	" " "
Martin McAllister	"	" " "
Sidney S Alden	"	" " "
John C Van Vorhis	"	" " "
Henry Shaulf	Corporal	" " "
Simeon Oatman	"	" " "
Ezra J Allman	"	" " "
Jas R Whitzel	"	" " "
Sylvester E Southard	"	" " "
Robert W Southard	"	" " "
Herry Chapin	"	" " "
Thos Armstrong	Private	" " "
Calvin Beal	"	" " "
Norral Balls	"	" " "
Franklin O Batch	"	" " "
Samuel A Buell	"	" " "
Lysander E Crandall	"	" " "
John Callahan	"	" " "
Jacob Caskey	"	" " "
Adam Dellman	"	" " "
Asa Faucett	"	" " "
Geo W Gardner	"	" " "
Thos C. Hunt	"	" " "
Levi Hartzell	"	" " "
Franklin Hickman	"	" " "
Orson J Hubbell	"	" " "
John Kinney	"	" " "
Abraham Krider	"	" " "

NAME.	RANK	REMARKS
Jacob Krider	Private	Discharged, expiration term service.
Benj F Myers	"	" " " "
John Main	"	" " " "
Eben Phinney	"	" " " "
Horace F Prouty	"	" " " "
Laufort T Romius	"	" " " "
Robert W Smith	"	" " " "
John E Southard	"	" " " "
Wesley A Seeley	"	" " " "
Hugh Underwood	"	" " " "
Wm. Varnly	"	" " " "
Geo M Wallis	"	" " " "
Andrew J. Wilson	"	" " " "
Wm C Wilgus	"	" " " "
Frank S Kauffman	Corporal	Discharged, for disability
Andrew J Smith	"	" " " "
David E Johnson	"	" " " "
David P Wallis	"	" " " "
Jos S Osgood	Teamster	" " "
Wm C Atkinson	Private	" " "
Jos Andrews	"	" " " "
Warren Britton	"	" " " "
Samuel Ballinger	"	" " " "
Aaron Clark	"	" " " "
Walter M. Crandle	"	Transferred to Invalid Corps
Wm H Drake	"	Discharged, for disability
Wm. Elliott	"	" " " "
Job S Goff	"	" " " "
Chas A Lyon	"	" " " "
Frank C May	"	" " " "
Edward L Moore	"	" " " "
Wm McDonald	"	" " " "
Orvil M McClintock	"	" " " "
Wm H Messick	"	" " " "
Jas Plimner	"	" " " "
Thos B Perkins	"	" " " "

NAME	RANK	REMARKS
Alfred A Riddell	Private	Discharged, for disability
Wm J Ruse	"	" " "
Theo. F. Ripley	"	" " "
Milton Southard	"	" " "
Mort D. Sanders	"	" " "
Wm Sautele	"	" " "
Amos F Sanders	"	" " "
Tim. F Smith	"	" " "
James Snyder	"	" " "
Quincy A Turner	"	" " "
Robert S Telley	"	" " "
John C. Vanderson	"	" " "
Wm Wallace	"	" " "
Wm. H. Winner	"	" " "
Frank Mantz	Corporal	Transferred to 96th Ohio
Nathan H. Alvord	Private	" " "
Henry Burnett	"	" " "
Isaac Ballinger	"	" " "
Franklin Brown	"	" " "
Jas. W. Brainard	"	" " "
Valentine Beaner	"	" " "
Absalom Brown	"	" " "
Amasa L. Clapp	"	" " "
Geo. T. Clapp	"	" " "
Daniel W Evans	"	" " "
Henry Frinkner	"	" " "
Edwin Grier	"	" " "
Edgar O Harvey	"	" " "
David P Hickart	"	" " "
Henry C. Hotchkiss	"	" " "
Edward Howard	"	" " "
Wm H. Len	"	" " "
Francis Mack	"	" " "
Luther C. Ponty	"	" " "
Fletcher D Richards	"	" " "
Cyrus A Rickards	"	" " "

NAME	RANK	REMARKS
SAMUEL STYRE	Private	Transferred to 96th Ohio
DANIEL DICKMAN	"	" " " "
HARRISON S. SOWER	"	" " " "
JOHN H. WASS	"	" " " "
JACOB A. WADERING	"	" " " "
HENRY B. RAFF	"	" " " "
JOSIAH THOMPSON	Sergeant	Died, wounds in battle, May 4, '63.
HIRAM W. ALLMAN	"	Died May 26th, 1863
JOSIAH K. BATCH	Private	Died April 5th, 1862
ALCINAS BALDWIN	"	Died May 5th, 1863, of wounds
BENJ. S. DOWNS	"	Died, Vicksburgh
MILO A. HOBERT	"	Died February 28th, 1862
LEONARD A. MITCHELL	"	Died February 7th, 1862
HENRY R. MARMON	"	Died March 22d, 1862
MARTIN W. MORRIS	"	Died May 5th, 1863
OLIVER MURDOCK	"	Died June 20th, 1863
RICHARD MARMON	"	Died May 26th, 1863
DANIEL H. RICE	"	Died February 23d, 1863
JASPER RASSALE	"	Died at St. Louis.
WM. SHAW	"	Died April 3d, 1862
LEONARD A. SOUTHARD	"	Died September 25th, 1862.
THOS. C. SUPLER	"	Died October 4th, 1863
JACOB STATE	"	Died March 29th, 1864
FRANK B. WALLARD	"	Died April 25th, 1862.
JOS. SOUTHARD	"	Died March 3d, 1864
GEO. HARRIS	"	Killed in battle May 1st, 1863.
ADAM C. VAN VORHIS	"	Killed in battle May 21st, 1863.

ERRATA.

1. The foregoing Roster has been printed from the final muster-rolls upon which the Companies of the Forty-Second were discharged from service. Such errors in names and dates as could be detected have been corrected. If others remain, it is the fault of the records.

2. On page 243, it is stated that, at Vermillionville, La., two Companies of the Regiment were distributed among the others, and that thenceforward the Forty-Second had only eight Companies. This is an error. The distribution of the two Companies took place as stated, but this arrangement was only temporary. During the Summer of 1864 the original arrangement was restored, and the Regiment included ten Companies at the time of its discharge from service.

THE END